GET REALLY RICH IN THE COMING SUPER METALS BOOM

D1419805

GET REALLY RICH IN THE ~~COMING~~ SUPER METALS BOOM

Gordon McLendon

PUBLISHED BY POCKET BOOKS NEW YORK

DEDICATION

Dedicated to my long-suffering, remarkable, famously moral, patient and incredibly loving father, and to my mother, who is not only all of that but carries with her a sweetness of disposition that has its own special importance in the lives of all whom she touches. Without the continually courageous and understanding help of my father, I believe I would have done little, and without my mother, nothing at all. Both of them I love unabashedly.

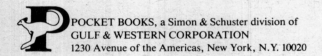 POCKET BOOKS, a Simon & Schuster division of
GULF & WESTERN CORPORATION
1230 Avenue of the Americas, New York, N.Y. 10020

Copyright © 1980, 1981 by Gordon McLendon

All rights reserved, including the right to reproduce
this book or portions thereof in any form whatsoever.
For information address

ISBN: 0-671-43225-7
      0-671-43202-8 Pbk

First Pocket Books printing April 1981

First Special printing October 1980

10 9 8 7 6 5 4 3 2 1

POCKET and colophon are trademarks of Simon & Schuster

Also available in Simon and Schuster hardcover edition.

Printed in the U.S.A.

Contents

Preface

If you've any doubt that an investment in strategic metals represents the same opportunity that gold did for you at $35.00 an ounce, or silver at less than $2.00 an ounce, consider having yourself melted down.

Salomon Brothers, in its annual review of alternative investments, points out that the mineral content of the human body—which includes some of the critical substances we'll be talking about—is now worth $7.28, compared to only $0.98 in 1970. That's a compounded average rate of return of 22 percent. Salomon Brothers adds dryly: "The prudent investor will note, of course, that Federal law currently prohibits purchase, sale or liquidation in any form of the mineral-bearing vehicle."

One London-based firm recently published a strategic metal index based upon a seven-year price performance measuring ten of the more important critical metals against the performance of other investments. The ten strange-sounding metals—in all of which you could have invested—were chromium, cobalt, columbium, magnesium, molybdenum, tungsten, silicon, indium, rhodium, and tantalum. The index shows that $100 invested in 1972 in these ten strategic metals would have increased to $821 at the end of 1979. That's a compounded average rate of return of 35.1 percent over seven years.

So there's no need to have yourself melted down. You can now invest directly in the strategic metals and substances themselves. That, in a phrase, is the news of this book. Until recently, the strategic metals field has largely been a closed shop, with metals moving most often from mine to refiner to user, with a broker sometimes in between. But now investing in these substances has become a practical possibility for the average investor; it has become so, if I may add a personal note, largely as the result of a two-year painful pioneering investment program in these esoteric metals undertaken by this writer.

One of my first experiments consisted of buying physical cobalt through a London broker who was not—at least then—a strategic metals specialist. The result turned out to be a minor loss, but the big loss was the considerable expenditure of time plus the frustration of dealing with an outpouring of paper couched in strange terms and using weights and measures that were then utterly alien to me—as they would be to most investors.

Indeed, before my cobalt exercise was consummated, my office was so inundated with paper related to its purchase that I could only recall the story of one of our more candid admirals who, in a moment of utter frustration during World War II, announced that as far as he could figure out, a U.S. Navy battleship was eligible for launching only when the papers pertaining to the building of the battleship equaled the ship's deadweight tonnage.

That's the way I felt about the amount of paper that accumulated during the cobalt deal, and so I finally sold the cobalt when I felt that the paperwork was equal in weight to the one metric ton of cobalt that I'd bought—exceeding the weight restrictions on the floor of my building! Had I had enough room to store more paper, I probably would have kept the cobalt, because cobalt, in this writer's opinion, has excellent profit potential.

Toward the end of the book, you'll see the McLendon Company's actual paperwork involved in some typical strategic metals transactions. But before we get there, you'll have learned how you can avoid all the beginner's learning pains that I went through.

It's sad that nowadays an investor has to go through all this trouble to make ends meet. Used to be that you could just invest in stocks and bonds and keep some money in a savings account for a rainy day. But not any more.

In fact, going back to that Salomon Brothers report on alternative investment returns in the decade from 1970 to 1980, these days the investor just *has* to learn to deal with tangibles—items like strategic metals, gold, diamonds, or coins—if he or she is going to have any chance at all of coming out of the battle to earn a living still in one piece.

During these ten years, when strategic metals have produced an almost hair-raising rate of profit, Salomon Brothers shows that gold and oil and silver as well as U.S. coins and Chinese ceramics and several other tangible investments were all going through the roof, but stocks and bonds were *right at the bottom of the list.*

In fact, we're going to present two tables right now, though we dearly hate tables. They show you, though, why you simply *must* diversify the vast bulk of your investments into tangibles and cut way down on any percentage you risk in paper investments like stocks and bonds. The two tables are easy to read. Table I shows that if you're in the 40 percent tax bracket and inflation is 15 percent, just to keep your standard of living at a break-even point you've got to make a return of 25 percent on your investments. Can you average that in the stock and bond market or in savings certificates or money market funds? Not by a long shot. Table II shows that if you were in that same 40 percent bracket and wanted to do a little better than break even, maybe turn an exorbitant 10 percent profit, you'd have had to make 44.2 percent on your investments for that year! Of course, if you're in a higher tax bracket and inflation rises over 15 percent, maybe you'd better not even look at the two tables because they'll have you wavering between the bottle and the pistol.

Even the poor guy in the 25 percent bracket has to earn nearly 19 percent on his money if he's just going to stay even with inflation.

Maybe melting ourselves down wasn't such a bad idea in the first place. Except that it's illegal. And so terminal.

TABLE I

Investment Returns Required to Maintain Constant Purchasing Power under Varying Inflation and Taxation Rates*

Taxation rates (%)	Inflation rates (%)																
	2.5%	5.0%	7.5%	10.0%	12.5%	15.0%	17.5%	20.0%	25.0%	30.0%	35.0%	40.0%	45.0%	50.0%	75.0%	100.0%	200.0%
0%	2.5	5.0	7.5	10.0	12.5	15.0	17.5	20.0	25.0	30.0	35.0	40.0	45.0	50.0	75.0	100.0	200.0
10%	2.8	5.6	8.3	11.1	13.9	16.7	19.4	22.2	27.8	33.3	38.9	44.4	50.0	55.6	83.3	111.1	222.2
20%	3.1	6.3	9.4	12.5	15.6	18.8	21.9	25.0	31.3	37.5	43.8	50.0	56.3	62.5	93.8	120.0	250.0
30%	3.6	7.1	10.7	14.3	17.9	21.4	25.0	28.6	35.7	42.9	50.0	57.1	64.3	71.4	107.1	142.9	285.7
40%	4.2	8.3	12.5	16.7	20.8	25.0	29.2	33.3	41.7	50.0	58.3	66.7	75.0	83.3	125.0	166.7	333.3
50%	5.0	10.0	15.0	20.0	25.0	30.0	35.0	40.0	50.0	60.0	70.0	80.0	90.0	100.0	150.0	200.0	400.0
60%	6.3	12.5	18.8	25.0	31.3	37.5	43.8	50.0	62.5	75.0	87.5	100.0	112.5	125.0	187.5	250.0	500.0
70%	8.3	16.7	25.0	33.3	41.7	50.0	58.3	66.7	83.3	100.0	116.7	133.3	150.0	166.7	250.0	333.3	666.7
80%	12.5	25.0	37.5	50.0	62.5	75.0	87.5	100.0	125.0	150.0	175.0	200.0	225.0	250.0	375.0	500.0	1000.0
90%	25.0	50.0	75.0	100.0	125.0	150.0	175.0	200.0	250.0	300.0	350.0	400.0	450.0	500.0	750.0	1000.0	2000.0

Taxation rates (%)

Inflation rates (%)

*Source: *World Money Analyst*, 1979.

TABLE II
Investment Returns Required to Make Real 10 Percent Profit under Varying Inflation and Taxation Rates*

Inflation rates (%)	2.5%	5.0%	7.5%	10.0%	12.5%	15.0%	17.5%	20.0%	25.0%	30.0%	35.0%	40.0%	45.0%	50.0%	75.0%	100.0%	200.0%
0%	12.8	15.5	18.3	21.0	23.8	26.5	29.3	32.0	37.5	43.0	48.5	54.0	59.5	65.0	92.5	120.0	230.0
10%	14.2	17.2	20.3	23.3	26.4	29.4	32.5	35.6	41.7	47.8	53.9	60.0	66.1	72.2	102.8	133.3	255.6
20%	15.9	19.4	22.8	26.3	29.7	33.1	36.6	40.0	46.9	53.8	60.6	67.5	74.4	81.3	115.6	150.0	287.6
30%	18.2	22.1	26.1	30.0	33.9	37.9	41.8	45.7	53.6	61.4	69.3	77.1	85.0	92.9	132.1	171.4	328.6
40%	21.3	25.8	30.4	35.0	39.6	44.2	48.8	53.3	62.5	71.7	80.8	90.0	99.2	108.3	154.0	200.0	383.3
50%	25.5	31.0	36.5	42.0	47.5	53.0	58.5	64.0	75.0	86.0	97.0	108.0	119.0	130.0	185.0	240.0	460.0
60%	31.9	38.8	45.6	52.5	59.4	66.3	73.1	80.0	93.8	107.5	121.3	135.0	148.8	162.5	231.3	300.0	575.0
70%	42.5	51.7	60.8	70.0	79.2	88.3	97.5	106.7	125.0	143.3	161.7	180.0	198.0	216.7	308.3	400.0	746.7
80%	63.8	77.5	91.3	105.0	118.8	132.5	146.3	160.0	187.5	215.0	242.5	270.0	297.5	325.0	462.5	600.0	1150.0
90%	127.5	155.5	182.5	210.0	237.5	265.0	292.5	320.0	375.0	430.0	485.0	540.0	595.0	650.0	925.0	1200.0	2300.0

Taxation rates (%)

Taxation rates (%)

Infaltion rates (%)

*Source: World Money Analyst, 1979.

No, there are easier ways, and whether you choose strategic metals or not, we're going to show you those ways. But we are going to emphasize strategic metals because you not only can get in on the ground floor in this new investment, you can actually enter through the basement—it's that new and foolproof—*if* you follow the advice in this book.

Just to give you an idea of what we will be talking about, photographs of some strategic metals—in different forms—follow the preface.

However tempting it may be to launch into an investment program in strategic metals right here and now (and of course you could turn to Chapter 5 and dive right into our first pages on this subject), it would be unwise. To do so would be a lot like doing a swan dive off the high board before having learned to swim. Sure, someone who *did* know the fundamentals might come to your rescue. But you might also drown, and nobody wants you to wind up at the bottom. Exactly the opposite, and that's the reason we're going to do something often overlooked in the dozens of other "how to" books on keeping afloat and even prospering financially.

If one is going to know where to go with his money, best he understand where he's *been,* and that's why we begin this book by summarizing the conditions which have brought us to the whole miserable economic mess in the United States and have prompted you to read this book. I feel that a slice of history is absolutely essential to anyone who wishes a larger piece of the financial pie for himself.

I'd like to add one further personal note.

Like Eddie Willers in Ayn Rand's prophetic novel, *Atlas Shrugged,* by 1970 I had a "sense of dread without reason . . . an immense, diffused apprehension, with no source or object." I determined to learn why I had this feeling of *Weltschmerz* and *Angst*—of slow disillusion and growing dread—to determine why, at least for me, the future of the United States no longer beckoned as openly and unimpededly as a stretch of Arizona highway.

Here is what I found out.

GORDON MCLENDON

ANTIMONY

BISMUTH
  Ingots and shots

CADMIUM
  Balls and sticks

CALCIUM

CHROMIUM
  Flake electrolytic

COBALT
  Electrolytic flake and crucible

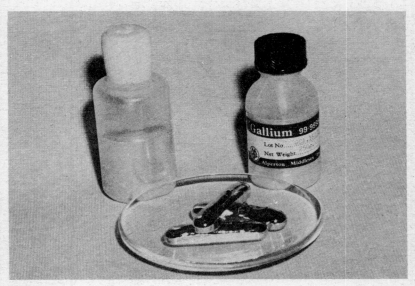

GALLIUM
Two squeeze labels; three ingots (25 grams)

GERMANIUM
Chunks; one-half round ingots; blocks

INDIUM
  Four ingots, wire; shots

MAGNESIUM
  Granules on watch glass

MANGANESE

MERCURY

MOLYBDENUM
Melt stock pellets; tubing; rod

SELENIUM
Granules on watch glass

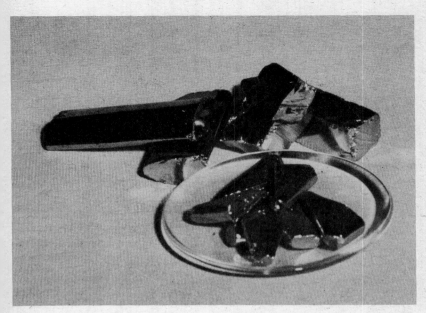

SILICON
  Boules; seeds

TUNGSTEN
  Crushed ingot; coiled wire (2 pcs); one straight wire on watch glass

1

Some Introductory Remarks

Perhaps this introduction is more important than the rest of the book.

On January 20, 1981, the nation's new President stood in front of the Capitol before untold television millions—with his hand on the Bible—and repeated after the Chief Justice of the United States, "I do solemnly swear that I will faithfully execute the office of President of the United States, and will to the best of my ability, *preserve,* protect and defend the Constitution of the United States." (My italics.) He so swore because those are the exact words that the Constitution specifies he must say when he is inaugurated.

That event is not unrelated to the subject of this book. How so? Bear with me for a moment.

In having so sworn, the new President has either (a) sworn to preserve a corpse or (b) admitted that he does not know what he is swearing to, despite the fact that the U.S. Constitution is the oldest written national constitution in operation in the world.

Among all the parts of the Constitution that he took oath to preserve, protect and defend is Article I, Section 10, a section of that venerable document which has never been changed, repealed or amended since it was first presented to the American people for ratification by the Constitutional Congress on September 17, 1789. Section 10 reads as follows: "No State shall . . . emit Bills of Credit; make any Thing but gold and silver Coin a Tender in Payment of Debts . . ."

Since much of the early part of this book has to do with the emitting of "Bills of Credit" by the federal government, allow me to restrict my comments on Section 10 only to its last part, whose language means that the President swears to preserve, protect, and defend a document that explicitly prohibits the states from authorizing anything but gold and silver coin as legal tender. Of course, I fully realize that other parts of the Constitution have been breached as well and, indeed, that may be as good a defense for steady lying as any politician needs to offer these days. It could also be that just because a man has his hands on the Bible when he swears to an untruth, it is no longer thought to be a sin but merely a violation of the Boy Scout oath.

But that old dog won't hunt with this writer. Not when a major part of the campaign of 1980 was fought on grounds largely dealing with the sorry condition of the economy of the United States.

All of this has a great deal to do with a book on strategic metals and about the way a prudent person can use these metals to make money. Money and metal are what this book is about and the best way to get a perspective on our subject is to zero in on the crucial fact that when this country began, the only basis for our money was supposed to be two of the strategic metals—gold and silver.

One of the founding fathers who had labored hard to produce the Constitution's historic set of rules for the conduct of a nation was Alexander Hamilton. He warned at that time, "to annul the use of either of the metals (gold and silver) as money, is to abridge the quality of circulating money."

Hamilton did not stand alone in his views.

Benjamin Franklin, whose first job as the owner of a print shop in Philadelphia was to print money for the Commonwealth of Pennsylvania, years before the drafting of the Constitution, knew full well the danger that the printing press represented to sound money.

James Madison, who would become known as "the father of the Constitution," who wrote nine of the first ten amendments to it (the Bill of Rights), and who would become our fourth President, had staunchly opposed the issuance of paper money while he was in the Virginia House of Delegates.

Thomas Jefferson, the third President, had already witnessed an earlier and nearly disastrous experience with paper money, when the thirteen colonies, operating under the Articles of Confederation, had attempted to finance their war with England by issuing paper currency, and the experience had been bitter. The new United States government later sought to "redeem" that old Continental currency at 100 to 1, but it was too late—all too many people had already papered their walls with it.

It is clear from Article I, Section 10 that the Constitution did not wish its republic to issue paper money. Article I, Section 8 of the Constitution quite specifically gave Congress the power to "*coin* money" and "regulate the Value thereof." Recognizing that the right to *coin*, not print, money was the only right to create money which had been given Congress by the Constitution, and after many notes and reports on this subject by Jefferson and Hamilton, Congress enacted the *Coinage* Act of 1792 (my italics), which provided for a bimetallic system, based on a dollar consisting of 371.25 grains of pure silver or 24.75 grains of pure gold, a ratio of 1:15. This act further provided for unlimited *coinage* by the U.S. Mint (to be established in Philadelphia) of both metals, and it designated only gold and silver coins to be minted.

What could have been more clear?

Even the staid old *Encyclopedia Britannica* observes

dryly: "It seems to have been the intention of the framers of the Constitution to prohibit issuance of paper money by the federal government . . ."

More than one event in our history demonstrated the insubstantiality—indeed, the danger—of paper money. In 1791, the first Bank of the United States, a kind of one-horse central bank, was created under an act of the new Congress, which then empowered this new federal bank to issue bank notes. These notes promptly depreciated, and the charter of the first "national bank" was not extended when it expired in 1811. Then, a second United States Bank was established in 1816; this bank was larger than the first one, but the result when it issued paper bank notes was the same, almost immediate depreciation, and the bank died in 1836 after President Andrew Jackson vetoed a bill to extend its charter.

America was not to have another national central bank for over three-quarters of a century, until 1913, when Congress created the Federal Reserve System (the "Fed") after spirited debate.

When you consider what has happened today to the worth of that paper money which the Fed has issued to you, you can readily decide for yourself whether the function of printing money should ever be given to the federal government.

Since U. S. courts first discovered what sport and ego-satisfaction could be had in re-writing the Constitution, many a tribunal has sought to satisfy political expediency by holding that Section 8 does not *forbid* "emitting bills of credit." That is true. Section 8 does not forbid Congress from doing anything else either, including hunting squirrels on the Capitol lawn. Section 8 is a *positive* section of 427 precisely-chosen words giving Congress 18 specific and affirmative powers.

But even granting that the wordage of Section 8 might be tortured sufficiently to permit the printing of paper money, is the meaning of "to coin money" in any way obtuse? Is that wordage of Section 10 providing that none of the states shall make anything but gold and silver coins a tender in payment of debts in any way confusing?

We might call to the witness box Karl Marx, who asserted in the *Communist Manifesto* that one general requisite in the establishment of a Communist state is: "Centralization of credit in the hands of the state, by means of a national bank with state capital and an exclusive monopoly."

One further point:

The founding fathers, in offering the Constitution for ratification that night of September 17, 1789, meant to create a republic, not a democracy. A republic is a form of government where the powers of the majority are exercised within a framework of constitutional restraints designed to guarantee the minority the enjoyment of certain individual or collective rights, such as freedom of speech and religion. Webster's *Dictionary* puts it most succinctly when it defines a republic as a "state where power is not directly in the hands of or subject to complete control by the people, in contrast to a democracy." Our forebears did not mean to establish the sort of "democracy" we have today, which, unlike a republic, offers little protection for property rights, one of which is our right to sound money, because money is most assuredly property.

It is small wonder, then, that when queried as to what the Constitutional Convention of 1787 had given the nation, Benjamin Franklin answered, "A republic, madam, if you can keep it."

When the new President put his hand on the Bible on January 20, 1981, and swore to preserve a corpse (for surely he is not swearing to preserve a document which he has not read), you may well wonder if we have kept anything at all—even honor itself.

2

The Way We Started

The United States has never been completely out of debt, and the changing size and character of that debt is the thread that will lead us from yesterday to today.

Again let me say that you could turn immediately to Chapter 5 and begin your study of investing in strategic metals, but I believe that you will find that perusing this part of the book first will give you a definite advantage. Among other things, you will understand why it is no longer possible, in the older sense, to *invest*—as one once did with stocks and bonds—and hope to keep abreast of government profligacy. And why the prudent man, since he cannot follow the rules of yesterday, must seek the safest *speculations* as an alternative.

In 1790, the new U.S. government had to assume a debt of $75 million which our colonies had run up in winning their freedom. But that didn't matter much. We were a sturdy, hard-working people—nine of ten Americans then lived on farms—and thrift was one of the greatest assets of our American forebears. They quickly reduced the government's $75 million debt to almost nothing.

Then along came the War of 1812, and again we went into

debt to win it—this time to the tune of $100 million. But once again our industrious forebears set busily to work to get rid of their onerous debt. They just about made it. In 1835, they had, like busy beavers, hacked their federal debt down to a mere $34,000. At that point, each of our 14 million forerunners owed two and a half cents each.

In 1860 another war hit us, our own Civil War, and the cost of fighting it once again pushed us into debt. This time it was a whopping (for that era) $2.5 billion. Our population was now 40 million, and so every person now owed $62.50.

In 1862, in order to finance the war, Congress passed the Legal Tender Act, creating "greenbacks," again stepping away from coinage. But it was exactly one year later, on February 25, 1863, as the Army of the Potomac lay cold, cheerless and in shambles along the Rappahannock following its bloody repulse at Fredericksburg in December, that the Congress passed the National Bank Act, the disastrous effects of which were not be become apparent for nearly a century. The Act established a system of nationally-chartered banks which were required to secure their own notes with U.S. government bonds. Henceforth, any U.S. administration unwilling to tax the people to cover its deficits, could and did sell its bonds to the banking system. For the first time, the government could now make money out of its own debt.

But Gen. Ulysses S. Grant, who had commanded the Union armies and became President after the war, responded sensitively to the problems of our currency. Grant survived terrible scandals, among them the infamous Crédit Mobilier under which the Union Pacific Railroad was fraudulently built, the discovery of the famous "whisky ring" which defrauded the Internal Revenue Service, the revelation that his Secretary of War, William W. Belknap, had taken bribes while participating in the whisky ring, and headlines revealing that others close to the White House had been involved in corrupt building activities of the Federal Board of Public Works. Add to all of that the attempt by tycoons Jay Gould and Jim Fisk to corner the gold market in

1869, and one can see that the General had more than his share of problems. It is a wonder that he had any time at all to keep his mind on the stability of our currency, but he did.

President Grant vetoed a legal tender act in 1874 which would have badly inflated the currency. Furthermore, it was he who fought successfully for passage of the Resumption Act of 1875, the wholehearted support of which led directly to the election of his successor, Rutherford B. Hayes. Under the Resumption Act, all of those greenbacks which had been issued by the Mint to finance the Civil War—and which were for the first time monetized by bonds—would be redeemed in 1879 in specie: in gold and silver. As a result, the greenbacks not only increased in value as soon as the Resumption Act was passed but, when finally redeemed in precious metal in 1879, became one of the few instances in history where a government's wartime issue of paper money was successfully restored to its citizens at face value.

At the end of the Civil War, our forebears once again returned to the fields and also, now, to the factories and mines, and by 1890 by hard labor they had whittled our U.S. government debt once more, this time from $2.5 billion to a little more than a billion dollars.

In fact, we worked so hard and so successfully that we kept the national debt at this comparatively modest figure until yet another great war came—World War I. This time we really had to dig deep into our pocketbooks to win. Victory in World War I left the nation in 1919 with—gadzooks!—a public debt of $24 billion. But the U.S. population was 106 million and each citizen owed $226 in 1920. That $226 was a lot, but not impossible.

This time, though, it would take more than a whittling knife. And those days of winning were hardly a time in which anyone worried about something as uninteresting as a national debt. For we had entered the Roaring Twenties—the era of fads, froth, and fiesta and of an infectious optimism which trumpeted that, if today was good, tomorrow would be even better.

Still, we went to work once again to reduce the debt of $24

billion that World War I had left us. President Warren
Harding was so concerned about it that he commanded his
trusted aide, Charles G. Dawes, to draw up "some sort of
yearly budget that we can operate on." Until 1921, unbelievably enough, the United States had never had a formal
budget.

Dawes' historic first budget was an expert job. It showed
that Harding could (and did) run the country for $3.5 billion a
year and that the debt could be reduced. And so it was—
somewhat—from the $24 billion of 1919 to only $16 billion in
1930. And that wasn't so bad, because now we had 123
million people and that meant that, dividing the debt among
us all, each one of us owed only $130. Bully! That was nearly
a hundred dollars less than each of us had owed at the end of
World War I.

How is it that our national debt has risen from $16 billion in
1930 to a published government figure of over $900 billion
only half a century later in 1980? Or, if you believe the
respected National Taxpayers' Union, to an actual national
debt of $9,033,000,000,000 (that's $9.033 trillion)—about
$40,000 for every man, woman, and child! How, indeed?

Well, one of the reasons was that Sections 8 and 10 of
Article I of our U.S. Constitution to which we referred in
Chapter 1 had kept us pretty well protected. With a few
minor detours here and there, we had stuck to our guns and,
while some paper money had rolled off the presses from time
to time, each paper dollar was pretty well backed by an equal
amount of gold (or, at times, silver) in our U.S. Treasury
vaults. Politicians in those earlier days all too often met
sharp resistance when they tried to order the Treasury to
print money willy-nilly without the necessary gold or silver
to back it up. That was true right up until President Roosevelt
abolished the gold standard in 1934—in fact, made it illegal
for Americans to own gold and ordered all Americans to turn
their gold in. Then, for really the first time, the government
was free to print money to its heart's content without
anything to back it up. Not that anybody had bothered to
amend Sections 8 or 10 of Article I—the two obnoxious

sections were just ignored, perhaps in the hopes that they would somehow go away.

The fact is that the United States had got off to a wonderful start in 1776. The men who wrote the Constitution, most of them religious men, were also both hardworking and brilliant. It and they enabled us to begin with a nearly totally free enterprise system. At least, it was the nearest thing to the laissez-faire capitalism first envisioned by old Adam Smith that the world has ever seen. Webster defines laissez-faire as "a doctrine opposing governmental interference in economic affairs beyond the minimum necessary for the maintenance of peace and property rights." In other words, under a laissez-faire ("let do") free enterprise system, which the Constitution tried to establish, the government would not be much more than a policeman protecting the citizens' property and civil rights. In the case of the United States, that meant that our government would keep to the function of enforcing the Constitution, the subsequent Bill of Rights, and any later constitutional amendments.

The Constitution is a marvelous document. If it has a single failure, it is the failure to tell us not to eat the daisies: the failure to provide language that would have prevented courts from trying to misinterpret language in the Constitution that is absolutely crystal clear to any man of common sense.

Certainly, we never had an *absolutely* free enterprise system. Human nature being what it is, politicians from the start handed out any number of special grants, favors, franchises, privileges, and protective tariffs which they could squeeze through political courts. But by and large it took more than a hundred years before the federal government took its first major step toward attempting to cripple the free enterprise system with a really whopping misinterpretation of the Constitution.

It is to this misinterpretation and its bitter consequences that we now turn. Along the way, we'll also take a quick look at some of the most prominent, and entertaining, events of our political and cultural past, to get a sense of how the country was behaving while the soundness of our economy was steadily being undermined.

Let's begin with the Andrew Jackson administration (1829–1837), where certain goings-on were good fodder for plenty of back-fence gossip. Jackson's opponents made much of the fact that the President had wed Mrs. Rachel Robards while she was still married to another man. This proved to be technically true; and even though the Jacksons were remarried immediately after her divorce became final, his opponents never let the issue die.

At the same time that such tomfoolery was kept in the public's eye, Jackson and his associates developed a theory of business cycles which contended that paper money was the villain that always caused successive periods of inflation and depression. The tough old Indian fighter from Tennessee and his cabinet believed that if paper money could be restricted and gold and silver increased in direct proportion to the amount of paper money issued, the inflation–depression cycle could at least be partially controlled. The soundness of that theory—its practice was defeated by Jackson's Congress, naturally—is by now almost too obvious for debate. Remember how Jackson in 1836 vetoed the second attempted U.S. central bank, the second Bank of the United States. Two years before, in 1834, he had registered the following protest:

> The bold effort the present bank made to control the Government, the distress it has wantonly produced . . . are but premonitions of the fate that awaits the American People should they be deluded into a perpetuation of this institution [The Bank of the United States], or the establishment of another like it.

For an interesting sidelight on American economic history, let's jump ahead now to 1848, when one of America's foremost free enterprisers, Horace Greeley ("Go west, young man"), owned the highly regarded New York *Tribune*. Doubtless unknown to Greeley, one of his editors was a socialist, who hired another socialist, a German, as the *Tribune*'s European political reporter—one Karl Marx. While on the *Tribune*'s payroll for 11 years, Marx, as we know, was busy both writing and codifying his history-making *Communist Manifesto,* which he published in 1848. In fact, Karl Marx remained on the New York *Tribune*'s payroll until Greeley, in a fit of budget cutting, attempted to reduce Marx's salary from ten dollars to five dollars per week. Marx, who knew a bit about money and the value of work, quit.

Here's another event (mentioned briefly earlier) that begins to take us more directly into our subject of strategic metals. On Black Friday—September 24, 1869—two famous promoters, Jim Fisk and Jay Gould, who already had gained control of the Erie Railroad thanks to shady government subsidies and the federal grant of a monopoly on their route, decided to try to corner the gold market. Fisk and Gould got the ear of President Ulysses S. Grant and—through an elaborate scheme which used Grant's brother-in-law and thus gained the President's innocent cooperation—very nearly succeeded. At the last minute, finally understanding the scam that Fisk and Gould had worked on (and through) him, Grant ordered the U.S. government itself to start selling gold in the open market and so broke the attempted Fisk–Gould corner at the eleventh hour.

As this little anecdote shows, however hard our forebears worked, they were neither dull nor dullards. There were peccadilloes and folderol galore, though perhaps not as many or as much as today, if only because the average person had to work so much harder and had less time to get into as much mischief. And our Congressmen and Senators, while by no means totally without a sense of financial self-improvement, had few government bureaus to hide behind and, besides that, still maintained a healthy fear of punishment by U.S. courts. What's more, many still cherished not only the concept of the United States as a republic but also the Constitution—including Sections 8 and 10 of Article I.

Still, our legislators soon began to get their licks in and the process of undermining the pillars of the American system began to gather steam. By July 4, 1876, the nation's centennial, a law was being considered that would ultimately give Presidents and Congresses the right to invest *all* power in the federal government. The law had its origins in the 1824 decision of U.S. Chief Justice John Marshall in the case of *Gibbons* vs. *Ogden*. In that classic decision, Marshall had denied to the State of New York the power to grant a steamboat company an exclusive franchise, ruling that "the authority of *Congress* is at all times adequate to meet . . . and to protect the national interests by securing the freedom of interstate commercial intercourse from local control" (my italics). In different words, states' rights—a power so explicitly desired by the Founding Fathers as they framed the Constitution—were dead. The state from now on had no right to rule on a franchise: only the *federal government* had the power to give or deny monopolies. Although the 1876 legislation failed, the Marshall decision eventually bore fruit in the 1887 passage of the Interstate Commerce Act, a law that gave enormous and unconstitutional *coercive* power to the federal government. Its enactment was, as the economist Alan Greenspan has put it, "ominous," for it led directly to the passage of the far more devastating Sherman Anti-Trust Act of 1890.

Just to give you an idea of the new power that the Interstate Commerce Act gave to the federal government to drive a spike into the body of the free enterprise system, take *Houston E. and W.T.R. Co.* vs. *United States*. In this decision, the Interstate Commerce Commission (ICC) found that railroad rates in Texas were far *lower* than the more "reasonable" rates which the ICC had decreed for all other states. Louisiana complained about the efficiency of Texas railroads, and the ICC forced Texas to *raise* its railroad rates and fares. Both passengers and shippers in that state were forced to pay higher rates than were economically sound in order to satisfy the artificial price set up by a government bureau.

The Interstate Commerce Act bred dozens of other government bureaus. Meanwhile, of course, life went on.

In 1858, in New York City, a future President of the United States was born who was later to do the free enterprise system great damage by putting the first teeth in the U.S. antitrust laws. But before that, as a young man he attempted to commit suicide one evening in Bar Harbor, Maine, over one of the most beautiful girls ever to come out of Boston, Alice Hathaway Lee. Young Theodore Roosevelt had become despondent because Alice had tried to date someone else.

In 1885, a man named Frank Barrett set a record by eating 2500 oysters in two and a half hours. That same year in Texas, Judge Roy Bean fined a dead man $100 for carrying a gun. Around this time, there was a strong movement in New York City to equip policemen with roller skates, the idea being that robbers on foot could be caught more quickly.

In 1896, the New York state legislature actually passed a law giving a man the right to whip any other man with whom his wife was having an argument. In 1887, New York was also asked to pass a law to close the open hole in the top of carriages through which passengers and drivers talked to one another, because drivers continued to swear at passengers. Mark Twain wrote a story in New York called *Pudd'nhead Wilson,* in which the criminal was identified by means of his fingerprints, which led police departments to begin to use fingerprinting.

Little noticed by an American public thoroughly enjoying the high jinks of the so-called Gay Nineties was the worst blow so far inflicted on the young nation's free-enterprise system: the enactment at the beginning of that dizzy decade of the Sherman Anti-Trust Act.

The horror of the Interstate Commerce Act, the Sherman Anti-Trust Act, and all the other anti–free enterprise laws that began to pop up before Congress was that some selfish businessmen had been the first to call upon Congress for the actions that led to the very laws that would ultimately victimize not only their competitors—and later themselves

—but the entire capitalistic system as well. A favor here, a subsidy there, a protective tariff to block off more efficient competition and thus raise prices to American consumers, a bribe to gain a forced government monopoly through some federal law or bureaucratic edict—here was where these short-sighted businessmen invariably aimed, looking for government sanctions that would permit them favored competitive status in the marketplace. For consciously or instinctively, that type of businessman has always understood that *no true monopoly can ever be achieved and sustained without the help of the government.* It was these clever connivers, this tiny percentage of "contrepreneurs," always the few bad apples present in any good barrel, who began to bring down the wrath of the people on business itself. Meanwhile, the fact that only *government,* and never the businessman, can create a *true* monopoly is a fact that was then and still is totally beyond the comprehension of the American public as a whole.

What has not been clear to the public (and least of all to Congressmen) is that there are two quite different types of monopoly, one of which benefits and one of which hurts the public. The first is the *earned* (or natural) monopoly, and the second is the government-sanctioned *true* monopoly. A businessman can earn a monopoly simply because he runs his business with such skill and delivers products to the public so cheaply that nobody can do a better job and deliver a comparable product for less. The second type of monopoly, deeply damaging to the public, is the one in which the businessman gains his monopoly not by his hard work, efficiency, or superiority of product and price, but rather because the government orders that no one else can open a competitive business to oppose him.

In the first case, of course, the businessman never enjoys the ill-gotten fruits of true monopoly because the moment his skill, product, or price is not right, any competitor is quite free to take a run at him—and will. In the United States, the sanctioned (or coercive) true monopoly is best illustrated in the government-sanctioned, coercive monopolies of the

U.S. Postal Service (one must resort to private express services these days if one needs to be certain that one's mail is delivered, particularly within any definite span of time) and AMTRAK. Another example has been the many monopoly airline routes sanctioned by the government until recently, when many such route monopolies became so unpopular they were politically dangerous to politicians in power. Again, for many years, the government-sanctioned monopolies given inefficiently operated radio stations to broadcast on AM radio's finest, farthest-reaching "clear channel" frequencies were little short of a national scandal—and, indeed, the media are so politically powerful that a number of these sanctioned clear-channel monopolies still exist after 60 years. The same sort of abuses have, to a lesser extent, carried over into government licensing of the better television channels, where far greater competition could easily have been made technically feasible, just as political pressures after many years forced an expansion of competition in radio by licensing daytime-only and directional radio stations. In October 1980, the *New York Times* reported the conclusion of a special task force of the Federal Communications Commission that "whatever economic power ABC, CBS and NBC possess is in large measure a result of commission policies that protected them from potential competitors."

In any case, to return to the Gay Nineties, little or no attention was given to Senator John Sherman of Ohio when, in 1890, he succeeded in getting Congress to plant its most powerful time bomb in the free enterprise machinery. Sherman's desire to centralize power in the federal government had been apparent for many years. As Chairman of the Senate Finance Committee, he had given earnest support to the Legal Tender Act and thus to substituting a federal banking system for the state system then existent.

Sherman's Anti-Trust Act, straight from the most confusing dreams of Alice in Wonderland, was represented as one with which the federal government could break up business monopolies that supposedly took advantage of the public. But its wording was such that every person who entered business in America became a potential criminal. If the prices he charged were too high, he could, at the whim of federal bureaucrats, be prosecuted for succeeding in an "intent to monopolize." On the other hand, if by extremely efficient operation his prices became too low to suit less able competitors, he was immediately subject to imprisonment for "restraint of trade" or "unfair competition." And what, one might ask, if he charged the same prices as his competition? Then the Justice Department could go after him on charges of conspiring with his competitors to fix prices.

The stated object of the law is to prevent "restraints of trade." We can put to one side the fact that the law applies only to business and not to labor unions. More important is the fact that nowhere does it specify just what the three critical words "restraints of trade" mean. Thus, as A. D. Neale has pointed out in his *The Antitrust Laws of the U.S.A.*, "the courts in the United States have been engaged ever since 1890 in deciding case by case exactly what the law proscribes. No broad definition can really unlock the meaning of the statute . . ."

Let us look at this far-from-simple issue of monopoly more closely.

As we have pointed out, wherever you see a true monopoly, it is a condition created solely by government through special laws, favors, and franchises given certain businessmen in return for untold, and almost always undisclosed, favors from those businessmen to people in government. As one instance, the government had played such a role in the railroad business for many years. The most aromatic and oft-cited example is that of the huge Central Pacific Railroad. Four corrupt financiers, headed by Jay Gould and Daniel Drew, were successful in using both influence and money in Washington to bribe their way into huge government land and money grants as well as to gain monopoly rail routes.

On the other hand, honest and hard-working businessmen, such as Commodore Cornelius Vanderbilt and James J. Hill, managed to create at least semimonopolies in the railroad field not by bribery but by the very excellence of their operational ability. The public benefited from the low passenger and freight rates on their railroads in the same way that it suffered from the high rates, ghastly service, and minimal safety standards of the government-created Central Pacific monopoly.

One of the most famous monopolies of all time was held by International Nickel of Canada. But the monopoly was made possible only because the management of International Nickel kept prices to the public so low—through sheer efficiency—that nobody could compete effectively. Such was monopoly *in* the public interest, not against it. The same was true of ALCOA—the Aluminum Corporation of America—which maintained a monopoly for very many years by maintaining their prices to customers at rock-bottom levels. ALCOA's final reward, thanks to Senator John Sherman and the foremost later advocate of the anti-trust laws, President Theodore Roosevelt, came from the famed Judge Learned Hand. He found ALCOA guilty of violating the antitrust laws because, he wrote, ALCOA so operated as "to embrace each new opportunity as it opened and to face each newcomer to the industry with a new competitive capacity already geared into a great organization, having the advantage of experience, trade connections, and an elite of personnel." In so unbelievably ruling, Judge Hand found ALCOA guilty of monopolization by superiority of skill and work—the very goal of every businessman and the heart of the American dream.

One more example of the disastrous effects of the Sherman Anti-Trust Act: seven executives of General Electric were sent to jail under this impossibly confusing law. During World War II, the U.S. Office of Price Administration—the OPA—fixed the prices that any business could charge for electrical gear. General Electric and 28 competitors obediently kept within the federally fixed price limits. Once the war ended, all the companies simply kept on charging identical prices. The government proceeded to indict the key officials of General Electric for price fixing. Who can see the logic here? It had been all right for the government to fix the prices but not for the affected businesses to continue to meet and keep the same prices after the government had stopped fixing them.

The Sherman Anti-Trust Act was not the only nasty little surprise that the year 1890 had for the capitalistic system. The other one came in the form of the McKinley Tariff Bill. This legislation provided a complicated schedule of specific and ad valorem duties on all manufactured goods imported from foreign countries. Not only did the bill predictably raise domestic prices enormously for the consumer (since U.S. companies no longer had to compete aggressively with foreign imports), but the revenue that the government had been getting from import duties was so badly reduced as to have a serious effect on U.S. government income.

But the real harm came from the Sherman Act, later to be strengthened as the Sherman–Clayton Anti-Trust Act and enforced so vigorously by President Theodore Roosevelt. We have noted the fact that Roosevelt was more than a moderate friend of labor and that labor is exempted from the antitrust laws, but that is no indictment of labor. Neither business *nor* labor should be subject to such ethereal legislation. The law tells the businessman that he must compete but that he must be careful not to win by too much, if at all. It also tells him that he must keep his prices low, but not too low, and tells him this without ever defining how low is "low." The antitrust laws, since not even a Philadelphia lawyer can possibly understand them, have the effect of making the businessman actually afraid to become *too* efficient. And in so doing, it deprives the consumer of full competition in the marketplace and the resultant lower prices.

Let us continue with this selected tour of America's foibles, economic, political and otherwise.

The U.S. Supreme Court, in 1896, had the good sense to declare any U.S. income tax unconstitutional. Such a tax had been tried briefly during the Civil War, abolished in 1872, then proposed again during the Gay Nineties while people were whooping it up and presumably had their minds elsewhere. Anyway, thank heavens, the Supreme Court's action ended any chance for such an unconstitutional tax.

But, in the 1890s, who the devil cared? What a time it was! New York's Bowery was so full of crooks that pickpockets did open battle with each other for the first crack at a passerby. The Boston Women's Rescue League hastened to take a survey of the fallen women to whom it was suddenly ministering in droves and promptly informed the U.S. public that more than 30 percent of these fallen women had, at one time or another, been bicycle riders. It was considered highly unfashionable for a young lady to say that her boyfriend was "intoxicated"; the proper word was "incapacitated."

The New York stage was at the height of its season in 1893 when that city's theatergoing public discovered a brand new and highly effective method of dramatic criticism. The audience at a Broadway play, bored beyond all patience, physically drove Mr. and Mrs. Wood, two celebrated actors, completely out of the Park Theatre, thus rather removing the need for reviews.

It was the beginning of the mauve decade, the wonderful years of gaslight and trolley cars and dark oak bars and whalebone corsets and cobblestones and Coney Island—days when, as Winston Churchill later said, the old world was in sunset and was fair to see.

The New York City Council passed a law making it a violation of the sanitary code to sleep in one's bathtub. The New York Police Department, however, was more worried about hordes of hogs that were wandering loose and clogging traffic in New York streets—thus presumably becoming the first roadhogs.

Indeed, the minds of most Americans were far removed from Washington. It was much more fun to read of the gorgeous new Floradora girls or Diamond Jim Brady's courtship of the matchlessly beautiful Lillian Russell. During one summer of that courtship, readers learned that Jim had arrived in Saratoga with 31 Japanese houseboys. One of them stole so many of his 50-cent cigars during the summer that the houseboy was able to open his own cigar store at the end of the season. Jim had given Lillian a carriage with solid silver trimmings, doeskin reins, a gold-plated bicycle, and a famous spaniel with an $1800 collar. Once Diamond Jim, in full view of spectators, laid a million dollars in cash in Lillian's lap and asked her to marry him. But she refused.

As for the six lovely and wonderful Floradora girls who performed their nightclub act each New York evening, they were all tall, flawless damsels perfectly matched in height, each wearing frilly, pleated walking costumes, great picture hats, and tapering black gloves, while carrying colorful parasols. All of New York fought to see them, and six millionaires sought to marry them. Dazzling Marie Gilman captured no less a prize than Wendell E. Corey, president of United States Steel, for which harmless adventure both Marie and Wendell were promptly fired. Stunning Marie Wilson accepted a stock-market tip from the partner of J. P. Morgan, quickly converted it into a million dollars, and then married multimillionaire Frederick Gebhardt. Agnes Wayburn took into tow the owner of a huge South African diamond mine. And Marjorie Relyea—a classic beauty— married Andrew Carnegie's nephew, who, however, got so excited before the girls came on one night that he dropped dead just before the curtain could rise. All over America, pretty school girls left home to join chorus lines.

With all this going on, who had time to worry about what was going on down in Washington? About the only thing that turned any attention toward the Potomac during the 1890s was a meteoric phenomenon named William Jennings Bryan, who had come blazing out of the West. On a blistering hot summer day in 1896, with delegates sweltering at the Democratic convention in Chicago, the silver-voiced "Boy Orator of the Platte" hypnotized the party with his famous "Cross of Gold" speech, perhaps the most famous oration since the Gettysburg Address. The speech was Bryan's battle cry in the struggle then being waged by the West for a silver standard rather than a gold standard. Little did Americans realize that had they stuck to a standard of *either* metal as the Constitution demanded, many of the country's economic woes that had just begun to grow serious at that time—and, indeed, are threatening to destroy it today— might have been avoided.

Let's turn now to our own century.

In 1908, Americans elected rotund William Howard Taft as their President. He had earlier been a judge and later was to become the only President ever to serve as Chief Justice of the United States. Although honest and able, Taft nonetheless *felt* unqualified to be President and as a result was never happy in the presidency. Fortunately, the "round gentleman," as White House servants called him affectionately, had a better-than-normal sense of humor. He needed *all* of that sense of humor, since on February 25, 1913, as a parting gift to him a few days before he left office, the Sixteenth Amendment was added to the Constitution of the United States, some 15 years after the U.S. Supreme Court had ruled that an income tax was unconstitutional. The income tax began with a normal rate of 1 percent on incomes over $4,000 with a surtax of 1 to 6 percent on taxable incomes over $20,000. The corporate rate was 1 percent. Fortunately, we were assured that the income tax would never go higher than that.

History does not record for us whether Taft was aware of the second general requisite of a Communist state that Marx had identified in the *Communist Manifesto:* a heavy progressive or graduated income tax.

The Federal Reserve Act also became law in 1913, under the administration of a new President, Woodrow Wilson. Its passage had been provoked by the financial panic of 1907, the "rich man's panic," which once again occurred as a result of government tampering with money markets and most particularly can be blamed on Theodore Roosevelt's general antagonism toward business (although his successor, Taft, was even more untrustful of successful businesses).

Entire books have been written about alleged conspiracies

surrounding the creation of the Federal Reserve System, conspiracies against the welfare of the nation. It is hardly necessary to go to such lengths to indict the Fed. The Owen–Glass Federal Reserve Act of 1913, in its preamble, describes one of its goals as the establishment of a flexible currency. The flexible (or rather elastic) quality of the currency was based, it seems, largely on private business IOUs (corporate loans) which the banks, all too often, took into their portfolios. The Act provided that the Fed would create money according to "the needs of trade." But that principle was steadily twisted to have a "needs of government" meaning. In the Federal Reserve, Congress had created an "engine" to pull along the inflation created by the government's continued deficit spending.

One of the primary excuses given for creation of the nation's first central bank since 1836 was that the nation needed it to help finance bankers in times of distress. Before the Fed's creation, however, private bankers had always been able to get together and help out brother bankers who deserved to be helped. That may explain the bitter fight U.S. banks waged against President Wilson's advocacy of the Federal Reserve Act. Like almost everything else that a government seeks to do, private business can do it better. It is no different here. The nation's monetary system would be better off under private operation, and as a result, the nation would be better off, too.

3

The Way We Are

The way we are is the way we weren't at the time Calvin Coolidge became President in 1924. Despite all of the new anti–free enterprise laws that had been created and the federal agencies that had been legislated into being, Washington was still a quiet, sleepy village as compared to the huge, nightmarish labyrinth of bureaus that make up the nation's capital today.

But if the Washington of Coolidge seemed somnolent, the rest of the nation didn't. Life was loud, lush, and luxuriant; Americans were still enjoying one of the longest, dizziest postwar victory celebrations in history. Hear again the words and names of an era: flivver, flapper, hip-flask, bathtub gin, Mah-Jongg, joy-riding, White Lightning, Ziegfeld, Lindbergh, whoopee, Dempsey, Tunney, Tilden, Babe Ruth, Bobby Jones, Chaplin and Fairbanks and Mary Pickford, bobbed hair, short skirts—and *margin*.

To economic sophisticates throughout America, and that included every shoe-shine boy on Wall Street, anybody not in the market was a very queer bird indeed. Wall Street appeared to be living proof of the maxim of that faddist philosopher of the Twenties, Émile Coué: "Every day in every way, we are getting better and better."

The New York stock market had taken off like a peg-legged man in a forest fire. Stocks rose at a dizzying rate, and almost everybody got into the game. It was easy: you could buy a piece of America's greatest companies for a tiny down payment—*margin*—and then, in only a few days or weeks, pay the rest from your profits as the value of your stock soared.

It seems an embodiment of the times that New York's mayor was a personable, dapper ex-songwriter, Jimmy Walker ("Will You Love Me in December as You Do in May?"), who loved dice, night clubs, and prize fighters. It was said that Texas Guinan ruled New York by night, and Jimmy by day. He was, perhaps, the perfect exemplar not merely of the New York era but also of the whole decade when Jimmy said, "To me, a reformer is a guy who rides through a sewer in a glass-bottom boat."

Who but some joy-killing eccentric would have paid any attention to the fact that the nation's newly created money masters at the Federal Reserve had increased the amount of money in circulation by a fantastic amount? With such affluence and confidence abounding, who could care that in the nine years from 1920 to 1929 the Fed had allowed the nation's spendable money supply (in those days, essentially currency in circulation plus other readily available alternatives to cash, such as bank accounts and Treasury securities) to increase by well over *60 percent?* It was ever so easy to let the money supply expand now. The Federal Reserve just kept lowering the amount of money that banks had to keep on hand as a reserve to protect depositors, thereby giving the banks ever more money to loan and speculators ever easier money to borrow and then spend for whatever they chose—most particularly, because it was the most fun, more money for margin.

In being thus able to manipulate bank reserve requirements like a yo-yo, to inflate the money supply and thus create inflation, the Fed (surely without intention) used that power to cause the very conditions that brought on the "Crash of '29" and the resultant Great Depression. I refer to

Fed practices of those years, any discussion of which would have seemed not only esoteric but downright uninteresting to the red-blooded investor: things like a wide-ranging purchase of acceptances (of time drafts or bills of exchange for payment when due), or open market purchase of government obligations (Treasury bills, bonds, notes, etc.), or ridiculously low rediscount rates for negotiable securities. A courageous few summed up all these practices as a "cheap money" policy debasing the national currency, but such a topic of conversation soon proved the easiest possible way to make oneself a crashing bore at any cocktail party in the Twenties.

Still the government, through the Federal Reserve, was only demonstrating once again that every major depression is a direct result (although sometimes taking many years before culminating in the final crash) of inflation directly caused by deliberate government foo-doodling with the nation's money. It was true in the collapse of 1837, and true also in that whing-dinger of a crash in 1873, which came about as a result of the federally inspired inflation during and immediately after the Civil War; and just as true in the depression of 1893, which followed the inflation that the government brought about by printing short-term silver certificates, or notes. The Sherman Silver Purchase Act of 1890 had directed the Treasury to buy 4.5 million ounces of unneeded silver each month (to the delight of silver producers) and to issue inflationary Treasury notes based on this silver.

Then, in the Roaring Twenties, we were heading for depression times again, but who was watching? President Warren Harding and his Vice-President, Calvin Coolidge, had presided over the first four years of the decade, having clobbered the Democratic team of James Cox and Franklin D. Roosevelt in 1920. No two men could have been more different than Harding and Coolidge.

Harding was friendly, simple, charming, gregarious, handsome, admittedly a ladies' man, perhaps well-meaning but none too bright and certainly unbelievably ill-informed.

In fact he was frighteningly incompetent, never quite able to grasp a problem, his mind cloudy and confused. His now notorious use, or misuse, of the English language was perhaps second only to that of movie producer Sam Goldwyn ("he was a milestone around everybody's neck"). Harding spoke of adhesion to treaties, of betrothment instead of betrothal. In tragic bewilderment, he found himself presiding over the nation's greatest scandal to date, Teapot Dome, which saw the disgrace of three members of his Cabinet and several of his closest friends. The Secretary of the Navy and the Attorney-General resigned. His Secretary of the Interior, Albert B. Fall, was sentenced to a year in jail and fined $100,000 for taking a bribe.

Even the easy-going, fun-loving Harding became both worried and despondent. He sought to escape Washington and tried to regain the nation's confidence by setting out with his wife on a nationwide speech-making tour in June 1923. However, the normally vigorous President fell ill with food poisoning on July 28 and, by the time his train reached San Francisco, was clearly exhausted. He developed pneumonia and, after seemingly on the way to recovery, suddenly died under highly mysterious circumstances. The official announcement called Harding's death a stroke, but the exact cause of the President's death has never been explained.

Calvin Coolidge was something else indeed. "Silent Cal's" chief prior claim to fame had been the breaking of a Boston police strike while mayor of that city.

He was, to say the least, an eccentric. He always had his hair cut while eating breakfast. He believed that the best government was the least government and proceeded to practice what he preached. Coolidge worked fewer hours and assumed fewer tasks than any other President before him. Painfully taciturn, he told the press curtly that he just handled the big problems. And because his schedule each day was not, to say the least, overly taxing, Coolidge became a practical joker. He would ring the bell at the front gate of the White House and then disappear before the sentry could reach the gate. Once, he walked up the long, brocaded train of a dress Mrs. Coolidge was trying on. Another time, just for the devilment of it, he created a terrible scene because a Secret Service man to whom he had given a dime to buy a five-cent magazine had forgotten to return the other nickel. In 1927, he invited some friends from Vermont to visit him and have dinner at the White House. His small-town friends, worried about their table manners in such august surroundings, jointly decided that the best policy was to watch the President and do everything that he did. When time finally came for the coffee course, to the surprise of his guests Coolidge promptly poured his coffee into a saucer. His guests did the same. Then the President added sugar and cream. The visitors did likewise. Coolidge then leaned over and gave his saucer to the cat, leaving his guests in both consternation and a predicament.

While the stock market zoomed on to incredible heights and the Federal Reserve continued to pour forth new money to feed the appetite of a happy populace, Coolidge spent most of his time rocking on the White House porch or wandering around the halls in his long nightshirt. When he chose not to run for a second full term in 1927, his one-sentence announcement was typically Coolidge. It said, only, "I do not choose to run for President in 1928."

Perhaps the public perception of Coolidge's personality and presidency was best shown by an incident that occurred some five years later, on January 5, 1933, in his sixtieth year. On that date, Jack Dempsey and a few friends were playing poker at the Algonquin Hotel in New York. Among the players was the great wit Wilson Mizner. During the poker game, the door to the room suddenly burst open and an excited assistant manager announced to the card game in a grave, hushed voice, "Gentlemen, Calvin Coolidge is dead."

Mizner never looked up from the table. "How can they tell?" he asked.

Of course, the stock market had crashed in October 1929, as the normal, natural, and inevitable consequence of the government's deliberate decade-long inflation of the U.S.

money supply. Beginning with a 31-point drop on October 23, 1929, the market in just over fourteen more trading days dropped from an average of 415 to 248—a plunge of more than 40 percent.

Like an earlier bubble in the South Seas, the 1929 bubble had not only burst but exploded. The long, dazzling boom was over.

The tulip was dead.

The economic policies of a desperate President Herbert Hoover, an earnest and hard-working man, flailed about like a catfish on a sandbank. Virtually everything he tried not only didn't work but actually made the depression worse. His well-meant creation of the Reconstruction Finance Corporation—the RFC—was a classic example of doing the wrong thing at the wrong time. It was an agency created to prop up *unsound* businesses and thus was simply a further jolt to what was left of the free enterprise machinery.

Even so, there *was* a lot left. The nation was still economically sound. We were still not only solvent but the dollar still *was* literally almost as good as gold. Left alone, the free marketplace would have righted itself, given time.

In fact, the United States had been making a slow but certain recovery from the recession when, in 1931, inflation and unbalanced budgets in Europe, plus unlimited currency issues and excessive borrowing by European nations from U.S. banks, resulted in the gigantic European financial collapse of that year. Hoover, with the support of both Senate and House leaders, quickly got a one-year moratorium on European debt payments to the United States, but it was too late. However, the critical point is this: America's capitalistic economy had begun to right itself within the remarkably short period of two years when the European crash suddenly stalled the movement toward recovery.

Also to the good was the fact that the nation then owed a public debt of only $16 billion ($132 per capita), which was far less than when the decade began.

But even if Hoover had known all the right answers, time was the one thing he did *not* have.

In 1931, amid a drought, with breadlines, soup kitchens, and apple sellers on every corner, with federal troops firing on bonus marchers and farmers sitting on their front porches to defend against foreclosures, it was election time again. Hoover, who only four years before had run on the prosperity ticket ("a chicken in every pot"), made the last of his classic list of mistakes: he decided to seek reelection.

Of course the Depression and the election weren't the only events that caught the public's attention. In that election year, fate also played a dirty trick on the underwear business. Back in 1932, every man wore an undershirt. It would have been undignified, unthinkable to be without one. But the hit motion picture of 1932 was *It Happened One Night*. In one scene of the movie, in a tourist court, Clark Gable took off his shirt in front of his leading lady, Claudette Colbert. Scandalously, there stood the handsome Gable nude from the waist up—wearing no undershirt! Women swooned with delight, and the undershirt business almost went under. Business dropped 50 percent in a single year.

The election year of 1931 was also the year of the Lindbergh kidnapping. It was the year that saw the passing of an era, as former President William Howard Taft died in Washington. It was also the year that the famous pioneer sports broadcaster Graham McNamee made the first nationwide broadcast of the Poughkeepsie Regatta—the Kentucky Derby of rowing. It was, in fact, the first time that the irrepressible McNamee had ever broadcast a rowing event. Over NBC radio, he excitedly reported to the nation from his broadcast booth near the finish line, an astonishing upset victory by the underdog MIT crew. Graham was not to discover until after he had gone off the air that, to his horror, the MIT crew not only had *not* won but had actually sunk halfway back down the Poughkeepsie river.

Was there an augury of the future in this blooper? Or was one of MIT's fun-loving competitors simply guilty of *augery?*

President Hoover's opponent in 1932 was the handsome, ambitious, brilliant speaker and former Assistant Secretary of the Navy and governor of New York, Franklin D.

Roosevelt. To his credit, Roosevelt refused to attack Hoover personally, saying that the nation should not tolerate abuse heaped upon the person of the President of the United States. Then again, Roosevelt knew that he didn't have to get personal.

Instead, the Democrats in 1932 focused their attention upon Republican waste and spending. A glittering array of Democratic slogans appeared, among them, ''Throw the Spenders Out!'' and ''Sound Currency at all Hazards!''

Roosevelt's campaign speeches followed that lead. After all, he pointed out, the Hoover administration had operated $462 million in the red the year before. (In the one year 1979, the government went into debt some $65.5 *billion*.) Roosevelt also lashed out at what he called the incredible Hoover public debt—all $16 billion of it.

''My friends,'' Roosevelt told the nation on the radio, ''I ask you very simply to assign to me the task of reducing the annual operating expenses of your national government. Any government, like a family, can for a year spend a little more than it earns. But you and I know that a continuation of that habit means the poorhouse. Let us have the courage to stop the deficits.''

To accomplish this, Roosevelt promised to stop the growth of government bureaus and to stick rigidly to the gold standard.

With 12 million unemployed, Roosevelt slaughtered Hoover at the polls. Quite suddenly, Americans had the NRA, the Blue Eagle, the New Deal.

They also had Roosevelt's announced opposition to further government bureaucracy and his devotion to the discipline of a gold-backed dollar.

Or did they?

By May 1933, less than two months after he took office, Roosevelt had accomplished passage of legislation ordering every American citizen, under threat of fine and imprisonment, to turn in all gold—coin, bullion, or gold certificates. Americans would be given other forms of currency as legal tender. Federal Reserve banks delivered the confiscated gold to the U.S. Treasury Department.

Almost immediately thereafter, Roosevelt announced abandonment of the gold standard.

With the citizenry safely stripped of all private gold, Roosevelt was free to devalue the dollar, and he quickly engineered the Gold Reserve Act of January 1934. Having done so, he promptly devalued the dollar by 50 percent.

The Gold Reserve Act of 1934 deserves more than passing note. It was nefarious in many respects. It did not merely confiscate the gold of all citizens in return for paper "gold certificates." Outrageously enough, in a country still financially sound and solvent, the Act provided, first, that these certificates, despite their title, were *not* redeemable in gold and, second, that the gold dollar the citizen could no longer have would be reduced to not more than 60 percent nor less than 50 percent of its former weight. That is what "devaluation" means. If you devalue a currency, perforce you must lessen its value against *something*. In this case, the dollar was not devalued against some other currency (as often happens in Europe), but devaluated (declared to be worth some percentage lower than before) against *gold*. It was small consolation that the Treasury announced a "stabilization fund" for the now weakened dollar, which fund would hold the "profit" made from the devaluation.

The Gold Reserve Act set forth what might be called a two-tier gold bullion standard. All U.S. paper certificates of indebtedness (currencies, notes, etc.) would henceforth not be redeemable in gold for American citizens but would be redeemable (at $35 an ounce) for all foreign central banks and governments upon demand. These governments and their central banks could then, if they wanted, pass on the U.S. gold to their own merchants, who had earned it through trade with U.S. businesses, or not pass it on, as the governments saw fit. Thus was the pattern set for the U.S. government to auction off in the seventies millions upon millions of ounces of this enormous hoard of embezzled gold—always auctions in which only foreigners could bid for this treasure seized from the American people by their government. It was one of the most blatant international larcenies in history. But the U.S. populace perceived its condition as being one of desperation, and thus it almost complacently accepted the rip-off as some sort of necessary price that the new administration was charging it to restore "prosperity for all."

It is vital to try to describe here the state of the nation and the mood of the people when Roosevelt took office. They were hungry; hundreds of banks had gone broke or had closed; and hundreds of thousands of individuals had lost their lifetime savings. Congress was confused, divided, helpless, in disrepute, and also utterly supine. The only person the people had confidence in was Roosevelt. They wanted a strong man, and they got one. For the first several months, at least, Roosevelt enjoyed every power of a dictator.

Far from opposing the new President, virtually every member of Congress was deliriously happy to hand him the problems and be directed by him at his whatever whim. Besides, to have opposed Roosevelt in those early months of his administration would have been political suicide, almost enough to risk a recall vote by a Congressman's constituency.

In the early months of his presidency, Roosevelt literally could send a bill to Congress for passage in the morning and find it on his desk for signature in the early afternoon.

During that first 99-day session of Congress in 1933, Roosevelt in fact had the sort of mandate that a future President will need if the United States is to remain a great—or even an important—nation; or, perhaps, even a nation! Actually, that future President will require even more power than did Roosevelt, for he will have to contend not only with a Congress as least as dazed as it was in 1933 but also with a court system that has become a national disgrace. No meaningful national reform, fiscal or otherwise, is possible without beginning at the judiciary.

Thomas Jefferson, in some ways as strict a Constitutionalist as James Madison, and determined that his country should remain a republic and not lapse into the doom that awaits any democracy, had opposed judicial review almost from the start, ever since Chief Justice John Marshall's landmark decision in *Marbury* vs. *Madison*. Jefferson rightfully took the position that Marshall's decision constituted a threat to peoples' liberties from that department of the government least subject to popular control.

James Madison had clearly felt equally uneasy even earlier when the Father of the Constitution said in 1788:

> . . . As the courts are generally the last in making the decision, it results to them, by refusing or not refusing to execute a law, to stamp it with its final character. This makes the Judiciary Department paramount in fact to the Legislature, which was *never intended and can never be proper*. (Italics are mine.)

Supreme Court Justice Felix Frankfurter, writing a century and a half later, had had the chance to see all of the fears of Jefferson and Madison become dreadful truth:

> People have been taught to believe that when the Supreme Court speaks it is not they who speak but the Constitution; whereas, of course, in so many vital cases, it is *they* who speak and *not* the Constitution. And I verily believe that this is what the country needs most to understand.

For by Frankfurter's time, the United States Supreme Court had already abandoned its Constitutional reason for existence, judicial review, for a new role as a court of *judicial activism*.

I should add that the preceding two paragraphs point to the very reason why, in this book on investing, we have begun with a slice of history before proceeding toward the potential riches to be made from strategic metals. The fact is, as I hope you are beginning to see, that in the long run, in a runaway government with no sensible restraint, there will be no sound dollar—and thus little likelihood of benefit to you, no matter how wisely you invest your money.

The capitalist machinery took other jarring shots during Roosevelt's first term in office.

Organized labor quickly seized its opportunity in the midst of the turmoil of the change of administrations, and aided by Roosevelt's determination to redistribute the wealth, dealt both business and the free enterprise system a blow from which they could not recover. It came in the form of the iniquitous Norris—LaGuardia Anti-Injunction Act of 1932, which curbed the power of the judiciary to employ its injunctive powers against unions for possible or probable future damages. That Act accomplished all that a union could ever desire: freedom to indulge in illegal activities, including violence, that would bankrupt a company before it could respond; the right to render unenforceable any contract that an employee might make with an employer not to join a union; and the capacity to apply union pressures against employers that left the latter no alternative but to cave in to union demands before the union decided to cave them in by other and now legal methods.

The fact that the act had taken away from every working man a fundamental *right*—his right to contract for his services with whomever he wished—seemed lost within the times. The succeeding Wagner Act of 1935, which gave to the union-dominated National Labor Relations Board (NLRB) virtually supreme powers and furthermore made it illegal for an employer to refuse collective bargaining, only put more frosting on labor's cake. No legislation since passed, including the Taft—Hartley Act of 1947, has been able to remedy the damage wrought by the Norris—LaGuardia Act. For since then, a strike has become all too often merely a period of rest the union desires before deciding that it is time to force the employer to accept pretty much whatever concessions the union had in mind in the first place. The vast majority of working people are not members of unions and are thus (like members of the unions themselves) damaged by the higher prices that helpless employers must pass on to the public as the result of coercive and uneconomic contracts. But this fact seems strangely lost upon the American people.

There were still more shocks to come in 1933. On May 12, a few simple but deadly amendments were tacked onto an agricultural act, authorizing the President to issue greenbacks, provide for free and unlimited coinage of silver, and take other measures to increase the quantity of money. The stated objective was to raise prices as a method of increasing prosperity. These addenda came to be known as "the inflation amendments."

Then there was the Banking Act of 1935, which—among other things—changed the organization and powers of the board of governors of the Federal Reserve System, giving it further powers to increase or decrease reserve requirements of member banks.

Meanwhile, other currents, big and small, were moving through the country. In 1936, Walt Disney, having labored like a mountain, brought forth a mouse named Mickey. John D. Rockefeller reached the age of 97 without a false tooth in his head. The biggest news story of the year came from London, involving a Baltimore beauty and King Edward VIII. As Big Ben tolled the hour on the night of December 11th, London's great Piccadilly Circus was abandoned, New York subways were empty in the rush hour, and from Sydney to Seattle, the world tuned in to hear King Edward give up his throne for "the woman I love." The highest paid gossip in the world was Walter Winchell, who said, "People who live in tin houses should not throw can openers." Of a girl's beauty, he said, "She looks better on the telephone." Winchell quoted Clarence Darrow as saying, "I don't believe in murder, but I've read many an obituary with pleasure." Later on, as war clouds loomed overhead, one of Winchell's prize cracks was that things were so confused in Washington, not even the German spies knew what was going on.

He had a point. For by 1936, Roosevelt had transformed Washington into a fairyland of government recovery bureaus—first, the National Recovery Administration (NRA); then, the Works Progress Administration (WPA), the Civilian Conservation Corps (CCC), the Home Owners' Land Corporation, the Farm Credit Corporation, and hundreds of others. There were so many government bureaus by 1936 that a salmon swimming up the Columbia River and trying to spawn passed under the jurisdiction of twelve different government agencies in the effort. The Department of Commerce had a National Committee on Wood Utilization, which itself had a subcommittee on uses for second-hand boxes and pieces of lumber. The personnel directory of the National Production Authority listed an Administrative Officer in the Administrative Services Division of the Office of the Assistant Administrator for Administration.

There were now and then some questions about why the United States was paying to build a huge university in Ethiopia, say, or about the logic being used in continuing the Commodity Credit Corporation, which had already lost billions since its establishment in 1933. (Similarly, in 1953 a few legislators no doubt also wondered on occasion why the federal government owned 23 rubber factories, railroads, a rum factory, sugar factories, a paint plant, a rope-making plant, a coffee-roasting plant, and hundreds of other businesses. All of them were operated at heavy losses each year.)

Some lawmakers were upset. The national budget was now $8.4 billion instead of the $4.6 billion it had been when Roosevelt took over. The federal debt, which had been $19.5 billion when Hoover left office, was now $33.8 billion.

Roosevelt's opponent at the polls in 1936 was Alf Landon, the "Kansas Coolidge." One of America's most respected magazines, the *Literary Digest,* predicted that Landon would win, with 370 electoral votes to Roosevelt's 161. Instead, the result was Roosevelt 523, Landon 8, *Literary Digest* (the most prominent news magazine of its day) out of business.

In 1938, the big radio programs were Myrt and Marge, the Goldbergs, the Voice of Experience, Col. Stoopnagle and

Budd, Tony Wons and his Scrapbook. Diego Rivera told intimates that Charlie Chaplin had given $50,000 to the Communist cause, and Chaplin's image with Americans suffered a heavy blow.

And by the late 1930s it was again dark all over the world. Germany's Weimar Republic was history; the Reichstag had been burned; Japan, already in Manchuria, was moving against China; the League of Nations was dying in Geneva; and fear lay heavy across Europe. Americans woke up mornings to hear the chilling reverberations of "Sieg Heils," made to sound even more ominous by shortwave distortion.

In Washington, the President had other problems. In October 1937, the stock market had crashed again. Administration critics said that this was the end of Roosevelt's "New Deal." The crisis was almost as great as that of 1932. Again, more than 10 million people were unemployed. Despite Roosevelt's alphabet soup of recovery bureaus, industrial production had suddenly gone down by nearly 35 percent. Apparently, that ol' debbil Depression had not been killed—merely stunned with $37.2 billion worth of knockout drops—and now the anesthesia was wearing off.

The Roosevelt position was terribly embarrassing. He had denounced Hoover, categorically, as a spendthrift, for refusing to cut taxes, and for his failure to balance the budget. Yet in 1938 the federal debt, as we have seen, had zoomed upward; taxes had reached a new all-time high; moreover, it cost the government $6.7 billion to pay for itself instead of the $4.6 billion it cost when Roosevelt took office.

The President relied on the theories of a British economist, John Maynard Keynes, who had made what some thought to be a great economic discovery. His theory was simply that a government debt is not like a private debt—that government could go into debt on a scale that would crush an individual or family. Keynes declared that a government debt was not a *national* debt at all but merely a debt of the *people* of the nation. The people of the nation owed the debt to the bondholders, and the bonds belonged to the people, so the people really owed a debt to themselves, and what was so wrong with that? Keynes' poisonous theory, the fallacy of which was

obvious to many,* came as manna from heaven to the
Roosevelt administration. For in 1938 Roosevelt needed to
justify spending far greater amounts of money to restimulate
the economy. That year was the most critical year Roosevelt
faced in the 13 years he held office.

What with the country having lapsed into deep recession
again, many Americans who only five years earlier had gone
along unquestioningly with Roosevelt's "New Deal"—out
of either confusion or desperation—were now beginning
publicly to question the "solutions" they had so eagerly
embraced in 1933.

In particular, blacks and other minorities, were openly
critical of what just yesterday had seemed like such a good
idea: the minimum-wage laws which arrived in 1938 as an
NRA by-product called the Fair Labor Standards Act.
Despite Washington bureaucrats, industry could only pay a
worker the wage that his productivity justified, and since the
productivity of many unskilled (and even some skilled)
workers did not justify the minimum hourly wage mandated
by the new law, factories had no choice but to lay off workers
rather than violate the law. Industrial production dropped
like a rock. Hundreds of thousands of workers whose
productive ability was worth less in hourly dollar value than
the wage that by federal law had to be paid them each hour
were simply dismissed. As usual, the minorities were first
and worst hit. Unskilled white and older workers were also
finding jobs scarce at the new artificially-fixed and
government-dictated wages at which cost, clearly, industry
found their employment unprofitable.

Then there was Social Security. By 1938 the Social
Security Act of 1935 was beginning to give many economists
migrainish second thoughts. What had perhaps seemed to

---

*Although the government owes its public debt to the bondholder and to the
holders of other federal securities, only a small fraction of the people hold any
government paper. Thus, the government debt is not one owed to the people, but
rather only to that tiny percentage who possess federal bonds or other such
federally backed obligations.

government accountants as a viable federal insurance system was not turning out that way at all. The Social Security system as originally set forth was to have been self-sustaining within 20 years. (Eighteen years later, the system would become part of an enormous new federal agency called the Department of Health, Education and Welfare.) But in the meantime new benefits, including cost-of-living escalations, had been voted, and the fresh taxes that were to pay for it all had not been levied. Over the years, the Act of 1935, which had provided for a system of federal old-age benefits for workers, a federal–state system of unemployment insurance, and federally financed aid to the states to help them provide public aid to dependent children plus the needy blind and aged, became a giant, unfunded federal albatross. By 1974, the government trust fund for the payment of Social Security benefits had little money on hand, and *more than $2.5 trillion in liabilities*.

That same year, Roger LeRoy Miller, writing in *Harper's Magazine*, called Social Security "the cruelest tax of all." As with the minimum wage, blacks and other minorities were the most adversely affected and the wealthy the least. That is because under the Act, the sooner you begin to work (and minorities have a shorter life span), the more you collect. Millions who have paid Social Security taxes will never collect a dime. As the birth rate in the United States continues to decline, and as people live longer and retire earlier, the number of older people to whom Social Security checks must be sent is increasing enormously, and the amount of money that must eventually be paid out by law is increasing almost exponentially. Social Security recipients will soon outnumber the workers who must pay them. At the beginning, most workers had the mistaken notion that their employer was paying dollar-for-dollar with the worker toward the old-age check and other "insurance" benefits he would get. Not so. It is, as always, the worker who pays. For the employer quite legally lists his contribution as simply another expense item, passing this increased cost of doing business onto the worker in the form of higher prices—

more inflation. It is, once again, the old story of the government attempting to operate a business—in this case an insurance business—and making its usual massively miserable mess. If Social Security were needed, wouldn't it have been so much better for the government simply to pass a law making it mandatory that every citizen carry old-age insurance with any one of hundreds of well-operated, sound U.S. insurance companies? Social Security is most assuredly the most costly and damaging welfare program ever foisted upon an unsuspecting American worker. Worst of all, the cost of this program is taken right out of his paycheck, in ever-increasing amounts each year.

Like all attempts to redistribute the wealth that have come along since the first timid attempts to tamper with the Constitution and convert the United States from a republic to a democracy, Social Security has backfired with a bang the equivalent of an economic hydrogen bomb.

But in 1938 the bomb had not yet gone off, and there was still time to speculate about whether the new minimum wage and the Social Security Act had been such good ideas after all. And for that matter, what about the 1932 Glass–Steagall Act, which seemed to most fiscal conservatives a sort of final nail in the coffin of a sound dollar? That act, in authorizing the substitution in bank reserve requirements of government securities for private notes and commercial paper—both of which had become quite scarce because of the Great Depression—clearly, to put it gently, placed the political needs of an administration ahead of the best interests of business. George Christy, longtime professor of finance at North Texas University, has declared the Glass-Steagall Act as one of his "three milestones to crisis" and declared that it was with this act that the government provided final permission to the Federal Reserve to begin treating the Treasury's debt as money and so to inflate limitlessly.

Clearly trouble was brewing. But there were still a few good laughs for a restless public.

In 1939, George Jessel was making his weekly radio

broadcast for a well-known hair-restoring product. Just as Jessel was telling a national radio audience that the hair restorer would make bald heads bloom like fragrant gardens, his wig slipped down over his nose and nearly smothered him. That same year the Broadway critics began to lay it on. Tallulah Bankhead opened in *Cleopatra*. Critic John Mason Brown wrote in the New York *Herald-Tribune* the next morning, "Last night, Tallulah Bankhead barged down the Nile as Cleopatra—and sank." About the play *Halfway to Hell,* drama critic Brooks Atkinson observed, "When Mr. Wilbur calls his play *Halfway to Hell,* he underestimates the distance." But the most incisive line of the year belonged to critic Eugene Field of the Boston *Globe*. When a famous star opened in Boston playing King Lear, Field wrote, "He plays the King as though someone had just led the ace."

Those bittersweet summer days of 1939 . . . The nights had never been kinder to the Riviera than in that pleasure-drenched summer. But as the brilliant, sunlit weather cascaded across the Continent, hopes for an equally glorious autumn turned to ashes. European intrigue burst into a sheet of flame. Suddenly, there were new words: Stuka, panzer, Messerschmitt, Rommel, Quisling, von Rundstedt, blitzkrieg, Danzig, Heinkel, and Deutschland, Deutschland.

At home, Roosevelt's problem of 1938—how to prime our business pump with more money—was gone. With the war in Europe, spending for U.S. defense and for lend-lease to our allies could be justified easily. Hoover's $4 billion budget for 1931 had become $9 billion. The federal debt of $16.8 billion in 1931 would pass $40 billion in 1939.

To meet new commitments to Britain, Roosevelt now began regulating American industrial production.

It is told that a young lady from the Middle West went to Washington and got a job in the capital's bureaucratic maze. Proud of herself, she wrote her parents, "I work in the data analysis group of the aptitude test sub-unit of the worker analysis section of the division of occupational analysis and management tables of the Bureau of Labor Utilization,

which is under the Office of Emergency Management.'' Of
course, her mother did the only sensible thing—and ordered
her to come home immediately.

Space had to be rented in 107 private buildings in 1938 to
house all the bureaucrats.

Dr. Alvin Hansen, an economics professor at Harvard,
had been brought to Washington to head the President's
economic program. Hansen was a wholehearted supporter
of the Keynesian theory that the size of a national debt had
no significance, since the people owed the money to themselves. A member of Hansen's staff publicly proclaimed that
in years to come the government might go into debt a
thousand billion dollars (one trillion) without being unduly
concerned.

Two other members of the President's intimate group of
advisers—Roosevelt's "Brain Trust"—also made themselves heard on the subject of government spending. Rex-
ford Tugwell and Leon Henderson both admitted that the
Roosevelt spending program up to 1938 had been a failure.
But they assigned the failure to an astonishing reason: the
President had spent on far too modest a scale. Tugwell said
that the President should have spent four times as much.

But it was all right, anyway, because by 1940 we were
indeed spending at such a rate.

There was nothing new about the government's tax-and-
borrow-and-spend formula. The first statesman to discover
it, Pericles, in the city-state of Athens some 2400 years ago,
produced a great prosperity built on war spending and
borrowing which, of course, finally ended in war, the death
of himself, and the ruin of Athens. But credit for refinement
of the tax-and-borrow-and-spend formula in its modern form
must be given to a gentleman named John Law, who lived in
France during the reign of Louis XV. Law produced the first
great bank-borrowing boom in history, the most fantastic
financial bubble ever conceived up to that day. With it, he
ruined France financially for many years and fled Paris with a
mob at his heels. So, in one form or another, it must always
be.

In recent times, for years a man named Harry Byrd sat like the conscience of America under the big clock above the main table in the United States Senate, watching the clock tick away the wasted hours, burning in frustration at congressional extravagance, and warning his colleagues that the time had come to stop. His own state of Virginia in 1951 was able to cut her tax rates 20 percent. The state had no cigarette tax. The legislature had simply looked over the apparatus of government and found that the state's business was being run by fifty departments, which were promptly reduced to eight. The way to stop spending, said the tough old Byrd from Virginia, was to stop.

But back to 1940, another election year, and Mr. Roosevelt handily defeated the immortal amateur, the Barefoot Boy from Wall Street, Wendell Willkie, who became the first presidential candidate in history ever to use the word "damn" in a public speech. As we moved into a new decade, the country was still at peace, yet Americans could almost hear the rumble of war from across the Atlantic. The United States tottered on the brink of the whirlpool but had not yet been dragged in. Col. Charles A. Lindbergh, Jr., America's greatest shining hero of the 1920s, was a voice crying into the wind. Unaware of Hitler's unspeakable atrocities against the Jews, Lindbergh warned Americans to avoid entanglement in what he called "another of Europe's age-old struggles."

Lindbergh was a conservative by upbringing. His father, Representative Charles Lindbergh, Sr., had been the fiercest of all congressmen in opposing the creation of the Federal Reserve System.* Now, his son, the Lone Eagle, was joined in his forebodings about America's entrance into the war by hard-bitten old General Hugh Johnson, once a New Deal advocate and now one of its bitterest critics. Johnson cautioned the country that when the United States meddled in Europe, we were "shooting craps with destiny."

---

*"From now on, depressions will be scientifically created," Representative Lindbergh, Sr., said in 1913.

The warnings were, of course, much too late. In Washington, spending was up to more than $13 billion from the $4.5 billion of ten years before. The federal debt had skyrocketed from $19.5 billion to over $49 billion in the eight years since Americans had been given a "New Deal."

In Europe, by mid-1940, Norway was gone, Denmark had fallen, and across the bright tulip fields of Holland, Dutch blood flowed like red wine. The death beaches of Dunkirk, which a moonlit May sky, together with light from the burning fields of North Flanders, had turned a murky yellow, were now German.

In Hollywood, meanwhile, the golden children of the West were in high form. On Broadway, the most talked-about star was Tallulah Bankhead. She told newspapers that her private life was "as pure as the driven slush." MGM's Howard Dietz remarked, "A day away from Tallulah is like a month in the country." Someone else said, "When vitamins get tired, they take her." Sex researcher Dr. Alfred C. Kinsey asked for an interview with Tallulah to discuss her habits in that field. She consented, but only on condition that she could ask Dr. Kinsey the same questions. That prompted Kinsey to drop the entire matter.

In late 1941, Franklin D. Roosevelt sent a note to Japan warning that any further Japanese advance toward Singapore would bring America into war against Japan. Pearl Harbor followed on December 7.

In 1942, government waste in spending brought forth many scandals. On the last day of the fiscal year, the Air Force was abruptly faced with the alternative of spending a million dollars or turning it back to Congress. The Air Force hastily bought 142 miles of chain-link fencing and 500 miles of barbed wire, most of it lying in storage for many years thereafter. Likewise, the Army found that on the last day of its fiscal year, it still had $45 million it must hurriedly spend. The Army forthwith purchased 1,250,000 raincoats, which used up the $45 million. Then the Army discovered that it already had on hand over a million raincoats. Worse, when the million and a quarter more raincoats arrived, they were found unsuitable for use.

The joke in currency around Washington was that a government efficiency expert had walked into an office one day to find two men who were doing absolutely nothing and had promptly fired one of them for duplication.

By 1942, government spending was $72.4 billion, compared to the $4.6 billion of 1932, only ten years earlier. And the wartime jag increased to $79 billion in 1943, $95 billion in 1944, and $98 billion in 1945.

If some had begun to think American spending was getting out of line, the newly organized United Nations (1942, by the U.S., China, Russia, and Great Britain) was ready to deal this country the most staggering financial blow it was ever to suffer. In early July 1944, officials of the United Nations, with understandably little fanfare, assembled government monetary officials representing its member nations at Bretton Woods, New Hampshire. There, although neither operation had been contemplated in the UN Charter, two new UN agencies were created. The first was the so-called World Bank, which was to recirculate the financial life's blood of member countries—with particular accent on that of the United States—into the arteries of poorer nations in such staggering billions as to defy the imagination. The second, the International Monetary Fund (IMF) established fixed exchange rates as part of a world monetary system, with the U.S. dollar as the key currency.

As Leonard Silk, the *New York Times* economics analyst, recently noted: "Other countries gained a competitive advantage over this country because the dollar was overvalued—until the collapse of the Bretton Woods system and depreciation of the dollar in the early 1970's. . . ."

One more item on the Bretton Woods system is to the point here. The *Times* of London declared in 1979 that Harry Dexter White—an obscure Treasury official who led the U.S. delegation—and John Maynard Keynes were, respectively, the American and the British intellectual architects of

the post-war monetary system put together at Bretton
Woods. Who was Harry Dexter White? In 1953, the then
Attorney General, Herbert Brownell, informed the nation
that Harry Dexter White was a Russian spy.

But in 1945, for America at least, the long war was finally
over. Few Americans gave attention to the fact that on
November 23, 1946, fighting had erupted in Asia between the
French and northern Indo-Chinese (Vietnam) troops. In
1945, America's vast fighting forces, scattered from Johan-
nesburg to Vladivostok and throughout every sea, could
come home.

There was, at war's end, a respite from tension—indeed, a
marvelous sense of beginning again. After all, wasn't the GI
bill going to give great numbers of American youth a chance
for what had been just a dream until now—a college education? And the new American optimism had other roots,
though we also might have had some nagging doubts about
Russian intentions. Didn't we have a fresh guarantee of
peace in our nuclear monopoly and in the new United
Nations, where all the major powers would get together and
talk away their problems?

Spending could now come down "to normal," wage and
price controls could end, and the free enterprise machinery
could begin functioning again without interference.

Or could it? For almost immediately there was a new
potential U.S. enemy. The traditional Russian push toward
warm water was on; and in China, communism spread like a
red stain down the Yangtze. It had been a brief, sunny return
to optimism. By 1946, the cold war had begun.

That year, without fanfare, Congress also abruptly passed
a law that, needed or not, provided the final "enabling
legislation" for the full conversion of our republic to a
democracy, or from free enterprise to socialism—or, for that
matter, to just about anything else the government wanted.
In passage of the Employment Act of 1946, Congress for the
first time made full employment the direct responsibility of
the federal government. The consequences of the act were
and still are virtually inconceivable in monetary, physical,

and moral dimension. In accepting the responsibility for attempting to maintain full employment, Congress was literally saying to its staff and bureaucracies: "Now, having taken this responsibility, just do whatever you have to do to keep a state of perpetual boom going." For the first time Uncle Sam had printed himself a blank check, and the cost of that carte blanche no one can say. For the Act also gave at least moral justification for any number of actions the government was then subsequently able to take with its new-found carte blanche to stimulate employment. In accepting the Employment Act without protest, the American people had arrived at that philosophical turning point where they apparently were quite willing to lay all their problems at the feet of the federal government and leave them there for solution. In its specific application to employment, the Act was staggering enough: Who among Americans living in the early part of this century, or the 1920s, or even the 1930s, ever thought that if times ever got really tough for a person—a tough old farmer, for example—he could just tell himself that the government was responsible and would look after everything?

The Employment Act of 1946 has been construed to mean full employment: If there aren't any jobs, you make the jobs, even if it means merely shuffling papers and getting a salary at the end of the week. The passage of this Act, which might have been better titled "The Ultimate Enabling Act," simply meant that all the weapons were in place by 1946 for whatever was yet necessary to finish the job on the republic—or even upon that amazingly durable free enterprise machine. If the Act had no philosophical limits, neither did it have practical boundary points. Philosophically, it said, if you have an energy problem, you create a Department of Energy (or anything else) to solve it; if you have an education problem, you create a Department of Education —or whatever.

And so 1946 set the tone for the years to come. The republic was dead. Long live democracy!

The Act had one other devastating effect, and it was moral

in nature. Writing of this legislation in his *A Time for Truth*, former Secretary of the Treasury William E. Simon said:

> In fact, no one can "run" an economic system. . . . But from FDR on, American Presidents have indeed "run" the economy. And since 1947 their performances have been faithfully recorded in the President's yearly Economic Report to Congress, in accordance with the Employment Act of 1946. Since that law requires that the state guarantee the American people "freedom from want," the President must rise once each year before Congress and solemnly proclaim that either (1) he is *about* to create prosperity and security for all or (2) he has *already* created prosperity and security for all. Those are the only two allowed alternatives. And that means essentially that America's Presidents have been legally mandated to engage in intellectual fraud.
>
> The citizen who wants to confront the history of this fraud need merely go to the library, ask for the President's yearly reports to Congress, and read them, from 1947 on.

As an "almost incredible" example, Simon cites President Lyndon B. Johnson as he was leaving office in January 1969:

> The nation is now in its 95th month of continuous economic advance. Both in strength and length, this prosperity is without parallel in our history. We have steered clear of the business-cycle recessions which for generations derailed us repeatedly from the path of growth and progress . . . No longer do we view our economic life as a relentless tide of ups and downs . . . No longer do we consider poverty and unemployment permanent landmarks on our economic scene.

It is because of legislation like the Employment Act of 1946, even though it might have been quite sufficient by itself, that the present writer would, like the distinguished Austrian economist and Nobel laureate Friedrich A. von Hayek, find himself in disagreement with the equally distinguished Nobel laureate Milton Friedman. Inflation in the

United States cannot be slowly phased down to any acceptable level over a period of years, as Friedman contends. The American people are much too spoiled to put up with five or six years of the pain necessary, even granted the disease were subject to cure by degree. The answer must and will come in a short, convulsive, and violent period of only a few months.

But back in 1948 the battles at home seemed far less weighty.

Fred Allen was fighting a tough new radio competitor called "Stop the Music." Fred, disgusted with his network management, cracked jokes about the vice-president in charge of Dixie cups. Fred remarked that the average bureaucrat was a form of executive fungus that attached itself to a desk and which, on a boat, would be called a barnacle. He described a conference of bureaucrats as a meeting at which a group of men who, singly being able to do nothing, agree collectively that nothing can be done.

The other big battle of 1948 was between Harry S. Truman and Thomas E. Dewey. Theodore Roosevelt's daughter Alice Roosevelt Longworth—with embarrassing accuracy—described Dewey as looking "like the little man atop the wedding cake." The election campaign set a record for verbal barbs. "The Old Curmudgeon," Democrat Harold Ickes (Secretary of the Interior from 1933 to 1943), said that the Republicans were suffering from "halitosis of the intellect" and described a prominent Republican as having "mental saddle sores." Ickes said that he was glad that Dewey had "thrown his diaper into the ring again." The Republicans had their own shafts to cast. One of the GOP favorites was "to err is Truman." When President Truman went to Key West for a vacation, one Republican wit said it would be the first time that Truman had known what key he was in. Truman jibed back by saying that a Republican economist was a man who wears a watch chain with a Phi Beta Kappa key at one end and no watch at the other.

But in the flashing, acrid wit of that campaign, observers could not overlook the fact that we were still spending $40 billion in a *peacetime* economy and that the federal debt had become an incredible $257 billion—nearly a quarter trillion more than it had been in 1930, only 18 years earlier. And these were the *published* government figures on our national debt; the *real* amount of the debt was quite another matter.

Then it was a new decade.

The early months of 1950 were quiet enough, but by late spring things got rolling. In May, an obscure Tennessee Senator named Estes Kefauver began televised Senate hearings investigating organized crime; suddenly, daytime TV had come into its own. As Kefauver paraded a motley series of witnesses before the midday cameras, more than 20 million people watched. One of the witnesses was perhaps the foremost figure in organized crime—Frank Costello. About the only crime that Costello admitted, though, was that he was "a friend of some politicians." And 1950 was bringing a torrent of new slang to the country, including at least one word that was to stay: *square*. About the worst thing anyone could call you in 1950 was a *cube*, which was the squarest kind of square.

And then, on June 25, 1950, North Korea invaded South Korea; President Truman, immediately following adoption of a UN resolution calling upon its member nations to resist the North Koreans, ordered American GIs to the remote Asian battlefield. It was a major undeclared war which was to last until July 27, 1953. For the second time in five years, the United States was at war, declared or not. And more spending could, and did, begin.

The presidential campaign in 1952 was not much of a race. The nation's wartime hero, Gen. Dwight D. Eisenhower, took his famous, radiant grin into battle against Democrat Adlai Stevenson. Young Senator John F. Kennedy, a very wealthy man himself, criticized Eisenhower sharply because "all his golfing pals are rich men he's met since 1945."

The Republican nominee for the vice-presidency, Richard M. Nixon, went before an enormous TV audience to defend himself against the charge that he had accepted improper campaign contributions. In his famous "Checkers" rebuttal,

Nixon completely won over the American people as he talked mostly about his little dog. And he remarked, ''My wife Pat and I have the satisfaction that every dime we've got is honestly ours. I should say this—that Pat doesn't have a mink coat, but she does have a good respectable Republican cloth coat.''

The vast TV audience had other special treats in 1952. It was the first time that the whole nation got to see political conventions—70 million watched. Covering the convention for CBS was a slim young commentator for CBS named Walter Cronkite. During and following the convention, Cronkite drew much criticism from his CBS bosses. They said that Walter talked way too much.

During the next years, liberal comedian Mort Sahl, who called himself the intellectual voice of the era (''which is a good measure of the era,'' Sahl said sarcastically) had a field day with his routines about the new Eisenhower administration. Commenting on the power of big business under Ike, Mort cracked, ''One of these days General Motors is going to get sore and cut the Government off without a penny. Incidentally, the Chase Manhattan Bank has itself a lot of subsidiaries, you know—West Germany, for one.'' About spies and the supposed Russian lead over the United States in missiles, Mort said, ''Maybe the Russians will steal all our secrets. . . . Then *they'll* be two years behind.'' Another Sahl stinger about Eisenhower's frequent golfing was, ''If you're in the administration, you have a lot of problems of policy, like whether or not to use an overlapping grip. And I wonder if it isn't legally possible to get a Taft–Hartley injunction that would make the President stay in the White House for 80 consecutive days?''

Federal spending—with the Korean War and built-in items like the interest on the national debt—had already jumped from $39.5 to nearly $70 billion in two years, and the federal debt was nearly $260 billion. In the short span of 100 years, each American's share of the debt had grown from $62.50 to nearly $1700, despite the huge increase in U.S. population.

And in the late summer of 1952, Russia horrified the West

by exploding the first Soviet "superbomb"—the hydrogen bomb—in Siberia; this came only 9 months after the United States had set off its first H bomb at Eniwetok Atoll in the Pacific.

Americans had developed a giant case of doomsday jitters. To avoid radiation fallout, Americans got all sorts of advice: shave dogs and cats to prevent their fur from becoming radioactive; use aluminum pajamas, lead girdles, and lead-foil brassieres. A patent-medicine company started to sell an "atomic shock cure," but was stopped by the U.S. Public Health Service when the active ingredients were discovered to be table salt, bicarbonate of soda, and plain water.

In 1953, Ike's new Secretary of Defense, Charles E. Wilson, formerly president of General Motors, became the frankest man ever to come to Washington. Commenting on Washington's bureaucratic red tape, "Engine Charlie" said, "No inanimate object in Washington will move from one place to another without a piece of paper that goes along telling someone where to move it." On trading with Russia, Wilson said, "I come from a long line of ancestors who believe you shouldn't sell firearms to the Indians." Wilson's Defense Department budget (some $40 billion a year) was 60 percent of all federal spending. (Today, defense expenditure is but 24 percent of U.S. spending.)

U.S. government spending in 1953 jumped back to over $74 billion. The federal debt passed $266 billion. And movie actor James Dean became the overnight hero of all youth, the first national symbol of youth's revolt against "the Establishment." His film *Rebel Without a Cause* set young males afire with desire to imitate him and young females afire with . . . just desire.

That spring, the great comedian Fred Allen was offered a one-week engagement in Las Vegas. Fred said that the hotel there really wanted him badly—that they had offered him $10,000 just to get on a train that was going to Las Vegas. But, Fred told reporters, he had refused.

"It would all go in taxes," he declared. "I'm just a middleman for the government."

And then, as an afterthought, Fred added: "As a matter of fact, let the government go to Las Vegas."

The U.S. national debt in 1953 was higher than the debts of all the other nations on earth put together. England owed only one-fourth as much; Russia only $49 billion, or less than one-fifth as much. France owed only some $10 billion—one twenty-seventh as much as the United States. The combined national debt of Germany and Japan, the two nations we had defeated in World War II, was only one-ninth as much as that of the United States. And yet that year the United States continued to send financial aid to 56 other nations, including England and France.

In 1954 our major cities experienced an explosion of savage, senseless teenage gang wars. By then, TV had changed the habits of a nation. To some it was an "electronic tranquilizer"; to radio's Fred Allen, "an idiot box, the light that failed." Fred said that "television is a triumph of equipment over people, and the minds that control it are so small that you could put them in the navel of a flea and still have room enough left for a network vice-president's heart." The year 1954 was also the end of Senator Joseph R. McCarthy's controversial witch-hunt for U.S. Communists, a hunt that many felt had come close to wrecking the American political system. The Wisconsin Senator, trying to establish un-Americanism in the Army while more than 20 million watched on TV, met his Waterloo in the Army's lawyer—elderly, soft-spoken Joseph Welch. Toward the end of the hearings, the committee's audience was applauding Welch, to McCarthy's bewilderment. Welch, at the finish, told McCarthy, "Until this moment, Senator, I think I never really gauged your cruelty or your recklessness. . . . You have done enough. Have you no sense of decency, sir, at long last? Have you left no sense of honor?"

To anyone who worried about our economy, the nation's favorite nightclub comedian, Joe E. Lewis, had some memorable lines. "I don't worry about all this talk about a depression," said Joe E. "Hell, I went broke in the boom." Another of Joe E.'s favorites was, "Ain't it a shame that a depression has to come along when things are so bad?"

Americans in 1954 paid no attention to the fact that in faraway Asian jungles the French had finally been beaten by northern Indochinese Communists on May 7, 1954, at a place

called Dienbienphu. The French withdrew from Vietnam
within two months, and on July 20, 1954, the Geneva accords
carved out of Indochina four new states: Cambodia, Laos,
and the two Vietnams. South Vietnam, small and weak,
fashioned from a thin shoreline strip alongside the South
China Sea, comprised parts of the former French Indochinese regions of Annam and Cochin China. First Truman, and then the new President, Dwight Eisenhower,
pledged to keep the Communists from taking over South
Vietnam. A leading hawk was Vice-President Nixon, who in
1954 was already advocating our bombing the North Vietnamese Reds in Indochina. Sen. John F. Kennedy had little
faith in the future of the new nation. In fact, upon returning
from a trip to Vietnam on April 6, 1954, young Kennedy was
critical of "predictions of confidence [in Vietnam] which
have lulled the American people."

In 1956 radio announcers were having their usual
"blooper" problems. A confused Andre Baruch one night on
NBC announced his sponsor as "Hands Hind Cream." On
another program the announcer blurted forth, "For the best
in beer, try Buppert's Rear." Still, the real topper that year is
credited to the old baseball star Boots Roffenberger. Being
interviewed on the Wheaties program, he was asked, "Now,
Boots, tell us what is your favorite breakfast, taken with
cream, sugar, and some sort of fruit?" Boots, missing the
whole point, looked the Wheaties announcer squarely in the
face and said, "Ham, eggs and a couple of bottles of beer."

Vice-President Nixon said, "Sincerity is the quality that
comes through on television."

The model of the year was statuesque beauty Suzy Parker,
as talkative as she was lovely. Speaking of her highly proper
Texas background, Suzy blurted: "Nothing unusual. I come
from an average Ku Klux Klan family."

A "new" motion picture process, 3-D, was sweeping the
country in something horrible called *Bwana Devil,* but the
fad was over almost as soon as it began, and the movie
industry said that 3-D now meant dead, dead, dead. Another
overnight hit was chlorophyll, a green substance extracted

from plants that instantly appeared on the market in nearly 100 new products and was supposed to make the breath and body smell totally fresh. Americans had already bought nearly $150 million in chlorophyll products when the authoritative *Journal of the American Medical Association,* a real killjoy, made a telling point: grazing goats all but lived on chlorophyll and smelled worse than almost anything. There was more: skirts went up and up, and when shorts weren't short enough, young girls rolled up the cuffs. Boys' hair was also undergoing a fashion revolution, and one prominent school in New England announced it would expel any boy with a ducktail haircut.

As for the ever-present, ever-growing federal debt, it now had come a long way since the Dismal Thirties—from $16.2 billion in 1930 to $271 billion in 1956. Federal spending under President Eisenhower during this relatively quiet year was $67 billion as against Herbert Hoover's $4.6 billion in 1932. Each American's share of the debt was some $1,750 in 1956, even by government figures. The sum had been $133 in 1932.

In 1957, as always in a peacetime year, more fads hit the nation's youth. The latest college craze was seeing how many students could get into a telephone booth. A *Life* photograph showed twenty-two California college boys crammed into one booth. And other photographs proved that forty students could be sardined into a Volkswagen.

The entertainment sensation of the 1950s was a wiggly youngster named Elvis Presley. In late 1956, he had appeared on the Ed Sullivan Show. After that first show, Sullivan concluded that Presley's bodily movements were so suggestive as to be vulgar. Sullivan said Presley was "unfit for a family audience" and barred Presley from his program. But once Sullivan heard from the nation's female teenagers, he for some reason changed his mind and signed Presley to three further shows for an unheard-of $50,000 each. Eddie Condon wrote in the New York *Journal American* that Elvis "behaved like a sex maniac in public," and quoted Jackie Gleason as saying, "I tell you flatly—he can't last."

In August 1958, the biggest of all the TV quiz shows was "Twenty-One." But, alas, after handsome young Columbia professor Charles Van Doren won $129,000, the New York District Attorney proved that the show was fixed. Contestants were "coached" in advance. What a disillusionment, particularly since mothers had begun telling their daughters that they should marry someone like Van Doren, not "an Elvis Presley."

Although Secretary of Defense Charlie Wilson had retired from government in 1957, he still had plenty to say. On the subject of political ethics, Charlie declared, "There's an old political saying: 'If your political opponent accuses you of being a liar, don't deny it. Accuse him of being a horse thief.' " But Charlie was at his best when speaking about himself: "I'm like the old dog behind the Iron Curtain. It came across to West Germany one day and met another dog. The two dogs talked it over. The first dog asked the other did he get enough to eat over in East Germany, and the answer was yes. Well, the first dog asked, was there anything over there in East Germany he didn't like? And his friend answered, 'Well, yes, I would like to bark when I want to.' "

It was already getting very late for barking. For one thing, it would not be much longer before Charlie Wilson's defense budget would take second place to an item called "welfare" in our national budget. In fact, the very *interest* on our national debt was beginning to approach the size of the defense budget. Although it was peacetime and the Korean War had been over for four years, our federal spending in 1958 alone was still a mind-boggling $69 billion. The debt had reached $271 billion. Instead of owing some $20 per *family,* as we had when the republic was founded, each *person* in each U.S. family now owed well over $2,000 as his or her part of the debt run up by the federal democracy.

At the end of the 1950s, Elizabeth Taylor and Rock Hudson were the number-one moneymakers at American movie boxoffices. Movie fans were soon aghast at the news that singing star Eddie Fisher had left Debbie Reynolds and family for Elizabeth—the hottest triangle of all the turbulent sixties. Even so, the most talked-about star was a foreign sexpot named Brigitte Bardot, whose most talked-about gown was simply a bedsheet which she wrapped around her body in any number of provocative ways. *Time* did not appreciate the Bardot talent in her first and biggest picture, *And God Created Woman:*

> Miss Bardot's picture opens with a shot that promises a good deal more than the picture delivers. There lies Brigitte, stretched from end to end of the Cinemascope screen, bottoms up and as bare as a censor's eyeball. In the hard sun of the Riviera her little round rear glows like a peach, and the camera lingers on the subject as if waiting for it to ripen. If sex is the object, the French have clearly sent a girl to do a woman's job.

Hula hoops were still big stuff, but the fad of Davy Crockett coonskin caps had seen its day.

Also having seen his most prominent day, at least on television, was veteran commentator Edward R. Murrow. One of TV's most talented but controversial commentators, Murrow had caused so many waves that his boss, CBS chief William Paley, finally moved him out of his prime-time position, saying "I just don't want this constant stomach ache Murrow gives me."

And, by that year of 1959, TV had become the biggest of all media. Before "the tube" came along, more than half of us were sound asleep before midnight, but 10 years later three-quarters of all Americans who owned TV sets were still awake watching the late-night shows of Steve Allen or Jack Paar.

And in money matters, there was a strange thing happening. Spending had traditionally gone *down* with the end of a war. Yet somehow, it *hadn't* with the end of the Korean War in 1953. Indeed, it had gone up. The Eisenhower budget of 1959–1960 just exceeded $80 billion, $6 billion *more* than during the Korean conflict. And the national debt had vaulted to nearly $285 billion. It was the beginning of something brand new in American financial experience:

peacetime deficits, and whoppers at that. Annual government spending was never to go down again thereafter; every year after 1960, peacetime or not, federal spending was constantly to increase, with the national debt mounting commensurately. Welfare was by far the fastest-growing item in our expanding national "budget."

Always before, peace had meant a time for reduction of spending and debt. Evidently, new factors now had intervened to maintain the debt at ever-higher levels. It could well have had something to do with one of the features (already noted earlier in our discussion) that Marx had identified as a likely characteristic of a Communist state: "Centralization of credit in the hands of the state, by means of a national bank with state capital and an exclusive monopoly."

The year 1961 brought with it a new President—the youthful Jack Kennedy—and the prettiest of all first ladies, raven-haired Jackie. Kennedy had won by only a narrow margin and only when his opponent, Richard Nixon, had made the mistake of consenting to nationwide TV debates with the highly photogenic young Massachusetts Senator. On most of the debates, Nixon's makeup man had left the Republican candidate looking like death warmed over.

Vice-President Lyndon Johnson soon returned from a trip to Vietnam and reported to Kennedy that "American combat troop involvement is not only not required, it is not desirable." But Kennedy now overlooked the lack of confidence he had expressed in the Vietnamese after his fact-finding mission seven years earlier, just as Johnson would later overlook his own doubts. Truman had been the first to send U.S. military advisers to South Vietnam (he had sent 35); Eisenhower had sent 500 more; now Kennedy not only sent 16,000, but also authorized U.S. helicopters to fire upon provocation. Just a year later, he was to send U.S. choppers on strafing missions. We were *really* in another undeclared war by then—and, later, before the end of the 1960s, we Americans would be trying to remember how and why we so quickly had got ourselves again into such a tragic, no-win entanglement. For the moment, though, at the beginning of the decade, most Americans either paid no attention to Vietnam or generally supported the U.S. attempt to check further Communist advances. After all, it would be a small war, easy to win—a good military exercise.

Meanwhile, angry black voices were suddenly speaking out against racism. While Rev. Martin Luther King, Jr., pleaded for nonviolence, the more militant Malcolm X told the nation: "It was stones yesterday, it will be hand grenades tomorrow and whatever else is available the next day. You should not feel that I am inciting anyone to violence. I am only warning of a powder-keg situation. You can take it or leave it."

Some black comics saw a bitter humor in the dangerous situation. Flip Wilson satirized, "We've got to do something about the Indians. The Indians aren't ready yet. Do you want to build a $50,000 home and have some guy put a wigwam next to it?"

Still, no matter that black storm clouds were gathering both at home and in Asia, Washington had never been more glamorous than it was under the good-looking young President and his First Lady. Each new party at the White House was more celebrity laden than the last. Most of the nation lived vicariously on the regal, star-studded doings of the vital young couple. And the new President was full of what Americans wanted most—optimism and hope. At his inaugural on January 20, 1961, had he not said: "So let us begin anew. Together let us explore the stars, conquer the deserts, eradicate disease, tap the ocean's depths and encourage the arts and commerce . . . the glow from that fire can truly light the world." And: "Ask not what your country can do for you, ask what you can do for your country."

Truly, never had the lights shone brighter in the nation's capital, never had the women seemed lovelier, the yachting on the Potomac so carefree, never had everything seemed about to be so glorious once again.

Yet it was but a year later that a sobered Kennedy told the nation with furrowed brow: "The responsibilities . . . are greater than I imagined them to be, and there are greater limitations upon our ability to bring about a favorable result. It is much easier to make the speeches than it is to make the judgments. . . ."

It had indeed been but a false dawn—a short lull before some of the darkest years in the history of the nation.

The new decade, in the peacetime year of 1961, when the U.S. government had only around 500 military "advisers" in Vietnam, brought spending to $81.5 billion for the year (greater than expenditures in 1943–1944 during World War II). The national debt was getting up there, too. It was nearly $290 billion.

Yet, even in 1963, the nation, at least on the face of it, did not seem that much changed. J. C. Penney (after *all* those years) was still selling 100,000 elastic-bound bloomers every year. A romantic new motion picture idol, Sean Connery, made *Doctor No,* and James Bond was an overnight sensation. Skirts were still climbing—finally to the point where there were almost no skirts at all, just legs and the new panty hose. Daring new topless evening gowns were seen at fashionable balls, and the backs of gowns were cut so far down as to expose a good part of the derrière itself. Drugs were becoming a major problem, and the flower children began to appear everywhere throughout the nation. Nikita Khrushchev visited the White House and made it clear on arrival that what he wanted most was to meet the stunning Jackie, who had taken Parisian fans by storm a few months earlier. In short order, brash and bright Cassius Clay would—amazingly—knock out Sonny Liston and become heavyweight champion, then for years to come making good his famous rhyme, "They all must fall in the round I call."

Richard Nixon was clearly finished in politics, it seemed, having been soundly beaten in 1962 for the governorship of California by incumbent Gov. Pat Brown. It was a race forced upon the former Vice-President by his party; he had not wanted to run. And when it ended, he told the press bitterly, "Well, now you won't have old Dick Nixon to kick around anymore."

American blacks had become ever more militant, and now

black comedians were the only ones who dared joke about the situation. Night club performer Jimmie Walker, on crime by blacks: "We doin' damn good in violent crime, but non-violent stuff we ain't no good at. I mean, when was the last time you saw a black investor or a black man get busted for jugglin' the bank books? Just once I'd like to walk down 125th Street and have a black brother lay a counterfeit dollar on me, a buck with a picture of Booker T. Now, what's the point of getting a black brother in the Supreme Court if we don't commit crimes classy enough to get there?"

The nation's blacks were not the only ones restive. Most of America's young, of all races, seemed suddenly to have turned both defiant and demonstrative. They seemed to protest everything, but most of all it was Vietnam.

But 1963 waited until November 22 for its climactic moment. In the brilliant sunshine of that Dallas noon, a slight, weak-chinned ex-Marine named Lee Harvey Oswald shot and killed President Kennedy during a parade. The nation was stunned, almost paralyzed with grief. Oswald had appeared in Children's Court at 13, and had been court-martialed twice in the Marine Corps, once for possessing a pistol and later on for picking a fight with his sergeant. He was sullen, suspicious, resentful, withdrawn, had failed in everything before that day: he had been fired from one job after another, failed in an attempt to get Russian citizenship, failed to get into Cuba, and had even earned the nickname "Ozzie Rabbit" from those who knew him during his undistinguished Marine Corps duty.

But Oswald did not fail with Kennedy. America's renewed likeness to Camelot, which for a moment in time had sparkled in the sun like a great flying fish, as suddenly disappeared once more into the depths.

The new President was Lyndon B. Johnson, who had earlier warned against the use of U.S. fighting forces in Vietnam.

America's debt climbed relentlessly. For the first time, in 1963, it passed the $300 billion mark—nearly $306 billion, in fact. And the year's federal spending was nearly $93 billion.

Some said ruefully that the spending might have been really serious had we been in a *declared* war.

The country could well have approached 1965 with a shiver: Were we really only five years into this awful decade? Malcolm X had been assassinated in 1964, and other marksmen of the decade were soon stalking other victims. President Johnson had overwhelmed Sen. Barry Goldwater in the election of 1964, and the Texan's "Great Society" was at least a good new White House theme, if never a fact.

Part of that Great Society proposal was LBJ's "War on Poverty." But was it not just such a "war" that had provoked the famous French economic theorist, Frederic Bastiat, to write:

See if the law takes away from some persons what belongs to them and gives it to other persons to whom it does not belong. See if the law benefits one citizen at the expense of another by doing what the citizen himself cannot without committing a crime.

Then abolish this law without delay, for it is not only an evil in itself, but it is also a fertile source for further evils because it invites reprisals. If such a law—which may not be an isolated case—is not abolished immediately, it will spread, multiply and develop into a system.

Meanwhile, Betty Friedan, a New York housewife, had written a book called *The Feminine Mystique*. The book was an ardent attack on the lowly role of women in the society. Not only was the book an instant success but it was one of the major triggers for a new movement called "Women's Liberation." Women everywhere began to do strange things. There was even a public brassiere-burning. And the Women's Lib movement was no mere fad, as American males were to find out soon enough.

There was much sympathy for the hippies and "love children" in many quarters. Playwright Lillian Hellman said, "God knows how many of them are fools . . . but they're a better generation than we were." The *Michigan*

Daily commented that "they took their tactics from Gandhi, their idealism from their philosophy class, and the money from Daddy." On the other hand, the irascible Groucho Marx growled, "Kids today are detestable. You couldn't give me another one . . . and kids aren't a minority if they're all yours and you have to wait for the car to get home to know your daughter hasn't got pregnancy or leprosy." Al Capp, who drew the *L'il Abner* comic strip, was just as severe: "I have no objection to any herd of semi-domesticated animals roaming the country, uttering their mating cries and scratching their pelts, as long as they avoid centers of civilization and congregate only in college auditoriums."

As the war in Vietnam picked up steam, so did the revolt of the nation's now often violent youth.

The 1965 budget, now LBJ's responsibility, was $96.5 billion, a close second only to 1945 ($98 billion), World War II's last year, when almost the entire resources and manpower of the nation had been devoted to the climax of a war that occupied the United States in every corner of the globe. Now, there was only tiny Vietnam. Not only that, but the federal debt in 1965 jumped all the way to $317 billion. It had been only a little over $1 billion in 1916—remember? And only $16 billion in 1930. There were some who tried to track down a quotation often attributed to Alexander Hamilton, to the effect that a capitalistic system was not one designed for purposes of making war, that capitalism would find waging war too expensive a proposition. But nobody could find his exact wordage, or where it had been said.

It was 1968. The ugly decade was almost over. But, then, on April 18, we had a warning of how tragic this particular year was to be. The first victim was the apostle of black nonviolence, Martin Luther King, Jr. Rev. King was assassinated in Memphis by 40-year-old James Earl Ray, a man who had a long jail record for burglaries, who once had stolen school lunch money from the teacher's desk, who couldn't look questioners in the eye, whose mother was an alcoholic, and whose father also had an arrest record for larceny and forgery. Both Ray's younger brothers had served reformatory time for robbery. And among his many antisocial views, Ray held a hatred for blacks. He was also still an escapee from the Missouri Penitentiary when he killed King.

The terrible sequence of assassinations was still not complete. Senator Robert Kennedy, the slain President's brother, was next. A 24-year-old Jordanian named Sirhan Sirhan emptied a revolver into the former Attorney-General at point-blank range just after he had finished a presidential campaign speech at a Los Angeles hotel on the night he won the California primary. Son of a violent father who had once burned Sirhan's feet with a hot iron, the young Jordanian hated Zionists and Jews as much as James Earl Ray despised blacks. Sirhan was also terribly resentful of the rich. Like Oswald, he had failed at most things he tried—including being a jockey. He talked a lot about returning to Jordan and becoming "somebody big." And if notoriety could make one big, Sirhan achieved his goal that June night in 1968.

What was happening in our America? Famous columnist Art Buchwald wrote that "to the rest of the world, the United States must look like a giant insane asylum, where the inmates have taken over."

The third victim in 1968—although not physically assassinated—was the President of the United States himself, Lyndon Johnson. He had fallen victim to a Vietnamese war he himself had warned against fourteen years earlier.

With the nation riven by dissent, LBJ had increased the number of U.S. troops in Vietnam to 510,000, but Gen. William Westmoreland, commander in Vietnam, was asking for 206,000 more. And then, suddenly, on January 24, 1968, the American public, which had been told that the Communist forces were all but whipped, realized they had been duped. The President had told Americans we were winning the war. But, astonishingly, as their Tet religious days began, the North Vietnamese launched an offensive that seemed to prove that they were just as strong as ever. Lyndon Johnson, it appeared, had been lying to us about the war all along.

Some 22 percent of Harvard's seniors voted to go to jail

rather than to Vietnam. When popularity polls began to show a comparative unknown, Senator Eugene McCarthy, hot on Johnson's heels in the race for the Democratic nomination, the President knew he was through. On the evening of March 31st, he stopped the U.S. bombing of North Vietnam and announced that he would not accept another term as President.

With both Bobby Kennedy and Lyndon Johnson out of the way, the road was paved for a Republican. It turned out to be none other than Richard Nixon, who turned in an incredible comeback. He edged out Hubert Humphrey by only a little more than 0.5 percent of the popular vote.

The political conventions had literally been a riot, both in the surrounding streets and the convention halls. Components of America's rebellious youth, incensed by the continuing war in Vietnam, formed the Youth International Party (the Yippies). The Yippies nominated a huge pig named Pigasus to oppose Hubert Humphrey at Chicago's Democratic convention. The Yippie's slogan was "Rise up and abandon the creeping meatball." And they chose as their major issue the subject of pay toilets.

Later, at their trial, the "Chicago Seven" became international symbols of youthful political rebellion.

British hairdresser Vidal Sassoon made the headlines when he was flown to Hollywood to style Mia Farrow's hair for the movie *Rosemary's Baby*. Sassoon's fee, $5,000, was an even one hundred times greater than his normal fee. The sex bomb of the 1960s was Raquel Welch, who made herself famous with an ever-so scantily-clad appearance in a terrible film called *One Million B.C.* Her dialogue consisted of exactly four unintelligible words.

Some of the biggest headlines of the year came as the immensely wealthy Greek shipowner Aristotle Onassis married Jackie Kennedy and gave her $5 million in jewelry the first year they were married. Professional athletes like Arnold Palmer, A. J. Foyt, and Mickey Mantle had begun to become big businessmen through both prize winnings and endorsements. In July 1969, the United States finally managed to fulfill Jack Kennedy's promise of a "man on the moon"—Neil Armstrong.

But once again, as before World War II, Charles A. Lindbergh sounded warning words. "Along with this development of space, we must protect the face of the earth. That's even more important." Environmentalists everywhere cheered.

The year 1968 brought the national debt perilously close to $350 billion. Government spending in 1968 was a staggering $148 billion. At least money men *thought* that that figure was staggering. It certainly seemed staggering then. To contemplate that the nation's *peacetime* spending would be more than $245 billion in a future 1975–1976 budget would have required either a Jules Verne–like imagination or a George Orwell–like capacity for horror beyond the ken of any comparatively sane economist of 1968.

In 1970, as promised, Nixon was gradually bringing American fighting men home. Nixon soon would cut the number of U.S. troops in Vietnam in half (from the late 1968 high of 536,000 plus 100,000 more in Thailand and Guam). But the public demand for a complete U.S. pullout grew ever more vehement.

Another kind of war, a social war, was raging in the country itself. The whole concept of marriage seemed to be collapsing. In college dorms across the country, male and female students cohabited, and now there were singles' vacations, singles' cruises, and singles' apartments. Parents everywhere were up in arms about morality (or the lack of it) among the young.

Everything was becoming computerized too, even dating. And the computer mistakes made wonderful newspaper copy. One computer attempting to match ideal partners picked a brother and a sister. In Albany, a hospital computer sent a woman a bill for $25 for a circumcision. Laughably worst of all, in Boston, only 72 hours before an election in which Mayor John Collins was running for the Senate, one of the city's computers, having been given no such instructions, nonetheless proceeded on its own to prepare, address, and mail 29,500 delinquent sewer tax notices. Mayor Collins lost the Senate nomination. The computer age was with us to stay, and Orwell's *1984* seemed closer each day.

Arthur Godfrey became a hero of the ecologists, refusing to do a detergent commercial the way he was asked to because, he said, he had discovered that detergents polluted lakes and streams. The U.S. ecology movement was growing by leaps and bounds, with American youth, as always, in the vanguard of the battle. The National Audubon Society proceeded to sue the Texas Parks and Wildlife Commission, attempting to prevent oyster shell dredging in the only remaining feeding ground of the fast-vanishing whooping crane.

As for the debt and the budget: not that it seemed to matter much anymore—since the numbers were getting beyond comprehension anyway—but in 1970 federal spending was more than $156 billion in that one year. And the government-calculated public debt had reached $371 billion.

As 1971 dawned, Americans had some diverting moments reading about the fight between Georgia Governor Lester Maddox and his old enemies, the Atlanta *Constitution* and the Atlanta *Journal*. Maddox threatened to sue the two papers on behalf of "all the good Christian people of Georgia who've been lied to all these years." Maddox called the editorial writers of the two papers "lying devils and dirty dogs." He removed *Constitution* and *Journal* vending machines from the capitol grounds.

Muhammad Ali (née Cassius Clay) was beaten for the first time. Joe Frazier whipped Ali and became the undisputed heavyweight champion of the world.

There was other news in sports. Off-track betting was legalized in New York, and bookies finally had gained some respectability. And Ping-Pong diplomacy came into being as members of an American table tennis team were allowed into Communist China for a week of exhibitions; they were the first Americans to enter mainland China as a group in over 15 years.

A major earthquake shook Los Angeles, bringing the first earthquake deaths in five years.

Although Nixon continued to withdraw GIs from Viet-

nam, the nation was still being torn by antiwar demon-
strations, now reaching their zenith. On May 3, 1971, police
in Washington arrested 7000 protestors, the largest lockup in
a single day in any one city in American history.

Nostalgia swept a nation longing for memories of less
troubled times. A facsimile edition of the 1897 Sears
Roebuck catalog was published with the thought that it might
sell some copies to libraries. But so strong was the nostalgia
craze that copies of the old catalog became a best-seller.
Over 200,000 copies were sold at $14.95 apiece.

In the late summer of 1971, President Nixon announced
what he called the most momentous monetary decision in the
history of the world. He devalued the American dollar (the
first time it had been done since Roosevelt), and he also shut
the gold window of the U.S. Treasury. Now, even *foreign*
debtors who had been converting U.S. paper money into
gold (President Charles de Gaulle of France was by far the
biggest "offender") were stuck with their U.S. paper
money. All they had was a promise to be paid *something* and
that something turned out to be even *more* paper.

In 1971, the Nixon administration spent nearly $164
billion. The federal debt had approached what then seemed
some sort of Rubicon—nearly $400 billion. It really *was* a
good thing that we weren't in some sort of *declared* war in
which we were forced to defend ourselves. One sick joke had
it that it was good that Americans had elected a sound,
conservative Republican administration which could control
the size of government, keep it from invading our personal
liberties, and prevent taxes from eating the population alive.
Lucky that it was not a Democratic administration, the sick
one said. Things might have been really expensive had that
been the case.

Another year of electoral politics arrived—1972. Seeking
reelection, President Nixon visited China and, among other
things, was treated to a Chinese ballet that was obviously a
propagandistic assault on "capitalistic imperialism."

It was the year of the big auto recalls. The four major U.S.
auto makers sold 5.3 million cars in the first half of the year,
but recalled 11.6 million others to repair possible defects.

Airline hijacking was at a new high—38 commercial jets were hijacked.

In a big sports surprise, chess suddenly came into its own. American Bobby Fischer won the world championship in Iceland by defeating Russian Boris Spassky in a battle of temperaments. Fischer's psychological warfare against Spassky was so effective that *Pravda* suggested he was using chemical and electronic aids to unbalance his Russian opponent. Teams of Icelandic scientists, armed with X-ray machines, smear cloths, and microscopes, spent three days investigating Russian charges. They dismantled both players' chairs, the lighting fixtures, and even the chess table itself. The final discovery: two dead flies. Fischer further infuriated his opponent by asking if anyone wanted an autopsy of the two flies. One French newspaper observed of Fischer: "An interesting fellow. You expect to loathe him, and then when you meet him, you really can."

The presidential election pitted Richard Nixon against Senator George McGovern of South Dakota. Having reduced the number of American troops in Vietnam to only 24,000, Nixon was a shoo-in. He won 49 states, losing only in Massachusetts and the District of Columbia. McGovern protested justly but in vain that Nixon's system for ending the Vietnam War—a steady withdrawal of troops—was something that the President could have accomplished just as easily by withdrawing them all at the beginning of his first term in 1969.

Senator William Proxmire of Wisconsin continued his ceaseless battle against what he called "senseless government spending." Proxmire attacked the Pentagon first. He pointed out that it had paid billions for a military cargo fleet (including the C-5A, which was used only three or four hours a day), but that now the government for some reason was spending tens of millions purchasing cargo space from *private* airlines. He said it was like the commuter who calls a taxi, leaving his paid-for car at home. He blasted federal water reclamation projects, pointing out that on some upper Colorado River programs it was costing more than $2,000 per acre to reclaim land worth some $100 an acre—land upon which only hay and forage crops could be grown. And he slapped at proposals to spend $20 billion to erect a defensive system against what he called "outdated Russian bombers," submitting that the real need was for an impenetrable defense against the far more destructive Russian intercontinental ballistic missiles.

The government's spending in 1972 jumped to $178 billion. The federal debt vaulted right over the Rubicon and went to $427 billion, a figure too large to comprehend. Other countries that traded with us were alarmed by the flood of paper money that we sent them—U.S. paper IOUs, for the first time absolutely unbacked by gold or any other tangible, other than, manifestly, a gigantic federal paper-making plant. But no foreign nation could figure out what to do about the worrisome situation. After all, the United States was the major consumer market for the world's other industrial nations. To refuse those U.S. paper dollars would seem suicidal for their own export industries (not to mention their politicians), and which nation could afford to do that? And some foreigners held it still true that if the United States sneezed, Europe (and Asia, too) caught a cold. Just France complained that the return to sanity could come only when the U.S. backed its currency again with gold. With no metal backing at all the U.S. Treasury was for the first time free to print unlimited quantities of paper money—IOU nothings.

In 1973, Nixon was again inaugurated. He had won, or had he? True enough, the peace accord with the North Vietnamese had been signed in January 1973, but there was a faint whiff of some trouble brewing somewhere. In mid-1972, there had been what Nixon's press secretary called a "third-rate burglary" at Democratic headquarters in the Watergate building in Washington. But the Democrats insisted on a full-scale investigation of what the Nixon aides called an insignificant non-event.

It was also the year of the housewife meat boycott. Lasting seven days, it laid an egg. Meat prices continued to rise. In Grand Island, Nebraska, a meat market sign read, "T-bones 59¢ a pound; with meat, $2.09 a pound."

The Indians lost again at Wounded Knee. In a latter-day uprising, Indians took over the town that was the site of the Sioux massacre in 1890. The fight between the Indians and U.S. Marshals and FBI stirred the nation but changed history very little.

And suddenly, something happened that *did* change the course of U.S. political history. In mid-1973, a venerable U.S. Senator, Sam Ervin of North Carolina, became a national folk hero as his Senate committee began hearings into that bizarre predawn break-in of Democratic headquarters at Watergate. Although the committee seemed to be on dead center for a long time, at last it began to gather speed. One witness almost casually let it be known that all conversations in the President's Oval Office were routinely *taped*. A stunned committee immediately set up an insistent clamor that they hear the tapes. We were on our way to the first resignation of a President in the history of the United States.

Under a relatively new accounting system, which the government called its "Unified Concept," spending for the 1973–1974 "fiscal year" (two daringly dignified words considering the circumstances) was nearly $232 billion, and there wasn't a hint of a war around on which such spending could be blamed. The precedent initially set following the Korean War was continuing: for the first time in the nation's history, spending continued upward in *peacetime*. And it was true of the federal debt, too. It leaped to over $468 billion.

Not only that. Our annual budget was approaching one-third of the entire U.S. gross national product. Furthermore, some renegade Congressmen were trumpeting that the real U.S. national debt, as opposed to the published one, actually exceeded $2.5 *trillion* dollars. The National Taxpayers Union put the figure at some $5,077,000,000,000 (that's five trillion seventy-seven billion). Since federal wealth cannot include private property (for accounting purposes, at least), there began to be a strong question as to whether or not some point might be reached where the national debt literally exceeded the value of all federally owned assets. Should that happen, it might provoke the distasteful use of a word heretofore reserved only for individuals: *bankruptcy!* The nationally respected accounting firm of Arthur Andersen— presumably on its own hook, at its own expense, and without Treasury thanks—actually attempted something of a trial audit of the financial position of the United States. The firm finally came up with two different national debt figures, the highest one being $2.46 trillion, and then timidly or not, noted that this figure was not derived from good accounting practice, which was doubtless correct. Their reasoning was that an item is not a liability or an asset *until it is due*. All that was due as of 1974 (as far as their study goes) was $416 billion. Nonetheless, to this writer, it appeared that the Andersen firm had taken on what was an impossible project to begin with and had ended the study in alarmed dismay at the unpleasant conclusions that seemed about to present themselves.

In 1974, the Watergate imbroglio continued to occupy the nation's attention. Had the President known of the burglary at Watergate before it was committed? Had he lied to the nation?

There were, of course, some other news items. Newspaper heiress Patricia Hearst was kidnapped by something calling itself the "Symbionese Liberation Army." To the surprise of everyone, Miss Hearst appeared to have joined the cause after her abduction—and was even photographed holding a submachine gun at a bank robbery. She vanished from sight, and for months thousands of peace officers somehow could not find a trace of her.

Muhammad Ali was number one again. After knocking out George Foreman to regain the heavyweight championship, Ali was discussing a $10 million offer to defend his title. He was asked, "Who is the promoter?" "Governments want me now," Ali replied with characteristic modesty, "not promoters."

By summer, President Nixon had lost his desperate fight to retain possession of the tapes of his Oval Office conversations. He had been counting on his appointees to the U.S.

Supreme Court to back him in his contention that the tapes should not be released. But the Court voted 9–0 that he must release them. The recordings played for Congressional investigators were in such conflict with what Nixon had told the nation that public confidence in the President was all but destroyed. Finally, on August 9, 1974, the man who had carried 49 states less than two years earlier sent an eleven-word message to the Secretary of State: "I hereby resign the Office of President of the United States."

To add to the nation's other woes, we were in the grip of a new economic disease that some called *stagflation*— inflation and recession at the same time. Unemployment mounted, and even the administration—now under the direction of new President Gerald Ford—admitted that we were in a recession.

Peacetime federal spending in 1974 was $268 billion. The federal debt had reached $486 billion.

With the dawn of 1975, Americans, for the first time since the early 1930s, were once again permitted to own gold. The U.S. Treasury, to prevent Americans from rushing to buy gold and thus pushing the price even higher, announced an auction of a small part of the U.S. gold hoard. The strategy worked, the price of gold was pushed down, and the anticipated rush for gold by U.S. citizens did not materialize at once. Nonetheless, the price of gold had already begun a steady, inexorable rise against the ever-depreciating dollar, beset by government waste and economic corruption not seen since the reign of the Emperor Diocletian (284–305 A.D.), whose almost exactly similar policies helped to finish off the Roman Empire in the fourth century. (We will return to Diocletian later.)

In the mid-1970s, tireless Secretary of State Henry Kissinger continued his jet "shuttle diplomacy" and managed to work out what was called an "interim peace accord" between the Israelis and the Egyptians. War, for the moment, seemed averted in the tinderbox Middle East. But, weeks later, violent religious conflicts broke out in Beirut between Christians and Moslems. The Communists were going all out to seize Portugal, which was suddenly in the grip of a revolution, and as Portugal gave Angola its independence, that country broke apart with three tribes fighting for leadership. Both Russia and Cuba committed troops to aid the Angolan Communist faction.

President Ford in mid-November of 1975 went to Paris for a five-nation meeting on the world economy. The announced intention of the meeting was to agree on ways "to end the worst worldwide recession in 40 years." Ford announced at the end of the short, three-day weekend meeting that all of the countries were in accord and that there was no question that the world was on its way back to prosperous days.

Has anything changed much in the five years since this pronouncement?

Not much. The national debt, certainly. Larger. Also more bureaus. The Department of Energy. The Department of Education. The Department of Health and Social Services. A return to stagflation. OPEC. But if it hadn't been OPEC, we'd have found another way to throw away our bucks. A different name for the President: Jimmy instead of Jerry. Now Ronald.

As to *coercive welfare,* which is the only correct term for any government welfare dictated by a truly democratic state, there has been much more of that too. Take a look, through the eyes of William Simon, at the example of AFDC—aid to families with dependent children. Simon points out that the number of AFDC recipients increased from some 2 million to 11 million in 1978 and that, in this respect, AFDC has been a federal invitation to fathers to abandon their families, directly or indirectly. Simon also deals with OSHA—the Occupational Safety and Health Agency—a massive monetary drain upon the country, an agency with virtual police powers over any American's office or plant and yet one that requires no search warrant. Still, the same Americans who scream the loudest at any invasion without warrant of homes or offices for searches by the FBI, the CIA, or the police force are almost uniformly without reaction when OSHA's victims are businessmen.

Simon's excellent *A Time For Truth* is must reading for those remaining among us who still have the will to fight, and one paragraph in particular sums up its powerful message:

> America is not a welfare state even in the old New Deal sense of the term. This country today is purely and simply a redistributionist state, endlessly shaking down Peter to pay Paul. Not orphaned Paul, not crippled Paul, not aged Paul, not black Paul, just *Paul*.

While no writer has yet dealt with the most fundamental cause of America's sharp drop in productivity during these last two decades, someone will ultimately treat the subject of governmental edicts that force selective or percentage hiring of business personnel for reason of physical attributes. Future study of edicts in this area will doubtless produce obvious and mathematically substantiable conclusions dispelling much of the confusion as to why this country's industrial and other types of productivity have so drastically declined.

At least one thing has not declined. Table III, showing the calculations for 1980 by the highly respected National Taxpayers Union, both breaks down the $9,033,000,000,000 (nine trillion thirty-three billion) that is our nation's present public debt, and also details those items comprising the personal liability of $112,910 that is the debt now owed by every American taxpayer.

In the light of all this—the increasing weakness of our money, the U.S. government's unrelentingly wrongheadedness in monetary policy, the ever-ballooning, astronomical size of our national debt and our spending, the proliferating cells of our horror-house bureaucracy—let us next consider our likely future and its implications for a prudent strategy of investment.

TABLE III
The National Debt for 1980*

Debt or liability item	Gross cost	Your share
Public debt	$ 721,000,000,000	$ 9,012
Accounts payable	$ 80,000,000,000	$ 1,000
Undelivered orders	$ 332,000,000,000	$ 4,150
Long-term contracts	$ 15,000,000,000	$ 187
Loan and credit guarantees	$ 209,000,000,000	$ 2,612
Insurance commitments	$1,733,000,000,000	$ 21,662
Annuity programs	$5,900,000,000,000	$ 73,750
Unadjudicated claims		
International commitments and		
other financial obligations	$ 43,000,000,000	$ 537
Total	$9,033,000,000,000	$112,910

*Source: National Taxpayers Union, 1980.

4

The Way We Will Be

It would, of course, be of great help to any of us planning an investment program in strategic metals or anything else if we *knew* to a certainty whether U.S. price inflation would remain at the present high levels or once again recede back to a single digit. So let us assay a look into the future. And just as we introduced in previous chapters matters not normally thought to be relevant to questions of investment, here too we must introduce considerations not generally applied to speculations about the future inflation rate.

It is the view of this writer that for the foreseeable future inflation not only will *average* in the double-digit range but that this situation *could well be* in the best interest of *any thinking man*. The reason for the latter assertion: Only if U.S. inflation remains at a double-digit average for several years to come will it be possible for our nation adequately to arm itself.

This appalling proposal—that the *judicious* man might do well to hope for continued high inflation for the foreseeable future—is made in the light of convincing evidence that, whatever modest economies may be politically achievable in our national budget, prudence demands that ever-greater sums be spent for national defense during the 1980s, sums far larger indeed than any ever before spent for that purpose in our history (or in that of any other nation).

As will be proven over the next few pages, the only politically acceptable way to finance such apparently vital but staggering sums for defense and meet the concomitant and resultant deficits—since, as we shall see, we will not or cannot cut most other federal expenditures—is, of course, to increase our money supply at an ever greater rate than is being done at present. For reasons to be stated shortly, I do not believe that we will in fact spend the sums necessary to reach a parity of armament with our main enemy. But *should* we do so, such an overwhelming expansion of the U.S. money supply without a parallel increase in *useful* domestic productivity in the capital goods area can only be inflationary in the most extreme. One might ask, why then pursue such a painful policy? The answer is no less painful. If we do not choose this road of extreme inflation toward achieving an appropriate national defense, then to paraphrase an oft-quoted statement of the late Gen. Hugh Johnson, we shoot craps with the destiny of the Western world. As George Will, an able columnist, has often written, there has never *been* détente with the Soviets and there is no prospect that there ever will be.

Were prudence to prevail, in view of seemingly incontrovertible facts concerning serious deficiencies in the country's defense capability, U.S. defense spending should increase much faster than the inflation rate, almost exponentially, not to *keep pace* with the Russians but at the outset at least to attempt to *overtake* them.

This is due to two factors:

1. In the decade of the 1970s, the USSR spent on their military forces nearly *a third of a trillion* dollars *over and above* the expenditures of the United States. Today the Soviets annually spend nearly $60 billion *more* on the military than the United States does.

2. The Soviets currently spend between 13 and 15 percent of their gross national product annually on the military. We

spend 5 percent. Even worse, Russia's defense spending is *real* military spending; ours is *not*. The U.S. military budget is calculated on the assumption that there will be an average of only 9 percent inflation for all defense next year. Who really believes such a percentage?

Former Undersecretary of the Navy James Woolsey, now a Washington attorney, writing in the Washington *Post*, states that if we continue to assume only a 9 percent inflation rate for our purposes of calculating a realistic defense budget, then: (1) we must forget all about the weapons programs that are so "undercosted" they have built-in cost overruns waiting to be discovered; (2) we must pretend that fuel prices will not increase above those of today; and (3) we must ignore the much-publicized problem of highly trained sergeants and technicians whose pay raise is—yet again— half or less of the increase in prices for what their families have to buy.

To quote Woolsey:

> Russian military spending which tops ours on the order of a third of a trillion dollars within a decade—affects U. S. capability— and U. S. will—to prevent the Russians from dominating the [Persian] Gulf and Finlandizing Europe and Japan. That third of a trillion dollars difference is one big reason why the Russians have four times the tanks we have and are producing tanks, guns and aircraft at two to three times the rate we are; why they begin construction of a new general-purpose submarine about once every five weeks while we start one once a year; and why they have 25 divisions equipped for chemical warfare, some of which are now playing an exhibition season against Afghan tribesmen.

Woolsey's guest column in the most influential newspaper of our nation's capital concludes by pointing out that the Soviet military budget exceeds ours today—and I believe ominously—by about the same percentage as Germany's exceeded Britain's in 1935.

Some 40 years ago, a liberal young author, just out of

Harvard College, wrote about England's disastrously low defense budget in a book entitled *Why England Slept*. John F. Kennedy said, "We should profit by the lesson of England and make U.S. democracy work." "We must make it work," he continued, "right now."

Yet later on, as President, he did little to ensure that this democracy (and we have evolved to a democracy in the United States) worked militarily, and far less than enough has been done since his presidency. Be that as it may, better that we take our chances battling the horror of hyperinflation than take the even more unacceptable alternative of letting the Russian bear gain a victory by forfeit. Some nations *have*, indeed, survived even *triple-digit* inflation—God forbid the average standard of living in those nations most clearly available for comparison: Chile, Brazil, Argentina, Israel—but no free nation's standard of living can survive slavery. Life in chains becomes unthinkable to anyone who has personally observed the quality of existence in those nations currently under Marxist servitude.

Yet the horror of inflation is a vivid one.

History reportedly records that following the disastrous German inflation in the Weimar Republic during the early 1920s—an inflation that drove the German people directly into the arms of Adolph Hitler a few years later—the Germans were asked in a national poll which of two terrible alternatives they would choose: another war or hyperinflation. The poll showed that the people would prefer to go to war again rather than once more subject themselves to the horrors of runaway inflation—and, sure enough, not many years later, they did exactly that: went back to war. (It is important here to note explicitly the difference between double- or even triple-digit inflation. Milton Friedman, during a recent speech in Montreal, cited one of his colleagues, Philip Cagan, as having declared that inflation graduates to hyperinflation—runaway inflation—when prices are increasing by more than 50 percent.)

I am sure I need not point out that the United States can hardly expect an increased productivity of useful goods to stem our inflation, certainly not so long as our welfare (or redistribution) system and tax structure force high price inflation on the people, and not so long as current regulations of the Equal Employment Opportunity Commission place U.S. industry under the less than competitively acceptable requirements concerning minority hiring percentages. To quote Edward Dennison of the U.S. Department of Commerce on the hard truth about our economy: "U.S. productivity has gone to pot since 1973." Or Archie McCardell, Chairman of International Harvester: "If present growth trends continue, total productivity in France and Germany will exceed that in the U.S. by 1985. And shortly after that, Japan and Canada will surpass us." James B. Farley, Chairman of Booz, Allen & Hamilton, says, "The U.S. record in technological innovation . . . has been so poor in recent years that in many aspects of innovation the Japanese and Europeans have taken the leadership mantle away from the U.S. . . . [We] expect that overall productivity growth in the United States between 1980 and 1990 is not likely to improve."

But why, in all innocence you may ask, is it not possible to cut government spending and so reduce our inflation, whatever our defense needs, whatever the facts about U.S. productivity? Alas, to turn around a Watergate expression, it is because the *democratic* system is *not* working, for all the reasons given in previous chapters.

British historian Alexander Trotter is quoted by a nationally syndicated columnist as saying that "A democracy cannot exist as a permanent form of government; it can only exist until the voters discover that they can vote themselves largesse from the public treasury." From then on, Trotter wrote, the majority always votes for the candidates promising the most until the democracy collapses because of loose fiscal policy.

Our federal pension laws furnish the perfect example of why an observation such as Trotter's is so terrifyingly accurate. Some background first. Today, five cents of every dollar spent by the government goes for federal civil or military pensions—not Social Security, but *pensions*. That five cents is double the amount of only 10 years ago because federal pensions are indexed to increase with the cost of living. In 1980, we will spend more than $26 billion on federal pensions; that amount will again double over the next 10 years to more than $50 billion. One hundred thousand federal retirees now are drawing pension benefits bigger *than the largest paycheck they ever got while working*, by U.S. government figures. What's more, federal retirement ages are lower than those in private industry, and thus there are workers who retire early enough to earn second, or even (rarely) third, pensions.

Surely a reform in our pension system must be made. Indeed, in July 1979, President Carter proposed a modest, even timid reform bill that would have saved only a relatively small amount. But so unpopular was that weak yet timely 1979 military pension-reform proposal that not only was it *not* passed but no Congressman had been found to act as the bill's sponsor. In other words, the President *couldn't even find a Congressman to introduce it*. No President, nor candidate for President, will tackle the American Legion, the Veterans of Foreign Wars, the Association of Government Employees and the innumerable other organizations involved in pensions.

Is this an example of a system that's working?

But the sum amounts to only 5 percent of the budget, doesn't it? Not really. Direct benefit payments to individuals—the pensions, Social Security, and various welfare benefits—make up 43 percent of the 1981 budget. No President will find it politically possible to appreciably cut that 43 percent of our budget.

But aren't other cuts possible?

To the 43 percent of the budget already accounted for, add the interest on our national debt—9 percent of the budget, and counting. No President can cut that at all. That's 52 percent together.

Now add national defense, which currently is 24 percent of the budget, and which should be *increased*, not cut. Considering only the current 24 percent for defense to continue, we've now accounted for 76 percent of our national budget. Consider for a moment the utter enormity of the spending cuts in other areas that would be necessary for us to rebuild our fighting forces adequately to protect American interests in all exigencies. The whole staggering immensity of the cost of resuscitating the United States militarily can perhaps best be set forth by the following example: The hourly cost of operation of our C-5 transport plane (the only one we have that can carry the two American tanks big enough to stand up to their Soviet counterpart) is $11,000. That means that the cost of flying just two tanks 10,000 miles to the Persian Gulf area is $221,000 *one* way. The return trip, whether or not the flight had an Iranian rescue mission ending, would cost still another $221,000. The Army has two other new weapons that only the C-5 is big enough to carry. Does this example shed any light on just how much we are talking about?

At the risk of redundancy, please note that I have spoken of huge amounts of money that *should* be spent for national defense—for national survival. I did not say *would* be spent. Prudence, in my opinion, may well *not* prevail. I regret to declare that I do not believe that these apparently necessary and highly inflationary sums *will* be spent. For—and this is the hardest statement of all for me to make—the writer sees nothing to indicate that the American citizenry in its present mood of complacent apathy has either the *will* to mandate the spending of these sums or the *steadfastness* or *understanding* (of our forebears, for instance) to undergo the hardship and sacrifice that must accompany the prolonged period of punishing inflation that appears necessary to put and keep our defense capability consonant with the growing arms capability of the Soviet Union.

Despite current media opinion, there is no swing toward conservatism in the United States; there is only *perceived* to be a swing. When a chief executive or a Congress actually gets around to attempting the reductions in our standard of living that will occur once we increase our *real* military spending to the level that a *prudent* government should effect, the proponents of such propositions will quickly find themselves squarely opposed to the *real* will—or lack of will—of a spoiled, selfish, mostly uninformed, and indolent average American voter. The vast majority of today's American electorate want conservatism only as a theory, and they want prudent government only so long as it does not in one iota affect their personal pleasure, income, or standard of living.

In this observer's opinion, the people of the United States are unlikely at any early date to develop the necessary will and resolution to move toward what appears to be prudent defense, unless one of three highly unlikely events occurs:

1. The Soviets attack the United States or one of its possessions.

2. The Russians take some action forcing the United States to think it must defend itself, such as an overt Soviet attack upon Western Europe, Saudi Arabia, or some other foreign land quite precious to us. In neither Saudi Arabia nor Western Europe could we, in our present state of military preparedness, present a *winning* defense, but we might, in a flight of false national pride, attempt to do so. (It should be emphasized here that veteran Western authorities on the Soviet Union believe the Russians regard their aggression in Afghanistan as no more than mere annexation of some adjoining land which quite correctly the United States both could not and did not choose to defend.)

3. Some sort of simple but unforeseeable *mistake* is made by one side or the other. Today's complex defense technology offers each day thousands of chances (and buttons) for human error—in planes, aboard ships, and on land.

The key issue here is the first possibility, which we will return to shortly. As to the second, there is every likelihood that when actually faced by a decision as to whether or not to react militarily to Soviet moves in an indefensible part of the world—where such action can mean nothing less than national suicide—our government will accept the bitter reality that we can only back away for the time being and prepare to resist another day.

But what about the possibility of direct military aggression by the Soviet Union? In my view, there is no reason to believe that the Soviet rulers have any intention of taking any overt military action that might provoke the United States to defend itself.

The people currently holding power in the USSR indicate every desire merely to continue to play us, both diplomatically and militarily, like an old fiddle. The Soviets appear quite prepared to continue their long-held strategy of taking two steps forward and one step back.

As if to prove the preceding point, on June 4, 1980, on the very heels of the Soviet invasion of Afghanistan, the Associated Press quoted Leonid Zamyatin, a senior official of the Soviet Communist Party's Central Committee, as saying that Moscow "is prepared to build relations with the United States on the principle of peaceful co-existence." That same Associated Press dispatch from Moscow reported that the Soviet Union had begun pressing a campaign aimed at moving toward what one Soviet commentator calls "a period of diplomacy after a period of anti-diplomacy."

Of course, as I already have suggested, prudence dictates that we try to match the Soviets militarily, if only because this writer could be wrong in his assumption that the Soviet leadership is not willing to risk an all-out shooting war. Indeed, the successor to Leonid Brezhnev may well be far more hawkish, far less cool and calculating, than the present Soviet leader. Let me hasten to add that mere defense for survival is hardly the *only* reason why expedience dictates that we present a strong military position for other nations to observe. No politician today seems to be taking issue with Teddy Roosevelt's long-ago warning that the best way to keep peace (and, as a natural corollary, it would seem, to keep needed allies from bolting one's side because of a perceived military impotence) is to "carry a big stick."

That said, I still hold that nuclear war with the Soviet Union is unlikely. Why should Russia wish to make war upon the United States at this time? The Soviets already have the basic world situation going their way.

First, consider the fact that Soviet leaders have a normal sense of self-preservation and do not wish to risk their own sudden death from either retaliatory nuclear attack or its resultant fallout (which would last for years).

Second, the Soviet Union wishes ultimately to control by fear alone a still productive America—a United States that can continue to help feed the Russian people, a U.S. that has its farms and great factories both intact, operating to whatever extent they may serve the best interests of the Soviet Union.

And, third, the Communists must realize that, given their present steady rate of progress and their continuing conquest by internal subversion of one nation after another (including the United States), their grand strategy is well along the path toward victory without direct military aggression.

As all this suggests, the Soviet leaders do not want us to move to that extraordinary rate of high inflation necessary to rearm adequately, nor—and this is the crux of the matter—do they need us to run the risks of such inflation. They are quite aware, as Table III at the end of Chapter 3 indicates, that the actual national debt of the United States is now nearing $10 trillion dollars. They are also quite aware that our annual national deficits, quite without any really meaningful or prudent increase in our military expenditures, will continue to be on such a monumental scale that either a further debilitating Latinization of the U.S. economy or an actual financial collapse will sooner or later come to pass simply because of our *present* profligacy of welfare and other nonproductive spending.

The Kremlin leaders know, in short, that on its present course the United States is headed straight for either desperately high double-digit inflation or actual runaway hyper-inflation. Either condition would satisfy the Politburo. The Soviets can easily enough deal with an Argentinian-style United States. If it is to be runaway inflation, the Soviets fully expect that it will lead to an internal revolution in the

United States, a bloody racial conflict as part of it all, and finally, at the end of that short but convulsive nightmare, the emergence of a totalitarian form of government with which they can readily strike a working relationship quite satisfactory to them.

This, then, is the grim scenario we face. It is recited here not to depress you but to enable you to plan your investment strategy correctly. Your investments should be planned with two possibilities in mind. In the rather unlikely event that Americans choose prudently to rearm, your portfolio needs to be planned in anticipation of extraordinary inflation. In the far more likely event that voters choose *not* to sacrifice and spend those hitherto unthinkable sums necessary for *real* defense (not for just months, but for an indeterminately long period), your investment strategy should assume an inflation rate that is high to the point of bearability, with the ever present possibility that such inflation will, sooner rather than later, graduate from indexed into runaway inflation.

Am I saying that I see no long-range hope for this country? Not quite.

While it is true that I see no hope for the prolonged existence of this democracy in its present convoluted form, I *can* conjure the hope that the traditional and enormous resilience of the American people united in adversity will bring forth a new leader who, given a fresh start, can guide us toward the republic that James Madison and his eminent colleagues in 1787 had every reason to believe was well delineated in the Constitution.

Others have projected different and happier resolutions to the grim economic situation of our country; but as pleased as I would be to find comfort in their views, I must say I cannot.

For example, I cannot believe that the William Simon who wrote *A Time for Truth* really *believes* in any serious possibility of the national metamorphosis necessary to translate his "three points for liberty" into reality: (1) that business in the likely time left for this system will rush its profits by the multimillions to the aid of liberty; or (2) that business will cease mindlessly subsidizing institutions of learning whose many departments are hostile to capitalism; or (3) that business money will flow away from "the media which serve as megaphones for anti-capitalist opinion and to media which are either pro-freedom or . . . capable of a fair and accurate treatment of pro-capitalist ideas, values and arguments." To move aggressively on these "three fronts," as Simon proposes, we must presume that the present dire state of our economy leaves time enough for the educational process that would be required to stimulate such decisive action. I cannot see any exigency that would so emotionally excite business that it would suddenly take up the cudgels to fight in time to be effective on these "fronts." Still none of the above prevents my applauding this keen observer for his admirable words and commendable, if wishful, objectives, objectives with which any businessman worth his salt should perforce agree, as I do.

It is no less easy to agree in principle with the six brilliant youngsters who wrote *The Incredible Bread Machine*. All of their proposals for bringing a new economic life to farmers and city dwellers alike are, it seems to me, well summed up by this one paragraph from their marvelous little study.

> Strike from the books all legislation that denies economic freedom to any individual and at least three-fourths of all the activities now undertaken by government would be eliminated. It is breathtaking to think what this simple approach would do to the apparatus of State control at all levels of government.

It would indeed be breathtaking, but it is just not going to happen under our present, highly advanced (or deteriorated) U.S. democracy.

So where do we go from here? Downhill, faster still I believe, and how much farther it is to the bottom none can say. Probably not too far, for if one reads the last days of Constantine, one can all but hear the same familiar cries of our present day reverberating from the crumbling walls of that other empire, echoing back to us from those centuries past—sounds of pain and fear all too alike those of an American struggling into the Eighties.

Despite material possessions that no other nation in

history has enjoyed, the confidence and faith so evident, as we saw earlier, in, say, the booming 1920s , has dwindled away. Those who look to the future do not, as they did then, look with hopeful hearts. Skepticism is the rule, and despair for the future not unusual. This change in the American moral and mental climate has not come about overnight. It has been a gradual thing, creeping upon us as each of our liberties was taken away one by one by the ever-reaching tentacles of a monstrous and bewildering system (how in *hell,* some still ask, did we ever come to this?) attempting to regulate our lives. Instead of the ebullient optimisim of the Twenties, disillusionment is now more the order of the day. Few Americans will deny an increasing disenchantment with our social system, an uneasy feeling that their entire life-style is slowly deteriorating and the very foundations of their social order giving way. Looking back over these 60 years, somehow the old American dream has taken upon itself the quality of a distant and remote mirage, now a life too far.

Yet let me close this portrait of the tomorrow toward which we are heading with a note of genuine optimism. Where this writer finds real hope is—as odd as the point may first appear—in the amazing advances still possible from U.S. military technology.

There is hope, of course, that a single weapon or more than one is now at hand with which we can literally overnight wrest from the Soviets the military capability to dominate land, sea, and sky. Whether there is or not, there is a real possibility, even a strong probability, that given any reasonable time at all, American technology will bring forth a weapon which the USSR cannot possibly match and cannot even steal.* The Soviet Union lags in the field of technology and continues to fall farther behind. With the advent of such devices as computer microchips, no bigger than a fingernail and containing a million elements, U.S. technology is capa-

---

*For simplicity's sake, this discussion has left to one side the whole issue of internal subversion, which unquestionably exists. To say otherwise would be to assume that U.S. intelligence forces are brighter than those, say, of the British, which housed for so many years the traitor H. A. R. (Kim) Philby, along with his KGB cohorts Guy Burgess and Donald McLean. Nor could any serious reader of

ble of bringing forth, far sooner than even the Kremlin masterminds might imagine, some marvelously advanced new weaponry. We speak of electronic and other weaponry that would make the U.S. and its NATO allies instantly capable of defeating any attempted Soviet blitzkrieg. Sophisticated new tactical and strategic sensors, precision-guided munitions, the high-energy laser and other directed-energy weapons, most particularly the charged-particle beam, which uses streams of charged electrons to create what amounts to a man-made lightning bolt—all give us every cause to hope for a real defensive—or, let's face it, even offensive—technological breakthrough for the United States.

Pentagon officials wisely express skepticism that directed-energy weapons of such importance as to afford virtually overnight superiority can be developed any time soon. But in the case of U.S. military technology, the present writer nonetheless maintains some optimism, unlike his gloom about the prospects for the U.S. economic scene.

Were we once again cast in a position of clear-cut military supremacy, everything that was once possible could be possible again!

Another great hope which this writer has for the United States rests in the very subject matter of this book: natural resources.

Nature has blessed this country with such an incredible abundance of coal, oil and other critical substances, most of them untapped, that, given strong national leadership, the development of these resources could result in a new capital productivity of such dimension as to produce a virtual economic rebirth.

---

the newspapers fail to see the stories of roughly comparable disclosures in Canada, West Germany, the Netherlands, France, and other countries. All of logic and contemporary history tells us that American security, no less than that of any other country, is infested with enemy agents buried in high places—"moles," as the language of espionage calls them. We need only recall the example of Harry Dexter White, mentioned earlier. Our best hope of unearthing the savage animals burrowing through our government is to restore to the FBI its originally mandated powers of counter-intelligence specifically enacted for the purpose of providing at least minimal protection from internal subversion.

In Alaska alone, for example only, over 100 million acres have been restricted from mineral exploration and development. Over 50 million acres in Alaska have been set aside as national monuments. Little of Alaska's land has ever been evaluated for mineral potential. This largest state in the Union has only two commercial mining operations of any dimension, one of them a coal mine and one a gold-dredging operation. Geologists rate as superb the potential of Alaska for chromite, nickel, cobalt, platinum and other key minerals. Yet only 17 percent of Alaska is even open to prospecting. It is an area far larger than France.

Almost the same situation exists throughout the remainder of the United States. Much of Idaho is already forbidden to modernization in that state's giant "Wilderness Area." In 1979, the Senate decided to legislate a new "River-of-No-Return Wilderness" in Idaho. In so doing, the Senate restricted access to a region of cobalt mineralization. This small cobalt area would have in no way prevented creation of the Senate's newest Idaho jungle.

Did the Senate consider that the United States had not produced a single pound of cobalt in either 1978 or 1979 and that cobalt is our single most vulnerable defense import?

Only the tiniest part of this nation's land has been given thorough geological analysis.

Modern technology makes possible the achievement of many, if not all, ecological goals while still permitting maximum utilization of the nation's resources.

Ecologists and environmentalists (most of them apparently unaware that any war other than that of the insect world rages around them) may some day be forced by a more realistic national minerals policy to recall that man got where he is today by conquering nature.

Without treating the question of whether or not similar strides might once again be made—this time by conquering the ecologists—it is nonetheless clear that a return to a sensible pragmatism in our approach toward development of this country's natural resources could also bring renewed hope for the future of this country.

5
The New Gold: Strategic Metals

In the following pages we will, whenever possible, be especially concerned with the situation of the beginning investor.

The first part of this book has, I hope, made the point that all paper money, over time, becomes valueless. Given the type of government now existing in the United States, it simply becomes worthless faster.

That is the reason the prudent investor and the conservative speculator (they are, today, in fact, one and the same), must seek the safety of durable tangibles—commodities that are not perishable and, indeed, have such durability that, unless they are subjected to severe abuse, they retain the form they had at time of purchase for long periods of time, sometimes forever. Paintings, drawings, books, carpets, antiques, stamps, precious stones, and many other commodities enjoy the advantage of durability if well cared for. Yet such commodities are risky bets as compared to the indefinite life span of most strategic metals and other elements as well as the eight metals that are separately categorized as "precious." Paintings and the associated items of either rarity or beauty have in many cases the value of being *collectibles*. But metals, in the form of rare coins and other rare objects, are still the *safest* of all the collectibles because of their generally far greater durability and *existence expectation*.

Thousands of ancient coins of the Greek, Roman, and even earlier periods, dating back to the first Lydian coinage in the seventh century B.C., not only still exist today and are highly valued collector's items but in a surprising number of instances can still be found in "mint condition," just as they were struck and without a scratch upon them.

Yet these ancient "numismatic" coins are not for the beginning investor who wishes to invest his or her where-withal in the safest possible area and achieve a rate of return that, at an average over many years, will be equal to or better than the rate of inflation in his or her country. They are collectors' items that require the counsel of knowledgeable experts in this highly specialized field. (I mention three of the world's best in my Acknowledgments.) The same necessity of learned counsel is true of older U.S. and European gold and silver coins, as well as of the few Russian platinum coins known to have been minted.

So too with regard to colored stones, which of all the collectibles mentioned so far have a durability that approaches (though does not equal) that of most metals. Like numismatic coins, whether ancient or modern, colored stones require either much study or the advice of a trusted expert before purchase.

All of which brings us to the question: Where should the beginning investor of modest means start? The answer, which may surprise you, is in the strategic metal of utmost versatility. In my view, the beginning investor should first invest in a metal that is one of the eight that can be classified as *both* strategic and precious—namely, gold.

Now, I am not an investment advisor, mainly because I am sufficiently occupied at this time with helping in the investments of our own rather large privately-held family partnership. Therefore, I can tell you only what I would do in what I consider an average circumstance, and what many thoughtful investors have already done.

With the recent introduction of South Africa's new one-tenth–ounce Krugerrand coin, it is now possible for even the most modest investor to become a holder of gold. With the price of gold at approximately $564 per ounce, this newest and smallest version of the world's most-recognized and widely accepted gold coin was selling at around or slightly less than $73 at most coin dealers at the time of this writing, January 1981.* It can be resold to any of thousands of recognized coin dealers throughout the nation and also at many banks, although I expect the coinage *premium* on this weight Krugerrand coin, if South Africa finds it popular enough to continue its mintage, perhaps to decline a bit.

The Krugerrand is what is generally referred to as a "bullion-type" gold coin. That is to say, its value rests largely upon the intrinsic value of its gold content and not upon any numismatic, or collector's, value (although with the very first of these coins, numismatic value, too, may develop in years to come). Although you pay a premium for a bullion-type gold coin (generally the cost of minting the gold into a coin plus a small profit to the dealer), you will generally get at least that amount of premium, and perhaps even more, back from a coin store or bank when you wish to sell the coin. At $73, the one-tenth–ounce Krugerrand was selling (at a moment when gold was at $564) at a premium of about 18 percent over its bullion gold content. Larger bullion-type gold coins—for instance, the one-quarter and one-half Krugerrands—sell at usually steadily diminishing premiums because more of them than of the one-tenth ounce are available. The full-ounce Krugerrands, Maple Leafs, and other comparable gold coins generally bear a premium of between 3 and 4 percent. (Although little counterfeiting goes on in bullion-type gold coins of 1 ounce or less, you of course should do as one ordinarily would do when buying any other merchandise of importance—purchase from a recognized

---

*The small investor also has available even cheaper gold coins—the two-and-a-half and the two peso Mexican gold pieces. The former contains .0683 percent gold and the latter .0482 percent. With the price of gold at $564, both coins were selling for below $50 each. Both have a ready resale market.

and well-established dealer whose reputation you have checked.)

The important point is that gold investment is at this writing within the reach of even that small saver with less than $100 to spend. Why is this important? Simply because any investment in gold bullion itself, given a sufficient period to appreciate in value, has historically been an individual's surest bet for at least maintaining his or her standard of living.

To illustrate: In 1920, with one-ounce of gold selling at $20.66, a man could sell or exchange that ounce of gold for a fine, tailor-made suit of clothes. Today, sixty years later, with gold around $564 an ounce as of this writing, that same ounce of gold has so survived the ravages of inflation that it still will purchase its owner the same or a better standard of living than it did six decades ago: an ounce of gold today, as in 1920, will still buy at least one and perhaps two fine suits of clothes.

Gold increased in value from $35 an ounce in 1934 to a high of around $850 per ounce in the early months of 1979. Like many another commodity, it is volatile in price on a day-to-day basis, but it generally has had an upward trend ever since the governments of the world permitted gold to circulate at a price fixed by the free market.*

George Bernard Shaw, a socialist, still was enough of a capitalist (as all smart socialists are) to recognize the value of gold. "You have to choose [as a voter] between trusting to the natural stability of gold and the honesty and intelligence of members of the government," Shaw wrote in *The Intelligent Woman's Guide to Socialism and Capitalism,* "and, with due respect for these gentlemen, I advise you, as long as the capitalist system lasts, to vote for gold."

---

*It is worth noting again that gold, like silver, is both a strategic *and* precious metal. Fourteen percent of gold is already used for industrial purposes. Its high electrical conductivity and high degree of corrosion resistance makes it much desired by industry for many plating uses, contacts, terminals, printed circuits, and semi-conductor systems. Space and defense programs use much gold in instrumentation, the reflection of infra-red radiation, vacuum tubes, etc. Its use in dentistry and jewelry is well known.

Except for staples like food and water, gold has been mankind's most accepted medium of exchange and the most dependable standard of value since the dawn of recorded history. Man's first use of gold as money as a standard of value came around 3000 B.C. in Egypt, and the first gold coins were probably struck during the reigns of either King Candaules or King Gyges in the early seventh century B.C.

Gold and silver (the latter to a somewhat lesser extent) were clearly the most recognized standards of material value during biblical times. The word "gold" is mentioned 417 times in the Bible, "golden" another 57, and "silver" 319 times.

Even the authoritative *Encyclopedia Britannica* (1961 edition) is quite clear on its opinion of gold as an investment:

> Gold has ceased to play an important role in the domestic monetary system of most countries, and the gold standard in its earlier and only authentic form may have passed forever, but gold is a tangible asset while fiduciary money is merely a more or less readily collectible promise. In a world of international skepticism, if not active distrust, gold . . . will long be more highly regarded than foreigners' promises subject to repudiation either by the promissors or their governments. Gold . . . possesses in pre-eminent degree the virtue of international vendibility. The prestige of gold is therefore still great enough to insure, for an indefinite period, its retention as international money. . . .

But this book is hardly meant to be a guide for the student of gold investment. Books dealing with that subject in detail, and silver investment as well, are readily available in bookstores. Suffice here to say that gold has served as the principal medium of exchange (as well as a strategic industrial commodity) throughout history because: (1) its value does not depend on a government fulfilling its promises, especially in times of crisis; (2) it is scarce; (3) it is portable; (4) it is easily divisible; (5) it is durable, and indeed for all practical purposes is indestructible and changeless in appearance; (6) it is desirable; and (7) it is impossible to counterfeit.

I spend this much time on gold because I would recommend to any investor that he keep a "core" holding of gold—a holding which he does not ever plan to trade—amounting to 10 percent of his investable funds. I would further recommend that he keep a minimum of another 10 or 15 percent of his portfolio in gold that he *does* plan to trade—to sell, taking the profits in his country's currency when the price seems most attractive, and later to buy again at a lower price. A seller of gold for currency may choose between trades to convert whatever currency he receives into another which he considers safer or appreciating more in worth. In so doing, he must always keep in mind that to convert and reconvert currencies from one to the other is not without *some* fixed cost built into the bid and asked prices.

The prudent investor will also have another 10 percent of his available investment funds in a "core" holding of another vital and strategic metal, silver—silver bullion or, preferably, U.S. silver coins minted in 1964 or earlier. Silver is a far more important industrial metal than gold and has the additional advantage of being in short supply. Most years more silver is consumed than is produced. Silver is not as universally accepted as a precious metal (by the world's central banks, for example), yet U.S. silver coins, unlike gold, remain legal tender in the United States. Every American investment portfolio should include that number of pre-1965 U.S. silver coins which you can afford, up to 10 percent of your investment holdings. These silver coins have, in my opinion, the opportunity for an even greater percentage appreciation than gold. Indeed, many investors buy silver coins from coin stores by the bag; generally such bags of coins have a face denomination of $1000. Non–U.S. readers would also do well to consider holding U.S. bullion silver coins or, at the very least, the nearest thing to a bullion-type silver coin (one with the very lowest possible premium) available in their countries. Members of other nationalities can easily acquire U.S. bullion-type coins (1964 and earlier) by buying nearest month U.S. futures in $1000-denominated bags of these coins and then taking delivery.

Summarizing, I would thus recommend that at any given time an "average" investor today should have some 30–35 percent of his or her savings always in, or earmarked for, ready investment in gold or silver.

A number of more affluent investors list a few *intelligently bought* low-carat diamonds as part of a basic portfolio, not merely because the diamond has also traditionally risen in value and maintained its purchasing power but also, more importantly, because of the diamond's high degree of portability. Although I agree with this view, I would still caution the investor who plans to put even the smallest percentage of rainy-day funds into diamonds that such a purchase be made only after the most careful study of these stones and even then only with expert consultative assistance. Under any circumstances, diamonds should be part of a *sine qua non* investment program only for the investor who has already taken care of the first two "must-do's": gold and silver.

It should also be said that every person needs to keep a modest sum in cash (international currency speculators, specialists in the field, can intelligently maintain larger sums). Ideally, one's cash or cash equivalents should be withdrawable on the shortest possible notice in order to be able to take advantage of bargains that may appear on a moment's notice. This is the reason that I prefer within the United States either bank call money (two-day dollars), a good money-market fund, or U.S. Treasury bills. (Call dollars may not be available to the average investor because banks normally will not sell them in any amount under a rather high minimum sum.)

Overseas, one's cash requirements should also be kept in a hard (Swiss or Singapore, for example) readily negotiable currency—call money, one-week time deposits, government paper, or whatever one chooses to be a foreign equivalent (for example, government-backed notes in the stabler foreign currencies) of the U.S. money market funds, most of which overseas placements pay excellent interest rates and, at least in the case of call (two-day) foreign currencies, are instantly withdrawable or transferable. (As an aside, I should note that the wise investor will generally keep one-half of his ready-cash requirement in U.S. dollar-denominated paper in the United States, and the other one-half abroad, "hedged" in the aforementioned types of foreign, ready-money investments. And, to further protect and diversify himself, he or she will maintain any foreign cash, cash equivalent, or other monetary holdings preferably divided equally within the better banks or, in the case of some chosen variety of foreign equivalent of our money-market funds, trustworthy brokerage firms in a number of different and stable foreign countries—for example only, Switzerland, Singapore, Hong Kong, and Australia.)

In a forthcoming book, a sequel to this work, I will present detailed recommendations for the investment of the remaining approximately 60 percent of one's investments. Here, however, I will focus on one key recommendation regarding that remaining 60 percent of your investment funds (and it is the end purpose of this book), namely, that you definitely earmark 10 or 15 percent of it for a new type of investment, a position in still another tangible—other strategic metals and elements.

Strategic metals, bought selectively and with the guidance of an able metals consultant are, I believe, both sound and the most promising investment opportunity since gold was selling at $35.00 per ounce and silver was less than $2.00 per ounce.

Strategic metals are precious ores and critical substances without which modern planes cannot fly, autos cannot run, television sets cannot function, advanced submarine manu-facture must cease, today's sophisticated electronics are impossible, and even a simple everyday, taken-for-granted item such as a battery just cannot be made.

These metals and other elements are all in *finite* supply. Their supply will one day be exhausted. As that supply diminishes, their prices must rise unless substitutes can be discovered for them. As the cost of mining these strategic elements rises, their prices must also respond by moving still further upward. In many cases, such as silicon and magnesium, one of the major costs is the fuel required to produce them, and fuel costs most certainly will continue to increase.

There are so far 105 known elements, many of them of critical importance, and the prices of some of them will increase explosively in the coming years. And new uses for them are being discovered every week. If some commodities can be called *collectibles*, the commodities that I group together as strategic metals can best be termed *indispensables*.

Learn all you can about these vital metals and other rare earth substances. Many of them are indeed the indispensables of life today. Without the strategic metals we must revert, if not to the Dark Ages, certainly to that unacceptably lower standard of living the world endured in those dim centuries before the Industrial Revolution of the eighteenth century.

Let's first look at the more than thirty major nonferrous metals—metals not containing or related to iron—from A (antimony) to Z (zirconium). Some of these metals have no known effective substitute—among them, chromium, germanium, and indium. Many are virtually essential to national defense: niobium (or columbium), cobalt, germanium, magnesium, molybdenum, titanium, tungsten, and vanadium.

Beyond the nonferrous metals are the more exotic precious (yet also strategic) metals. There are eight precious metals. Most people think only of gold, silver, platinum, and possibly palladium. Not many investors are familiar with rhodium (most expensive of all precious metals), iridium, ruthenium, and osmium (all found in small quantities in platinum ores).

Until very recently, the frontiers of strategic metals investing have been cloaked for the general public in a forbidding mystery and all but closed even to large, private investors. The writer has devoted much of the last two years attempting to explore this dark and hitherto almost uncharted land and to open it to the individual investor. I was told that it would not be made easy for me, and it has not been. Since their very discovery, these metals have gone from producer to user, directly from one to the other at first and today proceeding from producer (the mining company) to refiner to international mercantile brokers to user. But a series of personal trial investments in such metals as rhodium, aluminum, germanium, gallium, lead, and cobalt has been sufficiently successful to prove to me that there is considerable money to be made by individual investors in this new field.

What are some of the crucial facts concerning the use of strategic metals?

The United States must today import 64 percent of its nonferrous metals. We are wholly or in large part dependent upon foreign imports for at least twenty-three strategically vital minerals, many of whose major producers are sources of, shall we say, potentially precarious supply—for example, India, South Africa, Thailand, Zaire, Zambia, the Soviet Union, Turkey, Bolivia, China, and Zimbabwe (until recently, called Rhodesia). Virtually all of the world's mineral reserves of four key critical elements—chromium, vanadium, manganese, and platinum—are held by South Africa, Russia, and Zimbabwe.

We are now more dependent on foreign countries for our nonferrous metals than for oil and gas. This is also true of our allies. In 1979, the West German government set up a fund of nearly $400 million to help companies in that country stockpile vanadium, chromium, cobalt, asbestos, and manganese. To illustrate the indispensability of many strategic substances, the West German government has calculated that if for any reason it were suddenly deprived of 30 percent of its annual import of chromium, the entire West German GNP would drop by 25 percent.

NATO is deeply worried about the continued ability to obtain certain strategic metals; so is the U.S. Department of Defense. In June 1977, the United States set forth a "national mineral policy," President Carter describing our situation as "alarming."* Unfortunately, after more than three years, that program is foundering on the bureaucratic rocks of fourteen different government agencies, either through indifference, actual whitewash, or even—it is quite possible—active sabotage from enemy "moles" within our own government. The problem is simply desperate.

The United States has only 50 percent of the quantity of chromium and cobalt that it needs as a minimum in its national defense stockpile. In terms of quality, we do not have in our stockpiles the quality of cobalt, for instance, necessary to build the jet aircraft engines that we must have today. The result? We must import almost 100 percent of our cobalt. For the U.S. government, it is purely and simply a national security *crisis*. For investors, it is purely and simply an enormous investment *opportunity*.

Let's look at titanium as an example—lightweight, high strength, corrosion resistant, able to stand up to intense heat. The USSR, until recently a major supplier of titanium, has, at least for now, stopped exporting this vital defense metal. The Soviets are using their titanium internally for expanding aircraft production and, among many other military purposes, for the world's first all-titanium deep-running attack submarines which, precisely because the walls of the submarines can be built four times thicker than stainless steel, titanium being only one-quarter the weight of steel, can withstand the pressures of far greater depths than U.S. submarines can possibly reach, being far lighter and stronger than steel. Could you make money on titanium? Well, if you had bought stock 18 months ago in one of the three integrated U.S. producers of titanium, Ormet, you would have made a killing. Ormet (Oregon Metallurgical) has risen from $3 to

---

*Congressman James Santini, Chairman of the House Subcommittee on Mines and Mining, declared on September 18, 1980, that "recent evidence shows that USSR *acquisitions* . . . pose a new potential for . . . actual involvement in a 'Resource War' with the world's other superpower [my italics]." It is well known that the Russians are *importing* titanium, vanadium, lead, beryllium, tantalum, and lithium. Also, from politically sympathetic nations, they probably are covertly bringing in others of which we are unaware.

over $60 a share, where it seems overpriced for the time being. This writer holds a substantial position in quite another U.S. titanium producer. You would also have profited enormously over the last few years had you bought the physical product titanium and kept it in storage. Titanium has risen from a low of around $3 a kilogram to some $18 today, after peaking at $42.

Here we should note that one can safely enough take delivery of a few of the elements, but the buyer is much wiser to store them in a recognized, bonded warehouse equipped to cope with such matters as storage (the costs are surprisingly reasonable), chemical study, temperature, shipping, and such. The writer has often used the huge KLM Warehouse in Amsterdam. There are others, and your strategic metals broker (you simply must have one) can best handle your needs with respect to storage.

Perhaps the best way to grasp the full reality of strategic metals is to consider some of the stories of high adventure and romance that surround the strategic elements field. During bitter night fighting in the Six-Day War, the Israelis, according to a usually well-informed London metal dealer, encountered unexpected difficulty with Egyptian tanks in the Sinai. The war was over before Israeli intelligence could analyze a captured Russian-made Egyptian tank. Then the riddle was solved. The Soviet-built Egyptian tanks were equipped with a new type of night-sighting device, until that time unknown to the Israelis—a night-sighting device employing germanium.

Mercury for years was used in the manufacture of hats. It was not known for centuries, however, that mercury has a hallucinating effect if handled long enough: hence, the derivation of that old saying "mad as a hatter." Mercury, in addition, is one of the simplest metals to produce. All one needs is a kettle in which to boil the ore and a simple condenser. For this reason, many of the mercury mines in Mexico are run by only two people, working as a team in the hills. While one digs the ore, the other tends the boiling kettle. In two or three days, the two have produced a couple of flasks of liquid mercury, which they load onto their burro and take down to the nearest town. They sell the mercury and buy booze on which they get blind drunk. When the hangover has worn off, they must head up into the hills again. Hence, in Mexico one might assume a direct relationship between the price of mercury and the price of booze.

Another strategic metal, tin, may have cost Napoleon his empire. As *la Grande Armée* began its retreat from Moscow in October 1812, an unforeseeable disaster overtook the self-styled Emperor of the French. The buttons on the uniforms and greatcoats of his troops were all made of pure tin. As the dreadful cold steadily worsened in that frantic retreat, Mother Nature struck together with the Cossacks. When the temperature drops low enough pure tin often begins slowly to turn to gray dust. Suddenly (as battle-scarred metal dealers tell the tale), as battles raged in the unspeakable cold, all the tin buttons slowly began to disappear from the French uniforms, simply blowing away like sand. Greatcoats flew open; pants fell down. Think of fighting while freezing and trying to hold your pants up. Napoleon's retreat became a shambles, perhaps because of tin.

True, many—in fact, most—strategic metals also have important industrial *and* defense uses. Without manganese, our bones grow spongier and will break more easily. Again, without the new tungsten-tipped painless dental drills that can withstand the intense heat caused by drilling at high speeds, your every trip to the dentist would indeed be one you would remember forever.

What about zirconium? Without zirconium as an inner lining for reactors, there would be no such thing as nuclear power. (A tip: Investigate the zirconium situation before you buy it just yet. The United States is the major supplier of zirconium, but the Japanese, according to a press service report, have recently announced a new method of manufacturing it that halves the U.S. cost.)

Then we have cadmium . . . so toxic that it is thought to have wiped out whole populations. And arsenic . . . from the

Greek word *arsenikas,* which means male or virile, because the ancient Greeks believed that metals differed in sex. And the metal tellurium . . . a valuable alloy addition to steels, but to inhale the vapors from tellurium results in a monstrous garlic breath.

And more: Antimony, long used for women's eye shadow, among other things. Antimony can be poisonous. Monks used to take antimony to avoid the effects of fasting and were most often fatally poisoned. Beryllium, which can withstand melting to well over 1000°C and therefore is used in rocket nose cones. Aluminum, which was so rare when discovered in 1827 that the first samples cost more than $500 a pound and which is now so plentiful that it has been as low as 25 cents a pound. Cobalt, which takes its name from *kobold,* or evil spirit, because its poisonous ores were once terribly dangerous to mine. Osmium, the densest metal known—a bar of osmium the size of a brick weighs 56 pounds. Tantalum, used to replace bone in the human skull. And in delicate spinal operations, without yttrium, the surgeon would not be able to use a needle to kill the pain. Copper, one of the only two colored metals. The other is gold.

Then there is magnesium, vital in explosives and flash bulbs. Consider magnesium. A deficiency of magnesium can produce exactly the same effect as alcoholism: delirium tremens, the DTs. Gallium, a metal of significant use but which will melt if you hold it in your hand. Molybdenum, so important in boiler plate, rifle barrels, and filaments, discovered in 1778 but so difficult to produce that it was not until nearly two centuries later, in 1959, that a vessel could be invented in which to cool it.

A final anecdote: In the ABSCAM scandal of 1980 the federal agents offered merely cold, hard cash to garden-variety members of the House. But the Feds offered U.S. *Senator* Harrison Williams of New Jersey $10,000 in shares in a titanium mine, which he allegedly accepted. That's how important strategic metals have become. (By the way, the mine is now defunct and the shares worthless!)

Like most other worthwhile tangible investments (some of

which we mentioned at the beginning of this chapter), prices of the more readily tradable strategic metals and other elements are highly responsive to inflation. It is for this reason that tangible investments, strategic metals included, are often referred to as "alternative investment opportunities"—a polite way of saying that they represent an opportunity to escape depreciating paper money for the comparative safety of a nonperishable commodity, one less subject to either radical monetary or physical deterioration.

During the increased world price inflation in the year and a half from mid-1978 to early 1980, a majority of the active strategic metals more than doubled in price—a fair return on one's money by anyone's accounting.

But there is even greater potential in strategic metal investment than the already handsome current rate of return. The world's industrial nations have entered a recessionary period in which the output of many capital goods—cars, TV sets, airplanes, building materials, even kitchen equipment—is declining. This means that the manufacturers of these and thousands of other such familiar items should logically require far smaller amounts of the so-called base metals so common in their manufacture—lead, copper, zinc, iron, and tin, among others. Obviously, the prices of these base metals will drop as demand for them lessens.

Not so the price of most strategic metals. This price may even rise while the price of other base metals declines. How can this be?

Most strategic metals are by-products of the more familiar base metals. Thus, as the production of base metals decreases, so too the supply of strategic metals decreases— quite regardless of the fact that *demand* for these strategic by-products may be as great or greater than ever. In times of international tension, and the 1980s will surely be that, the price of the base metal zinc, used in nonessential capital goods, may drop sharply, as in fact it has, while the price of the strategic metal germanium, by-product of zinc refining, rises because of increased military demand. As noted earlier, germanium is a vital element in night-sighting devices, as the

Israelis presumably discovered during the Six-Day War. The result? While demand for zinc in industry may decline and its price likewise, the price of one of its by-products, germanium dioxide, has jumped sharply. I can add the personal note that this writer began to invest in germanium in mid-1979; the result has been most rewarding.

What holds for germanium similarly holds for iridium. Demand for its base origin platinum has reportedly been reduced by the normal decrease in industrial demand that usually accompanies any recession, however short. The result has been a reduction in the available supply of platinum's by-product, iridium, even more precipitately than in that of the main metal itself. Iridium (see a more detailed discussion in Appendix B), a key factor in the making of electrical contacts and jewelry, has increased in price from $240 per ounce on December 21, 1979, to $600 in January 1981.

The basic fact is that strategic metals for which there are no substitutes, nor even an inferior replacement, respond to shortages with understandably quick and huge increases in price. Is the price of a nonsubstitutable item like chromium to drop sharply because one of its basic users, the automobile industry, cuts back production? Not when the military forces of the world are stockpiling chromium for essential defense use in case of war.

Then, it would appear, all one needs do is buy one of these strategic elements, hold it for a reasonable period of time, and then rush to the bank with one's profits.

Not quite so, I regret to say. Even the reader who studies this book carefully needs the topical, inside information normally available only to the professional who trades strategic elements for his living and does *only* that. As we will discuss in more detail later, do not put your strategic commodities investments in the hands of someone who has five other business irons in the fire. Trading strategic commodities is a full-time business. Make no mistake about that.

In unusual cases, even a veteran trader who has specialized in the strategic field for years can get hurt. A rather well-known illustration of this point came out not so long ago. The head of a European mining firm, no mean chemist himself (or, perhaps, as it turned out, alchemist), had for many years been dealing in the tellurium market. He was quite aware that tellurium is never found in its pure state, but like so many other "strategics" is a by-product, in this case an offshoot of copper refining (and, in certain instances, is recoverable from lead and zinc deposits). Now, when one combines tellurium with certain steel and copper alloys, the resulting tough substance becomes much easier to "machine" into various products. Indeed, the ability to improve the machinability of many hard metals is by far the major use mankind has for tellurium; its use for chemical purposes is minor by comparison.

Our experienced merchant-chemist knew the limited chemical purposes of tellurium. Then, he came up with a brand new chemical use of this metal, a discovery that induced him to think he should try to corner the tellurium market, which he promptly attempted to do. Our hero had discovered that by combining tellurium with the element bismuth, one obtained bismuth–telluride, a strange new substance indeed. Joining a wire of bismuth–telluride with one of bismuth alone, one had only to put an electrical charge through the two joined wires and—the ends would freeze. Ahah! That should mean, he quickly grasped, that instead of having to use an ordinary gas-operated refrigerator (which was the type then used in most homes in his country), with the new type of wire his expertise had produced, Europe and then the world could be offered its first totally electronic refrigerator, its operation resting on his bismuth–telluride. That being the case, with the world having only a limited amount of tellurium, well—oh, jolly—if he bought all the tellurium in the world . . . what a demand would be created for it!

The result of the wishful squeeze on tellurium made the ill-fated attempt of robber barons Jay Gould and Jim Fisk to corner the gold market look like a successful heist at Fort Knox. What our friend had not taken into account—indeed, had not bothered to think about—was that gas-operated refrigerators are ten times *cheaper* than the bismuth–telluride models which his hired scientists assembled for him. To this day, bismuth–telluride still has only minor uses where a special freezing effect is desired.

So even people experienced in buying, selling, and working with strategic elements have made monumental blunders when their emotions, such as greed, got in the way or when, as in the case of our friend, they had not done their homework properly.

Actually, this story has more than one valuable lesson to offer both the trader and the investor. Don't try to do two things at the same time. The trader should stick to cool, reflective trading; the chemist to his own science; and the investor to conferences with a specialized strategic metals broker who is not at the same time trying to make other fortunes on the side peddling antique shoehorns, Krugerrand straddles, old English pewter, and other more esoteric items. Show me the man who offers you expert technically worded advice on strategics, colored stones, the currencies of obscure foreign nations, global geopolitical strategies that will quickly push the price of gold and silver up or down, and also offers a continuous, personal telephone answering service—and I will show you the man that I am not going to choose to be my broker in the strategic metal field.

The expert I employ in London to advise on my strategic metals purchases, sales, and lending or borrowing (the last being another beautiful little profit-making opportunity generally existent only in the minor metals field—we'll discuss it in the next chapter) does one thing and one thing alone: he gathers the most intelligence he can unearth on a given element and then submits it to his clients for their possible action. The result has been that my consultant has in the past months passed on to our company what have turned out to be highly profitable recommendations for the purchase of two metals that other would-be strategic metal advisers, offering and operating a virtual variety store of various investment bargains, have just now begun to discover.

At this point, let's look systematically at some elementary "dos and don'ts" for the individual considering his or her first investment in strategics:

1. Since the field is so new, and there are no Merrill-Lynches or E. F. Huttons, one ought to examine the past ventures of the primary stockholders of his trader's firm. What is the track record of the firm's major stockholders in the businesses they have previously owned?

2. Besides some agreed-upon and normal brokerage commission, what *other* expenses are you to be charged, such as telephone bills, postage, Xeroxing, etc.?

3. Is your trader available at any hour? Strategic metal trading is physically demanding since the markets are humming somewhere 24 hours a day; you don't want a broker who demands privacy for his favorite television shows while the news has just broken that the North Albanians have begun a surprise invasion of Zaire and Zambia, which means you now must decide what to do about your cobalt.

4. An odd-sounding warning to you: Try to be sure that you are not driving such a hard bargain with your broker that he isn't making a fair rate of return for doing business with you. A broker can't operate without making a profit any more than you can. To carry it one step further, unless he makes a *reasonable* profit, he can't buy or sell for you with the degree of efficiency you should expect. On the other hand, many brokers will try to set their commission structures so high that they earn money even if they have a base of only a handful of customers. So, another warning: Does the broker charge an inordinately high fee for his services? If so, better watch out, you could be doing business with an outfit that has insufficient capital to back their operation.

5. Was your broker ever the clown in a circus? An affirmative answer won't mean that he's not good. It's just that there are some weirdos in every business (and some quite successful ones, too), and it is always prudent to know as much as you can about a man to whom you plan to entrust your money. To be specific, there are some top people in the

strategic metals business—but there are a few clods and other oddballs that I would not touch with a 10-foot pole. Beware particularly of the character who talks so fast on the telephone and phrases everything he's saying so technically or metaphysically that you end up wishing you'd recorded the whole outpouring so that you could turn the tape over to Berlitz for interpretation. I once dealt with a trader like that in a strategic metals transaction. I was so new to the game that I assumed I was either too dumb to understand a perfectly simple Einsteinian explanation or not quick enough to follow rapid conversation—or that we had a bad line. Just why it didn't occur to me that I had once again run into a con man, since in younger years I held a near monopoly on hiring them, I cannot explain.

6. Examine carefully any strategic metals firm that offers to "make a market" within any unclear time span in any or most of the traded critical elements. "Making a market" means that a firm offering to do so is prepared at any time to offer you a price at which it will buy or sell your tungsten or silicon or whatever. To be as clear as possible, let's look at a specific example. The Swiss Bank Corporation makes a market in certain currencies, which is to say that at a given moment when the bank is open if you want to buy or sell, say, Swiss francs, you have but to call the bank and (barring some unusual circumstance) you'll be quoted a price at which the bank will either take the Swiss francs you own or sell you some of theirs. Now, I know at least one concern that puts forth representations (verbally and in regular weekly mailings) that seem to me to say to prospective customers that this firm makes a market in several of the strategics. But the only way in the world one can issue a standing offer to sell such war-related materials as germanium dioxide without carrying unlimited bankruptcy and fraud insurance (and this concern is, I hope, not given to fraud) is to set the prices at which one offers to buy and sell so high that it makes no difference if war breaks out while the offer is in the mail. Another way of saying this is that the broker must fix his "spread," the difference between the price at which he will

buy and the price at which he will sell a given commodity, with so ridiculously wide a margin between the two prices that, if you do business with him, you will doubtless start off far in the red if you buy from him and in all probability end equally far in the red if you sell to him. If Swiss producers (Switzerland being the world's primary supplier of gallium) decide without notice to increase the price of that metal materially, the broker who had offered to make a market in gallium would have little to worry about *if* he had built in a ridiculously high profit margin or spread when he first made (or, particularly, *mailed out*) such an offer. Otherwise, the offer is as dangerous as a theatrical agent mailing out a standing offer to deliver the services of Bo Derek as an actress one day before the premiere of *10*. Or at least, since to allow a metals offer made in the mails to stand indefinitely could only be the action of an inexperienced-in-the-field broker and a novice investor, as dangerous to the latter as a puppy on a new rug.

7.   Don't be afraid to ask plenty of questions. In the next chapter we're going to list some of the better questions to ask in a strategic metal trade. Here's an example: How soon will you receive your check after you sell? Behind this question, as you may have guessed, is a story. I bought a three-month futures contract in one of the key strategic metals—lead—on the London Metal Exchange (LME), then sold the lead a few days later for a whopping profit. Imagine my surprise when I found out that because of the rules of that exchange (this doesn't happen in the United States) one can't get paid until delivery day of the contract month. That is, if on January 2 or 3 you bought a contract to buy April zinc on the LME, and then three days later—January 5 or 6—sold it because the April zinc price had happily skyrocketed in those 72 hours, exchange regulations would still force you to wait until some designated "delivery day" in late *April* before you get paid. As a result, your profit isn't quite as exhilarating as it first seemed, since you have lost the right to earn interest on both your principal investment and the profit for all those many weeks (during which time you may gnash your teeth about

the fact that someone—possibly the broker, but I'm not sure—is living it up on money you've already spent for a special three month package trial offer being made by the hottest new psychiatrist in town).

8. Don't be afraid to tell your strategic metals broker that you didn't understand the answer he gave to your question. You may find out that he didn't understand either—your question *or* his answer—but at least you'll end up knowing *that*. And then, if you are still speaking to each other, you may be able to rephrase the question where the only answer he can give is a "yes" or "no." Even then, it wouldn't hurt to ask him to repeat your question to you. It is absolutely amazing how often people accept without protest an "adviser's" answer that has no relevance to the question asked. Once I asked a broker in New York, "Is there going to be any difficulty selling it when I get ready?" I received the absolutely astonishing answer, "Well, you've always got buyers and sellers in any market if you happen to pick the right time to move." I don't use him anymore.

9. For the sake of your broker's health and of your own pocketbook, write out your questions *before* any telephone call in which you are seeking various bits of key information and jot down the answer. You might wish to consult the questions to ask that are listed in this book.

10. Even if you hear on the QT from your friendly neighborhood scrap metal man that Thailand, Canada, China, and Australia, four of the world's biggest suppliers of tantalum, have formed a cartel and are going to dump a five-year supply on the market, don't rush to attempt a tantalum short. Shorting any metal is a dangerous game, made doubly so if you're a relatively unsophisticated trader, and made triply so if you're just entering the strategic metals field. Disregarding the obvious question of why four distant nations would discriminate against a nice middle-class guy like you in favor of the neighborhood strategic scrap dealer, just don't do any shorting until you've been around the track a lot of times, a year at least, and with strategic metals, maybe even longer. Better never than in Bellevue. I've had

many "short"–happy friends who ended up trying to trade with an unnerved broker from the padded pay booths at their local happy farms.

11. It is more than possible that a potential investor who reads this book will conclude that he now knows so much that he can just go it alone. Yes, I suppose that's possible. You *could* go it alone if, indeed, this book has been as fundamentally informative as I hope it will be. If I have provided you with a basic education in strategic metals trading, you should be able to get yourself a list of merchant brokers in London, Kinshasa, New York, and Kuala Lumpur who would take your order for metals in which their merchant houses have been speculating and even stockpiling. But I must warn you about one problem. You will find at least ten specialist brokers who concentrate on small different groups of strategics, and it is only in these strategics that their expertise lies. I can tell you from experience that these brokers do not give up real *secrets* every five minutes. If one has discovered a little gem, a nugget like the fact that Switzerland has just sold its total production of gallium for two years to the Saudis in return for oil, you can bet he won't hurry to tell his brother brokers because the situation, of course, would be a golden moment for someone to take a killing in gallium. The one specialist broker that you might choose, then, could easily not have had this essential information. That's why I recommend that you engage your own consultant—a person who acts as a "clearing house" between the buyer and the merchant broker. Believe me, there is a big difference, at any given moment, in the prices that various metals are quoted at by different houses. Of course, you can do as you think best, but personally I would opt to deal with the most reliable expert I could find.

Naturally, the trader—talking as he does to many different merchant-brokers each day, all of whom are peddling one metal or the other—picks up potentially important bits of information concerning any number of the various strategics, which crazy quilt of facts he may often be able to piece together into something meaningful. The trader may very well pick up some news concerning selenium, which is a by-product of copper, combine it with some news about germanium, which can be a copper by-product in certain cases, and deduce something that relates to the very product his client has been asking about, cadmium, which also has some of its recovery from copper ore. The new investor who chooses one specialist merchant-broker before asking help from an all-metals consultant has no chance at all to put together such facts.

Similarly, the trader may be able to tell his client that a new method of recovering scrap metal has been discovered with regard to titanium (where scrap recovery from machine-use of that metal is very important). That may well affect the trader's advice regarding his client's titanium. Or the trader may get news of a proposed government edict that will vastly affect stainless steel prices, which news will naturally relate, potentially at least, to the price of quite a number of the tradable strategic elements.

The writer should mention that the term "merchant-brokers" is not some idle characterization of certain businesses. Many firms falling into this category are tremendous companies. They don't just buy and sell for clients. They take positions of their own in the very metals they trade, and purchase and hold perfectly huge amounts of one, another, or many of the strategic metals. Some of the merchant-brokers even have substantial ownership position in the metal mines themselves. Not to mention that a producer will often, for many a reason (so as not to sell directly, for example) choose to use a merchant trading house as a go-between. Thus, it is important that we emphasize here the strategic and influential role that these big minor-metal investment houses play in the markets of almost every strategic metal that the writer discusses in this book. .

12. It is important for the investor who puts his money into one or another strategic metals through a broker and plans to consider the strategics for a possible permanent percentage of his portfolio, to keep up-to-date. The best way to do so after you're in the game, short of daily long talks

with traders in the marketplace, and perhaps even then, is to subscribe to and read either the *Metal Bulletin* or *Metals Week* or both, the addresses for both of which you will find at the close of this book under *Recommended Reading*.

13. Be sure the strategic metals firm you trade with really *is* a strategic metals firm. I say that because some firms offer their expertise to trade in a lot of these strategic metals, but the moment they get an order they hastily lay it off with a broker who actually specializes in strategic metals. It's slightly akin to the experience of buying a Deutschmark six-month time deposit (akin to a certificate of deposit in the United States) from a top Swiss bank and then later discovering that in accepting your offer the bank had simply acted as middlemen and two minutes later laid off the time deposit with some other bank in Germany. You thought you had the biggest bank in Switzerland standing behind your purchase, which naturally gave you a lot of confidence, and then you received your monthly statement only to discover that your Swiss bank was not legally responsible for a thing if your time deposit became worthless through the failure of the bank you purchased it from. This actually happens. Swiss banks, by that country's banking regulations, cannot carry even an overnight time deposit in another currency. They are just middlemen, taking a commission as your money whips through their hands on its way into the main bank in Bad Nauheim.

That's enough, and maybe too much, of that. I don't want you to begin thinking that the strategic metal game is Russian roulette with all the chambers loaded. Quite the contrary. It's the most promising new way to make money that I know of.

Mining techniques are improving all the time. But while the world's population and consumption of these critical elements is increasing by leaps and bounds, most strategic metal production cannot even begin to keep pace. Production of most strategic ores is *not* going up. Not only are these ores getting scarcer and harder to find in the earth's crust, they are becoming far more expensive to mine, what with the costs of labor and fuel and other business needs inflating every day. You can add to these conditions the fact that there aren't that many new mines opening anymore, even with the prices of many strategic metals going up like mad. Today's interest rates are such that the absolutely enormous capital investment required to buy new mine equipment and then operate it for months before any physical goodies start coming up out of the shaft has made more recent investors in many mines as discouraged as an alligator with a back itch.

If you want to get right down to it, there appear to be only three good ways to answer the shortage problem in strategics: (1) improved technology in scrap recovery techniques; (2) quickly finding substitutes for the scarcest metals; (3) recovering the treasure of minerals in seawater, below the floor of the sea, and in the rocks on the bottom. But if you'll examine these ostensible solutions, you'll see that there really are not three ways to meet the long-term scarcity problem in strategic metals. First, developing new technology that will recover more scrap more cheaply is all well and good, but each time you recover the scrap, you reduce the scrap still to be recovered. It is rather like saving the scraps from last night's supper: If it was a big feed the scraps could last you for two or three more meals, but then you've got to go out and find some new grist to stoke in the old mill. Secondly, as to developing substitutes, that's easier said than done: several of the finite strategic metals are readily replaceable but almost always by one or more of the other equally finite strategic substances. Mostly, it's like robbing Peter to pay Paul. You might say new ways of breeding fresh whooping cranes are getting tight. Finally, as for recovery of the strategics in and under the sea—well, first, I like to think once in a while of a few *good* things that will happen while I'm still around, and that just isn't one of them, at least until somebody solves cost equations of sea recovery that now would explode your pocket computer. Add to that the fact that the rights to sea recovery has somehow found itself in that hall of mirrors that calls itself the United Nations, and by the time their decision is finally acted on, we'll be likely to be studying remnants of the U.N. building in a 22nd-century sequel to *Planet of the Apes*.

In short, the amount of strategic metals around isn't going to increase much in the near future.

And don't think all the strategic metal markets are small. A few are, but you won't be trading in those. Many in fact have considerable volume, and it has been correctly pointed out, just as one example, that the combined production of two little-publicized metals, chromium and manganese, exceeds that of copper. Remember also that production always tries to keep pace with demand. Most authorities in the strategic metals field would agree that trading volume in strategic metals could already be approaching $50 billion a year. And that's *real* volume for the most part, not futures-market, paper-type Comex volume, because a substantial percentage of the transactions in strategic metals involve physical delivery, which in turn calls for what the British speak of as "prompt" (this is typical English gentility; it just means hard cash on the barrelhead when you buy or sell).

One of the questions I've been asked most frequently since people learned that I had become a genuine, certifiable strategic metals investor, is this: Where do you store all that stuff? That's not only a good but a logical question, since many—if not most—strategic metals are sold in minimum transaction amounts of *tons*. That takes up space. But that is one part of the strategic metal business that *isn't* a problem. Not unless you plan to hoard these metals as some do gold and silver, taking delivery and burying them in your back-yard, or in the flowerpot on your windowsill, or in your mattress. You can take personal possession of gold, silver, platinum and even palladium, all four of which this writer chooses to classify as metals both precious and strategic. You can also sock away a few of the purely strategics, like iridium, indium, osmium, rhenium and rhodium; I suppose the really hoard-happy could also find a way to salt away gallium and germanium. But to take personal possession of the others you will need a bulldozer to do a mighty big number on what has to be a West Texas–size backyard to begin with. If you are emotionally unable to cope with bonded warehouse storage of most of your physical strategic metal acquisitions, and simply must have personal possession of all your valuables, then the strategics market may not be for you. You could no doubt find a warehouse in your hometown, but you'd do better to take the heavier metals and keep them in one of a number of well-bonded specialized warehouses that are technically equipped to handle the storage of your metal, warehouses recommended by your merchant broker and with which he is accustomed to deal on a day-to-day basis; he will then take over and handle routinely the otherwise onerous paperwork involved with insurance, chemical testing, purity papers, storage costs, and other details, all of which together is a 10-ton drag if you try to go it on your own. Storage costs for even the heaviest material are generally surprisingly reasonable, I might add, and if you are worried about the theft of that minimum transactional unit of 5 tons of columbium on which you have agreed to take delivery, better get yourself a specialist shrink in paranoiac hoardery. Even the worst doom-and-gloomer doesn't lose a lot of sleep about whether someone's going to make off in the middle of the night with his minimum 1-ton buy of cadmium—whose toxic fumes would prevent a thief from melting it down. He'd be so sick he'd want to return it to the warehouse—if he could make it back!

There are fine warehouses in Rotterdam (I've stored a lot of valuable metal there; it's been impeccably and efficiently handled and never a smidgen stolen), London, Manchester, Singapore, Sydney, etc. Many of the warehouses are in free port areas, with all the freedom from governmental control, duties, and various taxes that free ports traditionally offer.

Although it's true that getting into many of the strategics now is like being able to reenter the gold and silver markets when they were $35 and less than $2 an ounce, respectively, don't expect overnight or even weekly miracles from your new metal acquisitions. Part of the reason is that investment in these metals is *so* new there aren't organized markets yet—no futures' markets, no coin shops, auctions, or even newspaper ads imploring you to rush down to one of your nearby scrap metal dealers and bring all that family tungsten and cobalt you've left hidden in the attic for so many years. That situation is perhaps a safeguard for you—that and the fact that the prices of strategics don't normally jump around on a day-to-day basis with the nervousness of a pregnant bride at a wedding. Not that some of them haven't and won't again jump hundreds of percent within a year after reports of a new use, the imminent danger of a world saber-rattling tournament, or fresh demand from some old market, or who knows what. Anyway, without the speculation existent in the highly organized gold, silver and soft commodity metals markets, you can't expect one of these staid and comparatively colorless old metals, which has lain peacefully in the earth for so many eons, suddenly to take off like a rocket. Refer to the price action histories and other details of each individual tradable strategic metal for a fuller analysis of their separate potentials. You will find these histories and capsule descriptions in Appendix B.

One of the most strategic and precious metals you won't find there is platinum, which is not listed because it's traded on the big exchanges. But platinum has some lovely and highly useful siblings who, although younger in years, contribute mightily to both U.S. industry and defense, the nicest three being palladium, iridium, and rhodium. For that reason alone, platinum should merit some attention in this book. It's one of the most important defense and industrial metals that's ever been, and it's going to keep getting more so because new and significant uses are being discovered for it almost by the hour.

Platinum's no newcomer. Platinum, not gold, has been *the* jewelry metal for centuries in Japan. Gold is just now beginning to come into jewelry fashion in Japan, but it will be ages before it begins to make inroads with the tradition-minded Japanese woman. To show you the importance of platinum, which most frequently costs more than gold, let's look at a current news event (in October 1980) you may have read about—the amazing treasure that they're now bringing up from the cruiser *Admiral Nakimov,* torpedoed off the island of Tsushima, near Kyushu, in 1905 during the Russo-Japanese War.

In what has already become an international diplomatic imbroglio between Moscow and Tokyo, Japanese divers, working in late 1980, have brought up—from a Russian ship, remember—sixteen platinum bars of 70 percent purity, a find of both enormous historical and intrinsic value.

The sixteen bars of platinum alone are intrinsically worth at least $2.4 million at today's prices and perhaps ten times again that much (or more) if auctioned off at any future Sotheby or Christie auction of international collectibles. But why platinum aboard a *Russian* cruiser during a war with the *Japanese?* It was apparently being transported to help finance the war. Historically fascinating! Czarist Russia was then evidently the only country in the world other than Japan to recognize platinum as a precious (and to the Russians, even monetary) metal. In fact, the Russians had, between 1828 and 1845, minted rubles of platinum, the first and only platinum coins known.

But there's more, much more to this wonderful story, not to mention the further treasure yet to come. The Japanese have been more than a little bit at odds with the Russians ever since the Soviets confiscated a good part of northern Japan at the end of World War II. The Russians, by virtue of a secret agreement between the Allies at Yalta,* had taken for themselves the entire southern half of the huge, mineral-rich island of Sakhalin, plus all of the fifty-six adjacent and

---

*Southern Sakhalin and the Kuriles were but another part of the enormous rewards which also included an agreement that Outer Mongolia should become independent—i.e., Russian—and the ceding of almost all of Eastern Europe to the USSR secretly promised the Russians at the Yalta Conference in February 1945, by Churchill and Roosevelt, in return for a promise by Russia to enter the war against Japan within "two or three months."

When the secret Yalta agreements became partially public in 1946, a storm of worldwide protest broke over the agreement by which an overly optimistic Winston Churchill and an ailing Roosevelt had unaccountably left the USSR dominant in Europe, the Chinese damaged by the loss of Outer Mongolia in the east, and the Japanese hopelessly Russian-dominated to their north (not to mention the vast Eastern European and other concessions).

strategic Kurile Islands. Given this background, the Japanese are now having the most fun they've had since, say, Saburo Kashiwara discovered sukiyaki. For in their work, off Tsushima Island, the Japanese treasure divers (actually, mostly British) are reported by the Associated Press to have located "a number of boxes in hold," which hold, according to meticulous Japanese records, *five thousand five hundred boxes of gold bars and coins worth almost four billion dollars at today's prices*. This marvelous little quirk of fate may well take its place in international history and may also turn out to be one of the most striking proofs of both Lenin's brilliance as a prophet and the effectiveness of his poisonous Communist philosophy and/or determination to subvert capitalism.

Boris M. Zinoviev, minister at the Soviet Embassy in Tokyo, obviously acting under orders from Moscow, is now busily asserting before the Japanese Foreign Ministry that the ship and the gold belong to the Soviet Union and that any further salvage work be attempted only upon permission from Moscow. Put this demand in the context of the other juicy facts that spice an already hearty Japanese enjoyment of the situation: (1) the Japanese sinking of the *Admiral Nakimov* not only gave the nearly exhausted Nipponese fleet the edge it needed to rally and throughly trounce the Russian Navy at the Battle of Tsushima, but the resultant Japanese victory caused such discontent in Moscow and St. Petersburg that it led directly to the Russian Revolution of 1905; (2) Ryoichi Sasakawa, one of the richest men in Japan, a strong behind-the-scenes force in the ruling Liberal Democratic Party and sponsor of the salvage operation, says the treasure, as soon as it is brought to the surface, could be worth *forty billion dollars* instead of four; (3) Sasakawa has offered to return his purportedly gigantic treasure to the Russians in exchange for all the territory (southern Sakhalin and the Kuriles) taken from Japan at the end of World War II, which territory has been a stumbling block of such major proportion in relations between Moscow and Tokyo that Japan, since the war, has doggedly refused to negotiate a treaty with Moscow until the land is returned; (4) with the alleged billions of dollars returned to Moscow, Sasakawa avers, the Russians would finally have the money to carry out their desperately desired Siberian development, now at a standstill awaiting Japanese financial aid; (6) the Japanese government is studying international marine law to see what effect the whole salvage project might have with respect to the severe economic sanctions that Japan has been exercising against Russia in protest against the invasion of Afghanistan; (7) the Japanese government, no doubt tongue-in-cheek, is fussing with the powerful 81-year-old Sasakawa,* once a convicted Japanese war criminal but now rapidly become a popular folk hero, about meddling in international diplomatic affairs; (8) strong rumors hinted that the Russians were sending another warship to put a boarding party aboard and seize control of Sasakawa's Singapore-built, special $10 million salvage barge. Bully, again! Bully, bully! What a grand thing is this true story about platinum and gold, which (as we pointed out earlier) are both strategic as well as precious metals, elements of great industrial and military importance.

This fascinating story, steadily growing ever more complex and fascinating as it unfolds so far away on the other side of the Pacific, comes at just the point where the writer intended to point out once again that the way to start moving into stragetic metals is *first* to put a substantial part of your investment funds into gold, or indeed *all* of it if you have less than $100, to begin a conservative yet certain-to-appreciate savings kitty.

But where does Comrade V. I. Lenin enter into all of this, and why can I say this episode promises to wind up another harsh proof for the United States of Lenin's misdirected perspicacity? For it's likely that any gold that the Soviets get their hands on will not wind up helping to pay for Siberian

---

*Sasakawa visited New York City in 1979 and donated 150 cherry trees to Central Park with the city's mayor, Ed Koch, at his side. There is no apparent truth to the story that Mayor Koch has cabled Sasakawa, asking for some of the ship's booty as a further gift to New York City, toward ameliorating the City's financial problems.

development, but rather will finance more Soviet missiles aimed at the United States or will buy American wheat to feed Soviet troops as they continue their slaughter of the Afghans.

Lenin boasted that gold (as money) was a capitalist snare and delusion, and that in the "workers' paradise" it would serve only to decorate public lavatories (which metaphorically was and is true as to gold's *internal* Russian use and its value in improving the lives of the Soviet working man). And recall Lenin's further and utterly correct prediction: that the best way to destroy the capitalist system was to debauch the currency.

There can be little doubt that Lenin, and Marx before him, had studied assiduously the fall of the Roman Empire, carefully noting that even before Emperor Diocletian accelerated in 284 A.D. those final actions necessary to finish off the empire (a process Constantine was to sustain with even more effectiveness when he rose to power in 324 A.D.), the Romans had discovered a neat trick. They could debauch the currency by slowly shaving their silver coins (another key strategic metal, silver), year by year, making them ever smaller and thinner, so slowly that surely the people would not notice. But they did. And just at the time the emperors had so reduced the silver content from nearly pure silver to less than 1 percent, remarkably enough the Roman empire died, an event studied with such care by historians that it is preserved for the United States today with the same attention to detail that we have given the exactly similar and steady debasement of our own coinage.

Fortunately for the reader, the government has not yet discovered a way to profit politically from the debasement of those strategic metals not used in coinage. And that is the whole reason for this book, and the reason you should get out of paper money and all coins that don't contain enough precious metal to give them intrinsic value. Unfortunately, we happen to be talking about most of the coins circulating anywhere in the world today.

The mischief, and eventual havoc, that is the punishment

meted out to those who debase their currency is not only inevitable but apparently without finite time limit.

The debasement of Roman silver coinage, which was in full swing between 260–280 A.D., is the perfect case in point. Believe it or not, the iniquity of what those long-dead Romans did to their coins 1700 years ago has cropped up in the summer of 1980 to haunt the British.

A Mr. Kilshaw, using a metal detector, unearthed a hoard of 7,000 Roman coins in a Lincolnshire field early in 1980. Kilshaw sought to keep his remarkable find for himself— thought to be worth at least $40,000, but a British coroner's jury heard about the discovery, and fined him for theft.

The case was appealed and went before British High Court Justice Dillon while I was in England in June of last year. The question before the court was: Could debased coins, varying from a high of 18 percent to a low of less than 1 percent silver, be legally ruled as a "treasure trove" and thus claimed by the Crown?

The issue before the court, the 7,000 coins not being pure silver, was whether "treasure trove" was limited to gold and silver articles, or extended also to base metals. If treasure trove was pure gold and silver, how pure did the metal have to be? Judge Dillon complained that not only was there no earlier court ruling as a precedent, but 100 percent silver coinage was almost unheard of. Even the finest, earliest Roman silver coins were only 99 percent silver.

Was any article, say a Roman iron helmet with a silver coating worn to 1/1000th of 1 percent silver, a treasure trove? The writer left England while Judge Dillon was still sleeping—or not sleeping—on that one.

The important point is: Why were the coins buried in the first place if they contained so little silver? The answer: Gresham's law, bad money driving good out of circulation, and the Roman hoarder's fear that the next time he got 7,000 Roman coins together they might not contain *even that much* silver—if *any*.

No less illustrative of the enduring and increasing value of strategic-precious metals is the fact that an effort will soon be made to reach and search the British cruiser *Edinburgh*, sunk in 1942 in the forbidding, frozen waters of the Barents Sea, 170 miles north of the Soviet Union's heavily-guarded northern submarine base at Murmansk. The *Edinburgh* was torpedoed to the bottom as it headed for the United States with five and a half tons of gold in payment for "lend-lease" military equipment for the Russians. The British salvage company which will go after the treasure has called it "one of the most difficult salvage operations ever." Doubtless the attempt would never be made were it not for the fact that the original 5.5 tons of gold, valued in 1942 at $6,500,000, is now worth over $100,000,000.

Reports from London indicate that the salvage company could receive as much as forty percent of the gold, with Britain getting one-third of the rest and the Soviet Union two-thirds. One idly speculates on whether or not the United States, to whom this gold was to be paid, should be concerned with proceedings.

To return to the major tradable and purely strategic metals with which the investor will likely be involved. They are itemized in the tables in Appendix A, together with the basic details an individual needs to know to begin asking his or her trader the appropriate questions. The writer has not listed any of the strategic metals for which organized commodity exchanges already exist. Extensive information on these exchange-traded metals is available from highly reliable U.S. and foreign brokerage houses.

The metals are divided into four groups: There are eighteen elements definitely feasible for individual investor trading. (To repeat, no organized exchanges exist for any of these metals.) There are six other strategic metals that are tradable but present significant physical difficulties in trading for the private investor. A third group consists of seven other strategic metals that, in the writer's opinion, present little or no profit opportunity at the time of this writing. The last group consists of three metals that are currently being investigated for future trading possibilities.

The eighteen elements feasible for immediate trading are

antimony, bismuth, cadmium, chromium, cobalt, columbium (niobium), gallium, germanium, indium, manganese,
mercury, molybdenum, selenium, silicon, tantalum,
titanium, tungsten and vanadium. The six elements that are
tradable but which offer practical problems are arsenic,
beryllium, iridium, magnesium, rhenium and rhodium.

The prospective investor is further urged to pay careful
attention to the element "profiles" in Appendix B, which
detail the sources of production, price histories, uses, derivation, and other salient facts concerning the twenty-seven
tradable metals (the eighteen that are immediately feasible
and the nine that currently present no profit opportunities).

It is unlikely that there will be many changes in these
tables over at least one year's time; however, as new uses or
new-found substitutes for some of the metals occur, any later
editions of this book will update the tables accordingly. In the
meantime, when you have arrived at the point where you are
actually discussing any of these metals with your chosen
trading concern, you should be careful to ask the firm if the
situation represented on the tables has in any way changed.

One cannot emphasize too strongly the necessity for
continuing intelligence if one is to trade strategic metals for
maximum profit. The discovery of how to substitute one
element in a major use of another can have an explosive
effect on the prices of both metals. One can see the picture
more easily if one visualizes the obvious effect on the price of
certain commodities if it were discovered tomorrow that by
some alchemy salt compounded with rice could instantly
replace gasoline as a fuel for automobiles. Ridiculous?
You're right. You and I both know that corn can't make
gasohol. Fact is, no less astonishing real-life discoveries are
being made by science almost by the day. Take this press
release of September 16, 1980, from NASA, announcing the
discovery of a new "super-metal":

LIGHTER THAN THE LIGHTEST. . .

STRONGER THAN THE STRONGEST.

IT'S SUPERMETAL!

QUESTION: What metal is lighter, stronger and stiffer than aluminum and carries a lifetime guarantee in space?

ANSWER: Supermetal! Aluminum or magnesium laced with thousands of hair-thin strands of graphite fibers . . .

Sandwiched between aluminum or magnesium, the feather-light graphite makes the finished materials stronger, about four times more rigid and up to 35 percent lighter.

Unlike other metals in space, the composite also provides thermal stability—remaining unaffected by heat or cold since graphite-metal . . . will not expand or contract significantly. . . .

The press release goes on to explain that supermetal resists solar radiation, is indestructible, and should function in space indefinitely. NASA further declares supermetal to be more than promising for the construction and automobile industries and for commercial aircraft with lighter and stronger structures.

Now, what does this startling press release mean for the future of the two strategic elements, aluminum and magnesium, used in its manufacture? And what about the effect upon metals currently believed to be virtually irreplaceable in aircraft—a metal such as titanium, for example? And what of molybdenum, also big in aerospace? Look at the tables and take note of the metals now so important to the construction industry. What effect will supermetal have on *their* prices? And what may it mean to the prices of strategic elements important to the automobile industry, particularly the U.S. auto companies?

And in this Buck Rogers world of ours, how soon will supermetal be replaced by some *newer* alloy employing other strategics?

And what buyers there are going to be, not only for the old faithful strategics, but for these new alloys as they come on stream. Saudi Arabia has let it be known—just for example—that it *wants* to spend billions in the huge, as yet relatively untapped strategic resources of Australia, and that's just one country. Need I tell you what the Saudis *can* spend? If that's necessary, let me point out that the OPEC

whom it was not possible to negotiate terms if the order was one that the trader's firm wanted badly enough—which is to say: if the order is big enough. There are always *some* circumstances under which nearly any trader in a negotiated market, which is what you have in the strategics, will offer some measure, sometimes a large measure, of the financing if you have excellent credit and will bargain with him (and if, indeed, he has sufficient financial backing to arrange the credit for you). Because there are no rules and regulations in strategic metal trading like those that govern such large commodity markets as the Comex, the Chicago Board of Trade, the LME, the New York Mercantile Exchange, the Winnipeg and Minneapolis commodity exchanges, etc., a buyer (should his order be sufficiently desirable to his broker) could conceivably even negotiate down payments, as well as any possible later margin calls, for even less money and/or better terms than the regulations of any of the organized exchanges permit. In short, trading the nonexchange strategic metals really *is* trading in a totally free market.

That has, as usual, several advantages for all concerned. The biggest one is that the governments of various countries either have not yet been able or cannot figure out how to play the tricky numbers on (usually unsuspecting) traders they have played so long within most of the organized exchanges. At least in the United States, these huge, organized commodity exchanges have rules and regulations that can be commanded to be changed on mere whim by the federal bureaucracy. It is by now no news to readers of this book that the writer regards any such government interference with the rights of individuals to do business or carry on their lives without harming others, within existing laws, as an attack repugnant to freedom itself.

Freedom—that is the name of the fight, isn't it? We are already in a war with the Soviet Union. It is not yet a shooting war. It is still a resources war. Yet if we do not win it, there may be little reason to worry about a shooting war. The Soviets will already have us.

Writing in the respected *Saturday Review*, Robert Moss reports that "Leonid Brezhnev told a secret meeting of the Warsaw Pact leaders in Prague in 1973 that the Soviet objective was world dominance by the year 1985, and that the control of Europe's sources of energy and raw materials would reduce it to the condition of a hostage to Moscow."

Soviet Major General A. N. Lagovskiy, in a book entitled *Strategy and Economics*, refers to United States reliance on certain strategic materials from foreign sources as the "weak link" in American military capability. The General then proceeds to lobby for a strong Soviet attempt to gain control of these strategic elements as a wedge toward *exerting influence on the well-being of the United States economy*.

The United States imports almost all of its chromium and cobalt from a limited number of foreign suppliers located primarily in central and southern Africa, an area of increasing political instability. South Africa alone provides the United States with a great part of its chromite, ferro-chromium, and platinum group metals, a big measure of its ferromanganese, and several other key metals. Zaire and, to a lesser extent, Zambia are the key sources of U.S. cobalt. Should supplies from South Africa become unavailable, the United States would be dependent on its second largest potential supplier of chromium and platinum group metals— none other than the Soviet Union.

David Kroft, a recognized specialist in mineral commodity analysis, points out that the Soviet Union needs hard currency to buy Western technology and goods. One way that the USSR can obtain this revenge and, at the same time, satisfy its strategic objectives, Kroft points out, is to resell to the West minerals obtained at low cost from countries either unfriendly toward, or boycotted by, Western nations. A classic example which he cites is the purported Soviet purchase of chromite from Rhodesia (now Zimbabwe)—for resale at a significantly higher price to the West.

Thus the economic noose created by our increasing dependency on foreign supplies of critical materials grows ever tighter.

Zaire and Zambia are perfect examples of our vulnerability. Together accounting for about 65 percent of the world's cobalt, these two African nations have agreed to establish a minicartel in an attempt to maintain the producer price of cobalt at $25 per pound in 1980.

A report to Congress by the Subcommittee on Mines and Mining in August 1980 admitted that the United States and its allies are dependent upon South African mineral supplies. Any interruption in these supplies would result in a disruption of our economy so severe that the President of the United States would have almost no other choice but to assume economic mobilization powers, impose resource-use priorities, and provide guidelines for domestic production capacity if possible. Neither the stockpile nor substitution would compensate even in the near term for the loss of South African mineral exports to the West. For the present, South African mineral-resources management maintains stability of contract and is motivated entirely by market objectives. Their minerals are available as noncartel commodities, thus providing a downward pressure on some of the producer-controlled mineral prices worldwide.

The "Resource War" is as full of arcane trickery and economic intrigue as the best of the spy novels. In 1978, the Russians were full well aware that 40 percent of all the world's cobalt comes from Zaire and, in fact, most of it from one mine in that country. It goes without saying that the Russians were also in full possession of advance knowledge of the fact that Katangese irregulars from their satellite in Angola would seize that mine. For weeks in advance of the invasion, Russia had been scouring the world for cobalt, buying up every available pound on the market. When the fighting erupted in Zaire, and mines were closed, an immediate worldwide shortage of cobalt developed. The spot price of cobalt shot up from $6.25 to $45.00 a pound. As the world's biggest consumer, the United States began scrambling like a cat on a hot tin roof in a desperate search for an alternate supply. There just happened to be one: the Soviet Union, which proceeded to sell to U. S. consumers at highly-inflated prices that had in fact been created by Russian agents in Dzerzhinsky Square in Moscow.

On the supply side, the Russians are equally brazen. Aware that the United States mines no chromium and that chromium is an irreplaceable ingredient in stainless steel for aircraft, during the Korean War the Russians embargoed all chromite exports to the United States. The Soviet Union was at that time the world's largest producer of chromium.

The Russians are also well aware of the political damage that can be done the United States through careful conduct of a Resource War. With other western nations also dependent upon key strategic metals for sustenance of their defense and well-being, the Soviet Union (to the extent that it can force the United States into competition for critical substances with its own allies) has the potential for creating havoc among friends.

Not to mention the fact that a Resource War is tailor-made for Russian military design.

From Moscow's vantage point, a Resource War is low-cost, has few casualties and allows them to maintain a profile low enough to avoid arousing the North Atlantic Treaty Organization.

Even government officials of the Carter administration could not present a rosy picture of U. S. strategic stockpiles.

Paul K. Kreuger, Assistant Associate Director of the Resources Preparedness Office, An Arm of the Federal Emergency Management Agency (in the time the poor fellow needs just to give his title, our stockpiles could diminish materially), allows that, "we might be able to stretch our titanium supplies out to eight, maybe nine months; cobalt could be stretched out to perhaps fifteen months."

Precisely, our chromium stockpile is but 18.8 percent of the national goal. The stockpile level of titanium is only 16.5 percent of the goal, that of cobalt 47.7 percent and that of nickel, zero.

Critics further maintain that the *quality* of many, if not most, of our stockpiled minerals is sub-standard.

And what amount of money would be required to build our stockpiles to the point of national adequacy?

Under President Carter, Congress appropriated such a small amount toward building our stockpiles that John D. Morgan, chief staff officer of the U. S. Bureau of Mines, estimated that it would take 60 years of such expenditures to accomplish the purpose.

"Whether we will have 60 years of peace before we need them, I don't know," observed Morgan.

The Russians are also well aware of what effect the outcome of the Resource War will have on our United States energy problem.

At present, oil imports make up only 40 percent of our national requirements. But should this war go against us, and the U. S. be cut off for any length of time from its supplies of such vital commodities as cobalt, chromium, rhenium, vanadium or manganese, for example, this country would in short order become dependent upon foreign sources not for 40 percent but for 75 percent or more of all our oil.

Why?

"If you can't get manganese, you can't make steel," says E. F. Andrews, vice-president of Allegheny-Ludlum Steel.

Without the strategic materials mentioned above, the United States could not manufacture that type of steel necessary to make the pipe required for drilling oil wells domestically, nor construct the barges for sufficient offshore drilling. We need not imagine what would be happening to the rest of U.S. industry at the same time.

Need we go on?

6

How to Buy and Sell Strategic Metals

Traders in gold and silver have it easier than those of us trading in strategic metals. They have only one price to contend with—the free market price. Those of us trying to tackle the strategic metals market have *two* prices: the free market price (which is usually the higher of the two) *and* the producer price. It is rarely the case with strategic metals (tungsten is one exception) that no producer, or group of them, can gain sufficient dominance to dictate a *producer price*. This dual pricing system is a problem sufficient in itself to lead you to seek out an expert's counsel before you begin trading in any of the strategic elements. It is vital that you understand the difference between the producer price and the free market price, and why this difference exists.

The usually higher free market price is the price that you and I are going to pay virtually every time we trade. But this is not due to an evil plot hatched by the large producers to separate you from your money. This system of dual pricing—usually a higher (free market) price for the little buyer and a lower (producer) price for the bigger fellow, the major consumer—is due simply to the nature of the mining business. After all, producers of strategic metals would make more money if they sold all their metal at the normally higher free market price, but remember that the basic business of these hard-working mining and refining folk is not that of being salesmen. They prefer to avoid marketing problems and sell directly to the big consumers, at a lower price, and stick to what they are best at, which is mining. Not that the producers or miners are so unsophisticated or selfless that they haven't often enough exploited their price-fixing possibilities. Still, the big producers do not control the *entire* supply of their product. Many smaller producers exist, and they sell their metal at whatever price the market will allow, which price becomes the free market price at which you and I can trade.

The free market price has several sources. One source is that global hodge-podge of small producers, some of them nearly mom-and-pop outfits, which for one reason or another cannot organize effectively enough either to fix a price themselves or find one or more big buyers with whom they might join to present, shall we say, a more compelling sales argument. Therefore, these disorganized small producers, together with many Soviet-bloc producers, perforce must end up selling or otherwise disposing of their metal to one or more international trading houses—wherever they can make the best deal. These big specialist mercantile houses then accumulate all of the odds and ends of, say, cadmium, and so come into possession of a supply not already contracted for by the large users, and, zingo, there's another place from which the free market place finally fixes itself. Or it may come from "outlaws"—major metal producers akin to certain OPEC counterparts, who sell any excess production during their slacker periods to any hungry consumer for whatever highest price the buyer will pay.

Once one understands that this dual pricing system exists, one can use it to great advantage. The relationship between the producer and free market prices will tell the knowledgeable trader a great deal. By keeping track of the two prices and observing the usual difference between them (again, the producer price generally being the lower), we may get valuable clues about the market. For instance, if the free market price sinks near to, or goes lower than, the producer price, you know at once that demand for the metal has either slackened, free market supplies have increased, or some highly unusual event has occurred. You must then determine why. When you discover the reason, the market may have tipped its hand and offered you a golden opportunity to buy or sell. Sometimes, you *can* buy cheaper than Big Steel.

For example, the falling demand may be caused by a lull in business activity. In this case, if you think the recessionary interval is about over, you may wish to take the opportunity to buy. Or the lull in business activity may be just the beginning, in which case you could want to sell before the price declines further (possibly drastically). Another possible reason for falling demand is a new-found substitute for the metal. Or speculators, as they occasionally do, have simply gone into a blue funk. If that's the case, you may wish to seize the opportunity to invest in the *substitute,* or take a holiday from trading the metal.

Now take the opposite case. If the free market price starts to go higher and higher against the producer price, you again may have several situations that could easily lead to further investment opportunities. Perhaps a new or unexpectedly large demand has been created for the metal since the producers last named a price and made commitments to sell their metal at that figure. The metal may, for instance, have become a substitute for some other more expensive metal. Or a much-publicized substitute possibility may have turned out to be an Edsel. This situation could present an excellent opportunity for purchasing the metal. On the other hand, speculators may be creating most of the new demand on the basis of news as ethereal as three straight days of no speeches by Castro or because of a sudden drop in the price of happy-hour martinis at their favorite London watering holes, which means that the demand will not last. In this case, the time is likely near for selling.

The important point of these examples is that *something* is causing the spread between the free market price and the producer price to change. Get the facts! Find out what has caused the spread to widen or narrow. Then you may be in a position to profit from the information.

Watching the spread between producer price and free market price is just one way to profit from strategic metals. Another advantage those trading in strategic metals have over gold and silver traders is the practice (briefly mentioned in the last chapter) of "lending out," and its natural corollary, "borrowing," both of which are often done with gold and silver. Lending your strategic metal is not only another way to profit from strategics, but is a common practice during periods of shortage.

Lending metal *is* as simple as it sounds.

But at first blush, lending your metal may seem as though you are selling it. Not really so. Let me explain. You have 100 kilograms of germanium that a consumer needs to borrow. You agree to loan it. What actually happens is this: The borrower agrees to purchase the germanium from you at the present market price and at the same time agrees to sell to you another 100 kilograms of germanium at the end of an agreed-upon period of time. The price at which you agree to buy back the germanium may be the same price at which you sold it to the borrower or it may be a lesser price. (There are even circumstances in which you might agree to buy back at a greater price, but this is a matter for consultation with a professional trader. Such sophisticated maneuvers take us far beyond the primer stage of trading in strategics.)

As you can see, what has actually happened is that the borrower has put up his money as collateral against your germanium. *He* has the germanium and you have the *money*. Now you put out the money at interest for the duration of the metal loan, at the end of which period you purchase 100 kilograms of germanium from the borrower (at a lower price, if your broker has been a good negotiator). What has all this done for you? Well, you have earned interest on the money; and, because the borrower had possession of the metal, you avoided the payment of storage and insurance costs.

Further, if you bought your metal back at a lesser price, you have, in addition to the goodies so far, made another tidy little profit.

In an actual loan of germanium made by myself, I had bought germanium in June 1980 at $645 per kilogram. At the time I loaned it (in October), the price was $840 per kilogram. I loaned it out at $840 for 14 days (during which time I both avoided the fees and put the borrower's cash to work), and I then bought it back at $840. The price today is somewhere around $920. Not only have I made a modest amount of money through the two-week loan, but there has also been an increase of over 40 percent in the metal price. I have now sold part of the metal and taken fine profits and will hold the rest of it for the time being. Please note that these fine profits were achieved in about four months.

In lending metals, there is an area where consultation with an experienced broker is especially important. If the metal is lent for a long period of time, you run the risk of seeing the price rise during that period. You, of course, would be unable to sell the metal until the loan period had ended and you had bought back your metal, as per your agreement with the borrower. You may have lost an opportunity to sell your metal at a profit. Further, as a remote and, we hope, academic point, if the borrower happened to go bankrupt during that period, you would never get your metal back, which would quash any opportunity to sell it at a profit. At the least, though, you would have the cash received for the metal at the time of the loan, and you would be earning interest on it. Obviously, in any such lending or borrowing transaction, the most thorough check of the borrower's credit rating and general reputation for responsibility is mandatory.

On the other hand, if the price of the metal drops while you have lent it to your borrower, in certain instances you actually could lose money. The price drop may have exceeded the return you earned on the money you took for collateral at the beginning of the loan.

I recall an incident in the recent past where one of the base,

non-ferrous strategic metals was in extremely short supply
and an investor reportedly had lent his metal out for months
at a price of $5,000 per day. Of course, the man had a lot of
something very basic and as scarce at that moment as weeds
in an elevator.

Gold and silver traders, touting the superiority of their
metal over the strategics we have been discussing, may point
out that there are places where they can now deposit their
gold and silver and be paid a small rate of interest by the
concern keeping their gold deposit on hand. Such an ar-
rangement is indeed possible. However, as even the gold and
silver traders acknowledge, the interest is small indeed.
Furthermore, gold and silver prices are far more volatile than
those of the average strategic metals. Strategic substances
just don't usually have a 10 percent up or down fluctuation in
a single day, as occasionally has been the case with gold and
silver. If you had your gold loaned out at some minimal rate
of interest and watched the price jump $30 or $40 a day while
you were helpless to sell, the small interest you were getting
wouldn't look like much, would it?

So much for the actual buying and selling of strategics and
the lending of strategics.

There is yet another and quite different way to put your
money into strategic metals: You can buy the stocks of many
companies that mine them or otherwise help produce them in
the process toward sale. Obviously, what you get here is a
piece of paper—a stock certificate—instead of a tangible like
the physical metal. Nonetheless, the stocks of some of the
companies with large holdings of strategics or which produce
large quantities of them and which are traded on one
exchange or another, or are sold over the counter, have gone
up remarkably in price. I hold shares in one company whose
stock is traded on the New York Stock Exchange, a company that has vast U.S. holdings of one of the most critical of
all the metals we have been discussing. That stock has risen
sensationally in just a few weeks. Some others have too.
Also available to the investor are a few mutual funds with at
least a reasonable percentage of their portfolios invested in

various companies having to do with the strategic metal field.

If purchase of stock is the route you choose to enter the field of critical metals, you will find fine opportunities on exchanges in the United States, Australia, South Africa, Canada, and several other countries. Such stock can also usually be shorted in the event you come into possession of information indicating that the particular metal around which a company is built is due for a big drop in price. And, of course, most big brokerage houses will sell such stock to a responsible customer at some reasonable margin.

Having said that, the writer must add that playing the stock market is not one of his favorite games, even when the stock involves a key strategic metal. I really do not like to put my company into the stock market beyond sums nominal to us. The problem is that no matter how promising a company's outlook may be, when you buy its stock you depend upon the management of the company. If the management is no good, that can foul up even the finest-looking company. On the other hand, if I have bought five tons of physical cobalt and have it stored waiting for inflation and other events to carry the price past an old high, I don't have management or mine disasters or labor disputes or any other type of manmade or natural disaster to worry about. And if you don't think that even the finest of strategic metal stocks can drop, go back and look at the South African gold stocks at the time the Communists overran Angola. Without exception, to the best of my memory, they all dropped like a rock, and I am told that hundreds of millions, if not billions, were lost. And all the while Angola was erupting like a volcano and South African gold issues seemed ready to go down for the third time off Cape Horn, the *holder* of physical gold was sleeping like a baby.

That brings us to the questions that you must ask a broker. Here is a key list of them. As you become skilled in the ways of strategics, you will no doubt want to add questions of your own.

1. Mr. Jones, I am interested in investigating the purchase of some cobalt. What can you tell me about the cobalt market right now?

2. Could you tell me the names of the two companies that are the biggest users of cobalt? I would like to contact them for some further information.

3. Are any substitutes for cobalt's main uses currently visible on the horizon?

4. What are the present free market and producer prices of cobalt? Do you see any significant change coming in that spread? If so, why?

5. If I bought the cobalt, where would you recommend I store it? How much would it cost me to store it?

6. Once the cobalt is in that warehouse you suggest, how do I find out how much I am going to have to pay for insurance?

7. If I buy 5 tons of cobalt, what sort of service or commission charge do you have.

8. Are there any other fees besides the service charge?

9. What is the minimum percentage of purity that cobalt dealers demand?

10. Could I buy less than the minimum tradable unit at some sort of premium over the normal selling price? If so, how much premium?

11. Wouldn't I have trouble selling such an odd lot on short notice? (Author's note: in my opinion you sure would.)

12. Do you think that there is any point in my buying, say, a quarter of a ton of cobalt now and adding to it little by little until I have a tradable unit of one ton? After all, there are a lot of us small investors around who have to get wet one toe at a time.

13. Does the cobalt market have enough liquidity so that I can sell on short notice if I have to?

14. Once I sell cobalt, how long do I have to wait before I get a check?

15. If I make a profit, what is your normal percentage of the profit?

16. Are any of your other clients buying cobalt at the moment? If so, why?

17. How many of them are selling cobalt? If so, why?

18. Are there political dangers in the countries of major supply of cobalt which might affect the price?

19. Could I ever short cobalt if I wanted to?

20. Do you sell futures in cobalt? If so, in what months?

21. Do you make a market in cobalt? Will you continue to do so?

22. How can I find out the daily price of cobalt without calling you every day?

23. How long have you personally been trading cobalt? Not strategic metals in general, I mean, but specifically cobalt?

24. Have you ever had a client lose money on cobalt? Tell me about it.

25. You may want to write me a letter about this, or maybe you have some printed material, but I would like to know more about the background of your company.

26. What other metals look good to you right at the moment?

27. How much cobalt would I have to buy in order for you to sell it to me on margin? What margin?

28. What would be my margin costs?

29. Are there any recent studies on cobalt that you think I should read?

30. What are today's buy and sell prices on cobalt?

31. Does your firm buy or sell cobalt for its own possession or trading purpose? What I mean is, does your firm act as both merchant and broker? Do you ever act as a producer's "agent" in selling cobalt or any other metal?

32. I've been told by Gordon McLendon not to get into any metal without asking about whether scrap recovery or recycling plays a big part in the free market price. Are either of these two big factors in the free market price of cobalt? If so, how big?

33. What is your home telephone number?

A number of those same questions should also be asked of a strategic metals consultant, should you—as I do—choose to retain one. An expert consultant need cost you no more than $250 and can make you many times that in a single transaction based on his advice.

(If you are in any doubt about how one finds either a good consultant or a broker to do the actual dealing, drop me a line in care of the publisher. Please include a self-addressed stamped envelope.)

Or, many of you may care to wait for the strategic metal "unit trusts" or mutual funds predicted to be on the horizon. I agree with Commodities Correspondent Michael Prest of the London *Times,* who said in November, 1980 that these will be the next stage.

The writer points out again that, unlike many of the base metals, such as zinc, copper, lead, nickel, etc., there are for the strategic metals profiled at the end of this book no organized future markets or "fixes," during which the market sets a specific price at a specific time. Traders do not sit or stand around a "pit" or a "ring" and scream for the attention of other dealers with fingers, arms, toes and sometimes tongues out to indicate offers to buy or sell. This is what you would observe if you were watching daily trading on the floor of New York's Commodity Exchange, or scores of other institutions in which members gather to buy or sell for themselves or for their clients. To use the word "organized" to describe these markets will seem to those viewing floor activity the most extreme prostitution of that word. Perhaps "organized mayhem" might be a better description, for the London "ring" is peopled each day by individual traders whose desperate facial expressions and wild gesticulations make behavior of the perfectly normal axe-murderer look like that of a headwaiter by comparison. And America's commodity "pits" are an assemblage of humanity that in its voracity and anger make the old-time pit bulldog resemble a well-curried poodle. This past year the writer observed proceedings of the organized Chinese Gold and Silver Society's trading floor from a balcony spectator's floor through glass, presumably bullet-proof. There was good reason to welcome the isolation. On the floor, Chinese traders wore neither shoes nor ties. Attempts at strangulation had been all too frequent to allow ties, and the shoe, a lethal weapon anyway, had wrought some of the quickest sex-changes known to man.

The market for those 31 metals which are listed in this book as offering at least some possibility for profit potential is a "negotiated" rather than an organized market. That is to say that buying and selling are conducted not in any one central place, but by telephoning each merchant known to deal in a given metal in order to ascertain which will offer the best price for buying or selling—in other words, where you can get the best bargain. To those who would prefer to shop at commodity supermarkets—the big brokerage houses— and to those with a "one stop does all" mentality, the strategic metals are much more difficult to trade. There is talk that futures markets may be organized for some of the metals with big free-market trading, but that is still down the road and perhaps quite a distance.

Since there are no organized markets in most of the strategics, the prices quoted are given only within a range: cobalt, for example, may be quoted on a given day at $21 to $22 per pound. Here, again, is why the investor needs a consultant who has the time to seek out the best prices.

A metal traded on one of the organized exchanges is said to have a *terminal* price, because at any point during the trading day that exchange can quote you an industry-accepted buy and sell price. The strategics without organized exchanges are referred to as *non-terminal,* since at no time of the day or night does there exist a price accepted by the market at large.

Be sure that you ask your broker in what form he is trading your metal. Germanium is widely traded as both germanium metal and germanium dioxide. Tellurium comes in lumps and powder, or stick form; cadmium can be traded as sticks or ingots. And there are major price differences between each form in which you buy or sell the metal. So, the beginning investor who waltzes into one of the major suppliers and announces only that he wants some germanium is apt to be greeted with a strange look indeed.

Familiarize yourself thoroughly with Table XV in Appendix A: "Amounts Normally Traded Among 31 Metals Available to Private Investors." What follows may be the most important advice we have to offer beginning investors in strategic metals: *BEWARE* the broker who offers you a lesser quantity than the normal trading amount, or unit, which we have listed in Table XV. Such a man is as dangerous as a Great Dane behind a meat counter. Although the minimums we have cited are those of a consensus of responsible metal merchants, such minimums can be changed by market conditions. If you are offered any amount of metal below our minimums, *check with a long-time metals specialist before you buy*. Merchant-brokers, and in fact the entire metals trade, by long custom, trade in certain fixed quantities of each metal, and often so packaged—in steel or other drums, in wooden boxes, in watertight containers, in flasks, in bags, and in several other ways. If you buy less than the normal trading unit, you will likely be paying a high premium for this smaller quantity and will be able to dispose of it only at a great discount. Take cobalt, for instance. Cobalt is packaged in half-ton steel drums, and the minimum normal trading unit is two such drums—one metric ton (2204 pounds). If someone offers to sell you half a drum (one-quarter of a ton), who is going to buy your half-drum? Or your washtub full, or whatever you use to store it in? Brokers are around these days offering sub-standard amounts of various metals at inflated prices—germanium, titanium, vanadium, antimony and tungsten, to mention just a few. The brokers do this in order to try to bring the cost of the metal down within reach of the investor, *no matter what it costs you in the end*. And, by the way, that's where you'll get it.

Be certain that the quality and purity of the metal you are purchasing is always at least the minimum purity or standard accepted by buyers. For example, magnesium should have a minimum of 99.8-99.9%, mercury nearly 99.99%, cadmium varies from 99.95% to 99.99% minimum purity, and gallium between 99.9% and 100% absolute purity, etc.

Do not assume that because there is a rise in the prices of any strategic metal there will necessarily be a corresponding fall in demand. By way of illustration, several of the strategics are used in the manufacture of an automobile. However, the amount of any individual strategic metal used in a car may represent only a few cents at most in the price of producing the car. Thus, that metal could double, treble, quadruple or more without affecting automobile production. In the same way, selenium is an important ingredient in the manufacture of photocopying machines. Yet the cost of the selenium is only the smallest fraction of the cost of the machine's manufacture. A material hike in its price should therefore have little effect, if any, upon the cost of, demand for or volume of copying machines produced, and thus little or none on the demand for selenium. The same can be said for the use of germanium in semiconductors, and many other strategics.

The prestigious *Times* of London reported in late November, 1980, that "it is widely accepted that many of these esoteric materials are underpriced at present, or at least that they offer considerable opportunities for capital gains." Still, strategic metals are not for the in-and-out, quick buck trader; any investor should think of them in terms of two or three year investments if he is looking for real capital gains. The one metal which might be an exception to this rule is magnesium. In fact, although newcomers to strategic brokerage field currently offer to sell or deliver to you magnesium with no strings or counsel, there is an important reason why time should play a factor in any investment you make in magnesium. Unless most carefully. packed, and kept under the finest of circumstances, magnesium will oxidize and sometimes in less than two years. That is the reason that this book includes magnesium under "metals tradable but with practicable difficulty." Magnesium is a metal meant to be *used* within some reasonable period of time and not stored as an heirloom.

Watch the scrap metal industry for clues on when many of the strategics are ready to increase in price. When industrial demand picks up (it has been quite soft during the last months of 1980), it is to scrap and recycled metal that industry generally turns as the most readily available source. That being true, the recent statement of Si Waksberg, one of the key officials of the National Association of Recycling Industries, could take on special significance. Waksberg said in an interview in mid-November, 1980, that the scrap trade is investing heavily in strategic metal scrap in expectation of considerably higher prices.

"The recovery processes required to salvage the exotic metals are extremely complex and costly, to say the least, because most arrive in the form of alloys," Waksberg declared. "Obviously, such investments would not be undertaken if the recycling industry didn't expect *much higher prices in the future.*" (Italics mine.) By the way, don't lose any sleep over the thought that the government in some remote time of dire need may confiscate your strategic metals. Yes, that *could* happen in the event of a national emergency in much the same way that the government can commandeer *anything* you own if it wishes—your house, your land, your business—even your gold.

But, exactly as was the case when the government did indeed call in all gold in 1934, in the event Washington developed an overnight desire for your particular metal, you would be paid as people were then—a fair market value in the very dollars that you were prepared to accept as profit when you bought the metal. Furthermore, at this point in the infancy of strategic metals trading, we individual investors are 50 country miles from accumulating enough to affect national security in any material way. And in the unlikely event this new free market grows so big that it does cramp Uncle Sam's style with regard to any of the strategics, you'll be very happy because it will mean that prices have been pushed so high that your recompense by the government will have you crying all the way from Rotterdam to the bank.

Addendum to Tomorrow

Was it only back on page 33 — only ninety years ago—that we had laid full siege to the republic with the passage of the Interstate Commerce Act and its savage offspring, the Sherman Anti-Trust Act?

How swiftly the bureaucracy has gnawed away at our vitals. For now, having assumed judicial power, a government *bureau* has begun to administer the anti-trust laws! On November 28, 1980, a mere Federal Trade Commission administrative law judge ruled that not only must one of America's large food companies divest itself of a recently acquired business, but also *turn over the recent profits of that business to the United States Treasury.*

The bureaucratic appointee ordered Beatrice Foods to undo its purchase of Tropicana Products on the ground that the acquisition, in 1978, had created an illegal, anticompetitive concentration in the frozen orange juice business.

And, astonishingly, the bureaucratic hearing examiner—in no way connected with the Department of Justice, actually invoked as his assigned reason a violation of the U.S. anti-trust laws, for 90 years a weapon jealously cherished by American *courts,* not bureaus.

This new attack on the flank of business from an unsuspected quarter further damages the capitalistic system, in so doing further driving investors away from business and into the arms of the alternative investments—the tangibles, all of them—gold, silver, and the strategic metals as well.

How far have we gone from Madison, Franklin and Jefferson's cherished sections 8 and 10 of Article I of the Constitution and the concept of sound money through gold and silver coinage!

Ralph Waldo Emerson wrote in his essay on "Wealth":

"The coin is a delicate meter of civil, social and moral changes . . . It is the finest barometer of social storms, and *announces revolutions*." (Italics mine.)

And now a new administration must begin the task of restoring public confidence in coins that are 87% copper and 13% nickel. It must confront an inflation that is far higher than the 10% that government figures show. That is so if for no other reason than that no official statistics on inflation reflect the deterioration in the quality of American products and services—poorly-made cars, a declining quality of education, homes more and more shabbily constructed, repair without merit—none of them included as depreciation factors in determining the actual rate of U.S. inflation.

It is against this forbidding backdrop that an administration must find the money, for instance only, to rebuild its stockpile of cobalt against an estimate by federal analysts that there is a 60% chance of further disruptions of supply from Zaire by 1984.

If you wish to gauge the quality of life in any society, look to the quality of its money, said Emerson.

And then to the increasing rate of its crime.

Those who would come to Washington having convinced themselves that Americans are now ready to partake of the bitter draught of self-sacrifice might do well to look at the difficulties of Britain's "iron lady," Margaret Thatcher, swept into power by a people who expressed themselves to be fed up with social excesses of a labor government. To take up cudgels against this fine schoolmarm with her quick and brilliant mind is no less difficult than to squelch the life of that first man to be executed in the Nevada gas chamber who, when asked his last request, replied simply, "a gas mask." Wilson Mizner wondered aloud how any state could execute a man with such a sense of humor. How could the British not love the lady who, when asked her definition of freedom, after only a second's pause, apparently ad-libbed so astonishingly, "I think freedom . . . might be the right to be unequal." Or fall out of love with the woman who had gone to Brighton to speak to a Tory gathering under such difficult circumstances? For as she spoke there, two thousand workers demonstrated against her outside the meeting hall in a cold, cutting rain, held back by cordons of British police. And who, when two of the workers somehow forced themselves into the hall shouting, "Maggie! Maggie! Out! Out! Out!" had replied with such unruffled warmth, "Oh, let them come in. It is always nicer where the Tories are, and it is raining outside."

That her tight-money program of austerity should not have endeared her to the more than two million now unemployed in Britain (the highest rate since the Depression of the '30s), nor to the hundreds of businesses that had gone bankrupt, was hardly surprising. But that she could lose the support of Britain's business establishment itself was unthinkable. How could these same industrialists who had cried for her leadership only 18 months before now declare themselves by newspaper poll to be more than 50 percent against her leadership? How could the *Daily Express* (and other newspapers) whose editorials had so vigorously supported her, put the case against her in a cartoon with the cruel heading, "Brother, can you spare a dime?"

After all, were these not the very businessmen to whom she had explained that, if Britain were to be a productive power again, the cathartic forces of capitalism must be allowed to purge that nation of those marginal and uneconomic businesses which had so unhealthily survived on the subsidies and inflationary policies of her predecessor Labor government? Had the *Financial Times* not pointed out that the inflation which had doubled to 22 percent during her first year in office had now receded to 15.4 percent?

Why, then, had her own Tories begun to rebel against her in the Parliament and force her against all vows to lower her government's interest rate from 17 to 14 percent, with yet lower rates demanded?

Still and all, *big business* turning against her? How could that be?

A tall, spare Austrian economist from Innsbruck, the all too often prophetic Nobel laureate Friedrich von Hayek, had said from the beginning that whatever the discipline of the British, Mrs. Thatcher would not be given the time to do the job in her country. When Milton Friedman had said that inflation in the United States could be phased out over five or six years, von Hayek had disagreed even more forcefully. The self-indulgent people of the United States would never put up with such a long period of inconvenience and unpleasantry, von Hayek insisted. He suggested that the situation in the United States would have to right itself in a much shorter period of time—perhaps six months of almost literal, violent convulsion.

It is within this threatening scenario that many of those aglow with what they perceive to be "a new conservatism" sweeping the land are just now arriving in Washington. Certain as they are that the light now so clearly visible at the end of the tunnel is no oncoming freight train, it would be heartless to point out to them that it might be their first glimpse of hell's fire.

Furthermore, any administration that sallies forth to attack Washington with the announced intention of eviscerating the personnel and power of a massive, deeply-entrenched and combative federal bureaucracy takes upon itself a fearful enemy indeed.

The encounter that must ensue conjures for this writer the image of an incident no less vivid than the dramatic denouement of James Michener's gripping *The Bridges at Toko-Ri*, as Michener's midwestern fighter pilot goes against his dreadful target:

> "Harry Brubaker's Banshee catapulted violently across the prow of the *Savo* and far into the sky . . . Then, as his eyes swept the empty sky in casual patterns . . . dead ahead they lay, bold and blunt and ugly. Tortured and convoluted, they twisted up at the two fleeting jets, the terrible mountains of Korea. Hidden among them, somewhere to the west, cowered the bridges of Toko-ri, gun-rimmed and waiting."

No less awesome and malignantly resentful, Washington's bureaucracy awaits the new administration's promised onslaught.

Which will survive?

Harry Brubaker did not.

APPENDIX A

Key Information About the Tradable Metals

TABLE I

ELEMENTS DEFINITELY FEASIBLE FOR INDIVIDUAL INVESTOR TRADING

1. Antimony
2. Bismuth
3. Cadmium
4. Chromium
5. Cobalt
6. Columbium (Niobium)
7. Gallium
8. Germanium
9. Indium
10. Manganese
11. Mercury
12. Molybdenum
13. Selenium
14. Silicon
15. Tantalum
16. Titanium
17. Tungsten
18. Vanadium

TABLE II

ELEMENTS UNDER OBSERVATION FOR POTENTIAL FUTURE TRADING POSSIBILITIES

1. Calcium
2. Hafnium
3. Scandium

TABLE III

ELEMENTS TRADABLE BY INVESTORS BUT PRESENTING PRACTICAL DIFFICULTIES

1. Arsenic
2. Beryllium
3. Iridium
4. Magnesium
5. Rhenium
6. Rhodium

TABLE IV

ELEMENTS PRESENTING NO PROFIT OPPORTUNITIES FOR INDIVIDUAL INVESTOR TRADING AS OF THIS WRITING

1. Cerium
2. Lithium
3. Osmium
4. Ruthenium
5. Sodium
6. Tellurium
7. Zirconium

TABLE V
_____

VOLUME OF TRADING ACTION

Heavy Volume of Trading	*Fair Amount Traded*
Bismuth	Antimony
Cadmium	Arsenic
Cobalt	Gallium
Molybdenum	Germanium
Titanium	Indium
Tungsten	Rhenium
Vanadium	Tantalum
	Tellurium

Next Most Often Traded	*Very Little, If Any, Trading*
Chromium	Beryllium
Magnesium	Cerium
Manganese	Iridium
Mercury	Lithium
Niobium (Columbium)	Osmium
Selenium	Rhodium
Silicon	Ruthenium
	Sodium
	Zirconium

TABLE VI
_____

EASE OF SUBSTITUTION

Substitutable—Within A Reasonably Short Time

Bismuth	Magnesium
Cadmium	Mercury
Columbium (Niobium)	Vanadium
Lithium	

Some Substitution Possible

Antimony	Silicon
Arsenic	Sodium
Beryllium	Tellurium
Gallium	Zirconium

Substitution Virtually Impossible

Cerium	Osmium
Chromium	Rhenium
Cobalt	Rhodium
Germanium	Ruthenium
Indium	Selenium
Iridium	Tantalum
Manganese	Titanium
Molybdenum	Tungsten

TABLE VII

SUPPLY DEPENDABILITY—DEGREE OF RISK TO WEST

Extremely Dependent

Chromium
Cobalt
Columbium (Niobium)
Iridium
Manganese
Osmium
Rhenium
Rhodium
Ruthenium
Vanadium

Moderate Dependence

Beryllium
Lithium
Tantalum
Titanium
Tungsten

Dependence Not a Vital Factor

Antimony
Arsenic
Bismuth
Cadmium
Cerium
Gallium
Germanium
Indium
Magnesium
Mercury
Molybdenum
Selenium
Silicon
Sodium
Tellurium
Zirconium

TABLE VIII

SUPPLY AND/OR PRICE DICTATED BY PRODUCER

Tightly Controlled	*Little or No Control*
Beryllium	Antimony
Columbium (Niobium)	Bismuth
Gallium	Cadmium
Lithium	Cobalt
Sodium	Indium
Zirconium	Iridium
	Molybdenum
Moderate Control	Osmium
Arsenic	Rhodium
Cerium	Ruthenium
Germanium	Silicon
Magnesium	Tantalum
Manganese	Titanium
Mercury	Tungsten
Rhenium	Vanadium
Selenium	
Tellurium	

TABLE IX

COST AND/OR STORAGE PROBLEMS

Substantial Problems	*Few or No Problems*
Arsenic	Antimony
Beryllium	Bismuth
Cerium	Cadmium
Gallium	Cobalt
Germanium	Iridium
Magnesium	Mercury
Manganese	Molybdenum
Sodium	Osmium
	Rhenium
Some Minor Problems	Rhodium
Chromium	Ruthenium
Columbium (Niobium)	Selenium
Indium	Silicon
Lithium	Tellurium
Tantalum	Titanium
Tungsten	Vanadium
	Zirconium

TABLE X

GROWTH IN USES

Rapidly Expanding	*Some Expansion*
Germanium	Beryllium
Magnesium	Cerium
Molybdenum	Chromium
Rhenium	Iridium
Silicon	Lithium
Tantalum	Manganese
Titanium	Mercury
	Osmium
Moderate Expansion	Rhodium
Cobalt	Ruthenium
Columbium (Niobium)	Sodium
Indium	
Tungsten	*Little or No Growth*
Vanadium	Antimony
Zirconium	Arsenic
	Bismuth
	Cadmium
	Gallium
	Selenium
	Tellurium

TABLE XI

USE IN TECHNOLOGY

Heavy Use in Technology	*Moderate Use in Technology*
Cobalt	Beryllium
Gallium	Cerium
Germanium	Columbium (Niobium)
Indium	Magnesium
Iridium	Molybdenum
Osmium	Silicon
Rhenium	Tellurium
Rhodium	Tungsten
Ruthenium	Vanadium
Selenium	Zirconium
Tantalum	
Titanium	

Some Use in Technology	Little Use in Technology
Antimony	Chromium
Arsenic	Manganese
Bismuth	
Cadmium	
Lithium	
Mercury	
Sodium	

TABLE XII

BASE METAL BY-PRODUCT

Most Often Produced as a By-Product

Antimony	Iridium
Beryllium	Osmium
Bismuth	Rhenium
Cadmium	Rhodium
Cobalt	Ruthenium
Gallium	Selenium
Germanium	Tellurium
Indium	

Least Often Produced as a By-Product

Arsenic	Molybdenum
Cerium	Silicon
Chromium	Sodium
Columbium (Niobium)	Tantalum
Lithium	Titanium
Magnesium	Tungsten
Manganese	Vanadium
Mercury	Zirconium

TABLE XIII

MILITARY RELATED DEMAND

Vital to Military	Moderate Use in Military
Cobalt	Columbium (Niobium)
Germanium	Lithium
Titanium	Magnesium
Tungsten	Molybdenum
	Vanadium
	Zirconium

Some Military Need
Cerium
Chromium
Gallium

Little Military Need

Antimony	Osmium
Arsenic	Rhenium
Beryllium	Rhodium
Bismuth	Ruthenium
Cadmium	Selenium
Indium	Silicon
Iridium	Sodium
Manganese	Tantalum
Mercury	Tellurium

TABLE XIV

ENERGY REQUIRED TO PRODUCE

Most Energy Required	*Little Energy Required*
Beryllium	Antimony
Gallium	Arsenic
Germanium	Bismuth
Magnesium	Iridium
Silicon	Lithium
Sodium	Mercury
Titanium	Osmium
Zirconium	Rhenium
	Rhodium
Moderate Energy Required	Ruthenium
Cadmium	Tantalum
Cerium	Tellurium
Chromium	Tungsten
Cobalt	
Columbium (Niobium)	
Indium	
Manganese	
Molybdenum	
Selenium	
Vanadium	

TABLE XV

AMOUNTS NORMALLY TRADED AMONG 31 METALS AVAILABLE TO PRIVATE INVESTORS

METAL	TYPICAL TRADING CONTRACT SIZE
Antimony	10-50 tons
Arsenic	5 tons
Beryllium	1-5 tons
Bismuth	1-5 tons
Cadmium	1, 5 or 10 tons
Cerium	1-5 tons
Chromium	5-10 tons
Cobalt	1, 5 or 10 tons
Columbium (Niobium)	5-10 tons
Gallium	100 kilograms
Germanium dioxide	100 kilograms
Indium	100-500 kilograms
Iridium	100 ounces
Lithium	10 tons
Magnesium	20, 50 or 100 tons
Manganese	100-500 tons
Mercury	50-100 flasks
Molybdenum	10 tons
Osmium	20-50 ounces
Rhenium	50-100 kilograms
Rhodium	100 ounces
Ruthenium	50-100 ounces
Selenium	1-5 tons
Silicon	5, 50 or 100 tons
Sodium	10, 20 or 50 tons
Tantalum	1-5 tons
Tellurium	1-5 tons
Titanium sponge	5-10 tons
Tungsten	25-50 tons
Vanadium	10 tons
Zirconium	5 tons

IMPORTS (NET) — % OF CONSUMPTION — 1977

	U.S.	EUROPEAN ECONOMIC COMMUNITY	JAPAN	COMMUNIST ECONOMIC SYSTEM
MANGANESE	98	100	99	3
COBALT	97	100	100	68
BAUXITE	91	97	100	28
CHROMIUM	91	100	98	2
ASBESTOS	85	90	98	1
NICKEL	70	100	100	13
ZINC	57	91	74	9
IRON ORE	48	82	100	5
SILVER	36	93	71	10
COPPER	13	100	97	4
LEAD	13	76	78	3
PHOSPHATE	MAJOR EXPORTER	99	100	23

SOURCE: U.S. Bureau of Mines

Source: *A White Paper,* Council on Economics and National Security (CENS), Washington, DC.

U.S. DEPENDENCE ON
FOREIGN SOURCES — 1979

MANGANESE

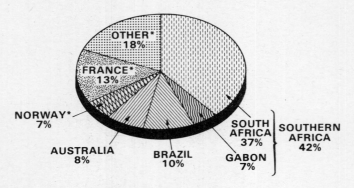

* = PROCESSING, NOT
   PRODUCING COUNTRIES

COBALT

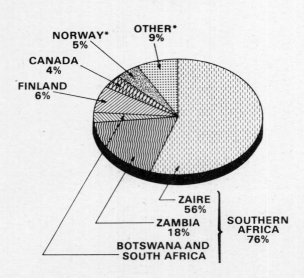

U.S. DEPENDENCE ON
FOREIGN SOURCES — 1979

PLATINUM

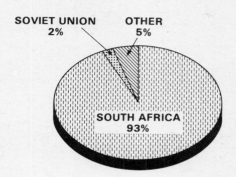

SOVIET UNION
2%

OTHER
5%

SOUTH AFRICA
93%

CHROMIUM

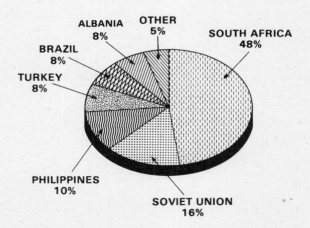

ALBANIA
8%

OTHER
5%

SOUTH AFRICA
48%

BRAZIL
8%

TURKEY
8%

PHILIPPINES
10%

SOVIET UNION
16%

U.S. NET IMPORT RELIANCE OF SELECTED MINERALS AND METALS AS A PERCENT OF CONSUMPTION IN 1979

MINERALS AND METALS[1]	NET IMPORT RELIANCE* AS A PERCENT OF APPARENT CONSUMPTION**	MAJOR FOREIGN SOURCES[2] (1975-1978)
	0% 25% 50% 75% 100%	
COLUMBIUM	100	BRAZIL (67), CANADA (9), THAILAND (7)
MICA (SHEET)	100	INDIA (80), BRAZIL (8), MADAGASCAR (3)
STRONTIUM	100	MEXICO (96), SPAIN (4)
TITANIUM (RUTILE)	100	AUSTRALIA (88), JAPAN (5), INDIA (4)
MANGANESE	98	GABON (23), SOUTH AFRICA (20), BRAZIL (18), FRANCE (11)
TANTALUM	96	THAILAND (31), CANADA (15), MALAYSIA (11), BRAZIL (4)
BAUXITE & ALUMINA	93	JAMAICA (33), AUSTRALIA (27), GUINEA (15), SURINAM (14)
CHROMIUM	90	SOUTH AFRICA (44), U.S.S.R. (12), S. RHODESIA (ZIMBABWE) (8), TURKEY (8)
COBALT	90	ZAIRE (41), BELG.-LUX. (19), ZAMBIA (10), FINLAND (7), CANADA (5)
PLATINUM – GROUP METALS	89	SOUTH AFRICA (50), U.S.S.R. (22), UNITED KINGDOM (12)
ASBESTOS	85	CANADA (96), SOUTH AFRICA (3)
TIN	81	MALAYSIA (55), THAILAND (16), INDONESIA (11), BOLIVIA (6)
NICKEL	77	CANADA (54), NORWAY (9), NEW CALEDONIA (8), DOMIN. REP. (6)
CADMIUM	66	CANADA (22), AUSTRALIA (15), MEXICO (13), BELG.-LUX. (12)
POTASSIUM	66	CANADA (94), ISRAEL (3)
MERCURY	62	ALGERIA (23), SPAIN (20), ITALY (17), CANADA (11), YUGOSLAVIA (9)
ZINC	62	CANADA (48), MEXICO (7), SPAIN (5), HONDURAS (3)
TUNGSTEN	59	CANADA (23), BOLIVIA (15), REP. OF KOREA (9)

Mineral	Net Import Reliance	Major Foreign Sources (%)
GOLD	56	CANADA (43), SWITZERLAND (20), U.S.S.R. (17)
TITANIUM (ILMENITE)	46	AUSTRALIA (55), CANADA (42)
SILVER	45	CANADA (37), MEXICO (24), PERU (15), UNITED KINGDOM (6)
ANTIMONY	43	SOUTH AFRICA (34), BOLIVIA (11), CHINA MAINLAND (9), MEXICO (9)
BARIUM	40	PERU (30), IRELAND (19), MEXICO (12), MOROCCO (9)
SELENIUM	40	CANADA (46), JAPAN (21), YUGOSLAVIA (10), MEXICO (6)
GYPSUM	33	CANADA (74), MEXICO (20), JAMAICA (4)
IRON ORE	28	CANADA (54), VENEZUELA (21), BRAZIL (12), LIBERIA (5)
IRON & STEEL SCRAP	(22)	NET EXPORTS
VANADIUM	25	SOUTH AFRICA (57), CHILE (25), U.S.S.R. (6)
COPPER	13	CANADA (25), CHILE (24), ZAMBIA (15), PERU (12)
IRON & STEEL PRODUCTS	11	JAPAN (43), EUROPE (37), CANADA (10)
SULFUR	11	CANADA (55), MEXICO (45)
CEMENT	10	CANADA (50), MEXICO (10), NORWAY (7), BAHAMAS (7)
SALT	9	CANADA (34), MEXICO (26), BAHAMAS (26)
ALUMINUM	8	CANADA (60)
LEAD	8	CANADA (28), MEXICO (25), PERU (17), HONDURAS (9), AUSTRALIA (7)
PUMICE & VOLCANIC CINDER	4	GREECE (82), ITALY (18)

0%   25%   50%   75%   100%

*NET IMPORT RELIANCE = IMPORTS-EXPORTS
+ADJUSTMENTS FOR GOV'T AND INDUSTRY STOCK CHANGES

**APPARENT CONSUMPTION = U.S. PRIMARY
+SECONDARY PRODUCTION + NET IMPORT RELIANCE.

APRIL 1980

[1] SUBSTANTIAL QUANTITIES ARE IMPORTED FOR FLUORSPAR, GRAPHITE, RHENIUM AND ZIRCON. DATA WITHHELD TO AVOID DISCLOSING COMPANY PROPRIETARY DATA.

[2] SOURCES SHOWN ARE POINTS OF SHIPMENT TO THE U.S. AND ARE NOT NECESSARILY THE INITIAL SOURCES OF THE MATERIAL.

BUREAU OF MINES, U.S. DEPARTMENT OF THE INTERIOR
(IMPORT-EXPORT DATA FROM BUREAU OF THE CENSUS)

U.S.S.R. NET IMPORT RELIANCE OF
SELECTED MINERALS AND METALS AS A
PERCENT OF CONSUMPTION IN 1978

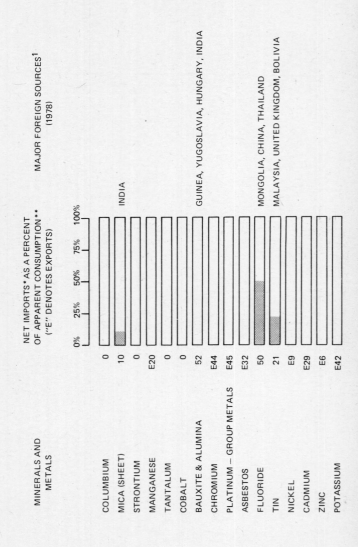

MINERALS AND METALS	NET IMPORTS* AS A PERCENT OF APPARENT CONSUMPTION** ("E" DENOTES EXPORTS)	MAJOR FOREIGN SOURCES[1] (1978)
COLUMBIUM	0	
MICA (SHEET)	10	INDIA
STRONTIUM	0	
MANGANESE	E20	
TANTALUM	0	
COBALT	0	
BAUXITE & ALUMINA	52	GUINEA, YUGOSLAVIA, HUNGARY, INDIA
CHROMIUM	E44	
PLATINUM – GROUP METALS	E45	
ASBESTOS	E32	
FLUORIDE	50	MONGOLIA, CHINA, THAILAND
TIN	21	MALAYSIA, UNITED KINGDOM, BOLIVIA
NICKEL	E9	
CADMIUM	E29	
ZINC	E6	
POTASSIUM	E42	

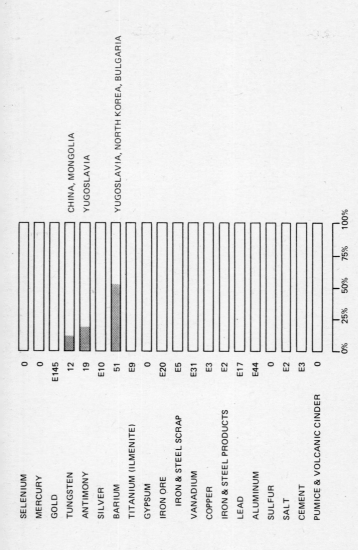

SELENIUM 0
MERCURY 0
GOLD E145
TUNGSTEN 12 CHINA, MONGOLIA
ANTIMONY 19 YUGOSLAVIA
SILVER E10
BARIUM 51 YUGOSLAVIA, NORTH KOREA, BULGARIA
TITANIUM (ILMENITE) E9
GYPSUM 0
IRON ORE E20
IRON & STEEL SCRAP E5
VANADIUM E31
COPPER E3
IRON & STEEL PRODUCTS E2
LEAD E17
ALUMINUM E44
SULFUR 0
SALT E2
CEMENT E3
PUMICE & VOLCANIC CINDER 0

0% 25% 50% 75% 100%

1SOURCES SHOWN ARE POINTS OF SHIPMENT TO
THE U.S.S.R. AND ARE NOT NECESSARILY THE
INITIAL SOURCES OF THE MATERIAL

MARCH-1979

*NET IMPORTS = IMPORTS-EXPORTS

**APPARENT CONSUMPTION = DOMESTIC MINE
OUTPUT + NET IMPORTS

BUREAU OF MINES, U.S. DEPARTMENT OF THE INTERIOR

Information Profiles
on 31 Important Metals

The prices and figures in these profiles are based on the best information available.

NOTE FOR POTENTIAL INVESTORS:

Any prices quoted for the following 31 strategic metals are subject to negotiation, just as in real estate. Because there is no organized marketplace for these metals—no "exchange"—prices quoted either herein or in any trade publication may remain the same for weeks, months or longer, unlike gold, silver or other metals traded on a daily basis by large brokerage houses. It is for this very reason, however, that the potential for such large profits (again, as in real estate) exists. The very fact that investors in these metals recognize that periods of slack demand may occur, and that they are willing to stand pat during such periods in anticipation of handsome profits when changing conditions accelerate demand, is the reason that trading in these metals can offer such unusual rewards. This market is not one for the "day-trader," or even short-term speculator, nor for any one else who does not plan an investment of either medium or longer term. If you think you might need to withdraw your investment on short notice, simply do not seek the opportunities of the strategic metals field.

ANTIMONY (Sb)

The auto industry uses a lot of this metal to make batteries.
However, the lead-antimony cells may well be phased out in
favor of newer batteries that are harder to charge but a lot
lighter. Also a good fire-retardant used in carpets, plastics
and power cable insulation. China has far and away most of
the metallic element, more properly called a metalloid.
Widely traded, mostly in heavy ingots. But the market is
highly speculative and prices swoop and dive like a drunken
swallow. Derived from the ore, stibnite, which gives the
element its symbol. The Bible says Jezebel painted her eyes
with stibium—antimony—and its use in cosmetics continues
to this day. The name is thought to come from the Greek anti
monos—"against one who dwells alone." Many medieval
monks poisoned themselves by eating antimony to help them
fast longer. Perhaps a more accurate interpretation: "a metal
seldom found alone."

Price 1971-1980	U.S. $ per metric ton
1971	1200.00
1972	900.00
1973	1100.00
1974	3600.00
1975	2700.00
1976	3000.00
1977	3100.00
1978	2000.00
1979	2600.00
1980	3300.00
Nov. 1980	3175.00

World Production	Percentage
China	27
Soviet Union	15
France	14
Belgium	6
United States	5
Rest of the world	33

Total World Production:

32,820 metric tons

ARSENIC (As)

Deadly compounds used to poison pests. Or people. Therefore packed in sealed drums marked with skull and crossbones. Other uses include metal refining and removing colors from glass. Increases hardness of lead and corrosion resistance of copper. Producers competitive with each other but control prices tightly. Merchants rarely deal in pure metal. They prefer the oxide, a white powder. Mexicans have the most, followed by Russians and French. Named, though, by the Greeks, who have virtually none. Called arsenikos—male—in belief that metals had gender.

Price 1974-1980	Pounds Sterling per metric ton
1974	1800.00
1975	1780.00
1976	2400.00
1977	2950.00
1978	2950.00
1979	2700.00
1980	2700.00
Nov. 1980	3000.00

World Production	Percentage
Mexico	25
Soviet Union	20
France	16
Namibia	12
Sweden	11
United States	7
Rest of the world	9

Total World Production:

37,000 metric tons

BERYLLIUM (Be)

Traded mainly in 5 percent alloy, beryllium-copper. It's used for everything from springs and electrical contacts to boat propellors. Pure beryllium rarely traded—it's highly toxic and not very useful, but hard enough to scratch glass. Strong, light, it resists corrosion. Almost no free market; producers set the price and not much produced each year. While Brazil is largest single supplier, 7 out of every 10 tons come from somewhere else. The ore, beryl, is easily refined. But fooling around with beryllium can give you a nasty little number called berylliosis, which is a cross between syphilis and cancer, and you may not spot the symptoms for 25 years.

Price 1970-1980	U.S. $ per short ton unit of BeO
1970	38.00
1971	35.00
1972	30.00
1973	30.00
1974	30.00
1975	30.00
1976	37.00
1977	37.00
1978	37.00
1979	37.00
1980	37.00
Nov. 1980	80.00

World Production	Percentage
Brazil	24
Argentina	6
Zambia	4
Australia	3
Rest of the world	63

Total World Production:

127 short tons

BISMUTH (Bi)

Aside from the jokes about its use in France as a laxative (where it has all but ruined French digestive tracts), big sales in drug store products still exist. Heavy use also in tools that make airplanes. Melded with some aluminum metal mixes, makes many products easier to mill. Many, many uses, including one in sprinkler systems. Gold bugs should love bismuth; it's important in smelting gold and silver ores. Market very active. Price as erratic as a crooked congressman at election time. No shortage for years to come. Keep watching bismuth but only buy and sell on the advice of an expert trader.

Price 1970-1980	U.S. $ per lb.
1970	8.20
1971	6.00
1972	3.00
1973	4.00
1974	8.00
1975	7.50
1976	5.00
1977	4.75
1978	2.40
1979	1.90
1980	2.40
Nov. 1980	2.00

World Production	Percentage
Australia	22
Japan	17
Bolivia	17
Mexico	15
Peru	13
South Korea	4
Canada	4
Rest of the world	8

Total World Production:

4,050 metric tons

CADMIUM (Cd)

Easy to trade, because there's plenty of it, and for all of cadmium's uses a substitute strategic element is available. Be careful when you're trading, whether you buy it in stick or ball form. Certain consumers want only sticks, others want only balls. Being a by-product of zinc, whenever zinc production drops, all things being equal, cadmium ought to go up in price. But new supplies keep coming on the market. Cadmium is highly toxic but still much used for such items as galvanized steel, zinc die casting, plating, etc. Brokers like to trade cadmium at free market prices, and if you follow it closely enough, a lot of money could be made here.

Price 1970-1980	U.S. $ per lb.
1970	4.80
1971	2.20
1972	1.50
1973	3.45
1974	4.00
1975	2.10
1976	1.45
1977	2.80
1978	1.75
1979	3.00
1980	2.10
Nov. 1980	1.95

World Production	Percentage
Soviet Union	16
Japan	14
United States	11
Canada	8
Belgium	8
West Germany	7
Rest of the world	36

Total World Production:
18,512 metric tons

CERIUM (Ce)

Most abundant of the metals from the rare-earth substances. When traded at all, is bought and sold as "mischmetal." Used in petrochemical and glass industries. Also in compounds as filters and in lighter flints too. Lots of new uses in prospect, anyone of which could make the price shoot up. U.S. in good shape, having the big part of world reserves. Found in a number of minerals in North Carolina. Mostly goes directly from producer to user, although veteran professionals who have nothing else to do but watch cerium have occasionally turned a free market profit. It's sure not to turn one for you yet, though.

Price 1974-1980	Pounds Sterling per kilogram of mischmetal
1974	2.10
1975	2.10
1976	2.10
1977	3.30
1978	3.30
1979	3.30
1980	3.30
Nov. 1980	3.35

World Production	Percentage
Australia	32
India	20
United States	18
Malaysia	13
Brazil	10
Rest of the world	7

Total World Production:

11,900 short tons

CHROMIUM (Cr)

Chromium is essential in stainless steel manufacture, not to mention other special steels. You see plenty of it on automobiles and on your table as knives and forks. Used to plate many items. Only .000002 of an inch needed for a brilliant surface. Vital to industry. U.S. produces none. Thought to be major deposits in Alaska on environmentally-protected land. U.S. stockpile woefully inadequate. If South Africa, Zimbabwe and Turkey suddenly vanished into Soviet orbit, we'd have to beg for our chromite from the USSR. There are a few other small sources, but all put together they can't begin to fill U.S. demand. Chromium has increased in price sixfold in 8 years. Similar in many of its steel uses to vanadium and manganese.

Price 1972-1980	Pounds Sterling per Kilogram chromium contained
1972	.26
1973	.27
1974	.33
1975	.85
1976	.80
1977	1.00
1978	.80
1979	.85
1980	1.05
Nov. 1980	1.00

World Production	Percentage
South Africa	34
Soviet Union	23
Albania	9
Turkey	6
Zimbabwe	6
Finland	6
Rest of the world	16

Total World Production:

9,650,000 metric tons

COBALT (Co)

The writer has bought cobalt on the theory that it has nowhere to go but up. It hit $40 a pound in 1979 and in December, 1980 around $21-$22. It's a perfectly vital metal in armaments, and if there is even a hint of further trouble in Shaba province (Zaire being by far the biggest cobalt supplier), the price could take off like the lead dog at a coon hunt. Currently indispensable for jet aircraft engines. Tough as tungsten in retaining its cutting edge at a red heat. U. S. produced not one ounce of cobalt in 1978 or 1979, due to environmentalists. Cobalt is U.S.'s major Achilles heel among metals vital to defense. U.S. dependent for over 98 percent of its consumption. Source of beautiful blue colors—for instance, cobalt ores were used to produce the lovely blue color of Ming dynasty porcelain. The Vitamin B_{12} you take is the only vitamin known to contain a heavy metal—cobalt. You also get cobalt in a lot of foods. Traders somehow find a way to get cobalt to sell, so there is always an active free market.

Price 1970-1980	U.S. $ per lb.
1970	.80
1971	.80
1972	2.30
1973	2.50
1974	2.80
1975	4.00
1976	4.25
1977	4.90
1978	5.75
1979	40.00
1980	24.00
Nov. 1980	21.00

World Production	Percentage
Zaire	34
New Caledonia	13
Soviet Union	13
Australia	11
Zambia	7
Rest of the world	22

Total World Production:

30,250 metric tons

COLUMBIUM (NIOBIUM) (Cb) (Nb)

Columbium comes from the same ore as tantalum. Brazil about runs the show, producing nearly three-quarters of the world's output. What with Brazil's big international debt, they can be expected to try to keep the price pegged high. It currently is sitting on an all time high, having come from $1 a pound to $11 in ten years. Major use in steels. Also in heavy building such as skyscrapers and in bridges. Most prominent new use for columbium is in making the steel for pipelines. Vanadium and molybdenum could be substituted in pipelines, but the writer believes columbium has a low downside risk and intends to buy some the moment the price has a momentary setback. U. S. totally dependent on foreign countries for columbium.

Price 1970-1980	U.S. $ per lb. oxide
1970	1.10
1971	1.10
1972	1.00
1973	1.20
1974	1.50
1975	2.00
1976	2.80
1977	2.90
1978	2.90
1979	3.80
1980	11.50
Nov. 1980	10.00

World Production	Percentage
Brazil	73
Canada	8
Nigeria	4
Rest of the world	15

Total World Production:

25,900 metric tons

GALLIUM (Ga)

Bluish-white metal with such a low melting point that it will melt in your hand. It's used to make those trick spoons where you stir your coffee, then look down—and there's no spoon left. Although originally discovered in a remote mine high in the picturesque Pyrenees, the Swiss control the supply, as cool as a pawnbroker's smile; United States second. By-product of zinc and aluminum ores. Biggest uses in high technology electronics. Also substantial use in measuring instruments. In some forms, helpful in bone cancer study: any cancerous portion of bone will absorb Gallium 72 and so can be quickly caught. Trading activity not big but easy to do, and one of few metals you can take home and hoard. Writer has a little gallium, at this writing, because he doesn't think production will keep up with demand.

Price 1974-1980	U.S. $ per kilogram
1974	450.00
1975	400.00
1976	310.00
1977	250.00
1978	250.00
1979	330.00
1980	380.00
Nov. 1980	490.00

World Production	Percentage
Switzerland	62
United States	29
Japan	3
Rest of the world	6

Total World Production:

30,500 kilograms

GERMANIUM (Ge)

Germanium is one fine metal. Comes from copper or zinc. Marketed as either germanium metal or germanium dioxide. The writer got into the market at the right time. It has gone from $400 per kilo in 1979 to $900 in October 1980. International tensions aren't likely to lessen, and germanium's a must for night-sighting devices. An even bigger application is in electronics (semi-conductors—Texas Instruments currently biggest germanium consumer). Not an extremely active metal but a good one to trade. Soviet bloc countries are now limiting exports, and western nations should begin stockpiling. Unfortunately, some early brokers in the game missed the boat on this one. Naturally, having taken a handsome profit on it recently, I like germanium.

Price 1973-1980	U.S. $ per kilogram
1973	200.00
1974	375.00
1975	360.00
1976	210.00
1977	200.00
1978	230.00
1979	400.00
1980	600.00
Nov. 1980	885.00

World Production	Percentage
Zaire	26
United States	18
Namibia	8
Canada	8
Rest of the world	40

Total World Production:

195,500 lbs.

INDIUM (In)

Due to the recession, indium's price is off from an all-time high in January 1980. Still, it has come from $2.10 in 1970 to its November 1980 price of $14.50. That's some rate of return! The free market is small but pretty active, and you should keep up with indium. By-product of lead and zinc, and cost of producing indium going up rapidly, plus fact that zinc being mined nowadays is yielding much less indium. Traded in both ingot and bar form. Portable enough to salt some away in the old backyard. Important in technological uses in electronics, only problem being that electronics industry is moving so fast that it keeps finding substitutes for substitutes every other day. World inflation likely to continue high, and therefore indium ought to keep pace.

Price 1970-1980	U.S. $ per Troy ounce
1970	2.10
1971	1.90
1972	2.00
1973	2.00
1974	2.00
1975	5.50
1976	5.00
1977	9.60
1978	10.00
1979	12.00
1980	19.50
Nov. 1980	14.50

World Production	Percentage
Belgium	21
United States	20
Japan	12
Soviet Union	11
Canada	8
Rest of the world	28

Total World Production:

1,750,000 Troy ounces

IRIDIUM (Ir)

Another one you can store in your safety deposit box. A mighty beautiful child of platinum, much more beautiful and almost a direct substitute for its radiant mother metal. So hard it's doubtful even a diamond could scratch it, and it won't show a speck of rust after a million years in a sunken ship. Extremely high melting point (over 2400°C) and may have many new uses in the future. Another USSR-South Africa near monopoly. Expensive, market thin, but because cheaper than platinum or rhodium likely to be big in Japanese platinum jewelry. So reflective it makes a mirror look cloudy. Writer missed buying iridium at its lowest, but am considering some right now and will hold for profits that have to come with the big inflation.

Price 1970-1980	U.S. $ per Troy ounce
1970	155.00
1971	150.00
1972	160.00
1973	220.00
1974	390.00
1975	475.00
1976	325.00
1977	300.00
1978	250.00
1979	235.00
1980	235.00
Nov. 1980	600.00

World Production	Percentage
Soviet Union	65
South Africa	25
Canada	10

Total World Production:

8,100 Troy ounces

LITHIUM (Li)

About the lousiest metal a new strategic metal investor could choose for a starting point. Lightest alkali metal. Soft and white. In a flame test, lithium gives off a brilliant crimson. Rarely used, just as rarely traded. Keep it dry, it doesn't like water. Used only in the form of salts, never in a metallic form. Very sophisticated uses in aircraft. Small amounts used for producing very light alloys since lithium lightest of all metal elements. In specialized alloys, increases tensile strength and resistance to corrosion. U. S. in fine shape. Is major world supplier. Has enormous reserves. A Texas company reportedly world's biggest producer by far. Try to forget if you're new in strategics.

Price 1974-1980	U.S. $ per lb.
1974	11.00
1975	11.00
1976	11.00
1977	11.00
1978	11.00
1979	11.00
1980	11.00
Nov. 1980	10.00

World Production	Percentage
United States	37
Brazil	26
Portugal	10
Soviet Union	9
Mozambique	6
Argentina	6
China	3
Rest of the world	3

Total World Production:

10,750 metric tons

MAGNESIUM (Mg)

Like silicon, the energy required to make magnesium is by far the largest part of its cost. There's a lot of it since these days it's most common source is salt water. It is very important in titanium production (and titanium is of course big). One of its biggest uses is in today's small car industry, because both light and cheaper than its competitors. GM, Chrysler, and Ford have all put some magnesium in their cars. Volkswagen's Beetle has had a magnesium engine block ever since the war, and all today's models have either a magnesium crankcase or gearbox. World's lightest structural metal. Used for portable items such as luggage; also machine parts, and lots of consumer products, such as fireworks and flash photography. One of the nicest metals around, and one of these days it's going to take off like a blistered man in a pepper patch. Keep in touch with your broker on this one. Also, be sure it's in your diet, or your bones will get spongy.

Price 1970-1980	U.S. $ per metric ton
1970	850,00
1971	800.00
1972	600.00
1973	750.00
1974	1250.00
1975	1900.00
1976	1700.00
1977	2000.00
1978	2000.00
1979	2300.00
1980	2750.00
Nov. 1980	2645.00

World Production	Percentage
United States	42
Soviet Union	28
Norway	15
Japan	4
Italy	4
France	4
Rest of the world	3

Total World Production:

259,000 metric tons

MANGANESE (Mn)

Much confusion in early days between this metal and magnesium since both derived from Magnesian stone. Most important for industry, and if Russia and South Africa ever got together and wanted to put the screws on this country, manganese would be a good place to start. We have to import over 95 percent of this element that is so critical in making steel. That goes for iron too. Beaucoup other industrial uses—batteries, dyes, dozens of products use it. Has a huge market, and no single producer can fix its price. Producers mostly sell directly to users, so difficult for private investor to get in as a free market buyer. But get to know it; technology advancing as it is, who knows that manganese won't be tomorrow's fairhaired boy.

Price 1970-1980	U.S. $ per metric ton
1970	550.00
1971	580.00
1972	600.00
1973	900.00
1974	1100.00
1975	1400.00
1976	1450.00
1977	1450.00
1978	1450.00
1979	1350.00
1980	1500.00
Nov. 1980	1550.00

World Production	Percentage
Soviet Union	38
South Africa	24
Gabon	8
India	8
Australia	6
China	4
Rest of the world	12

Total World Production:

22,500,000 metric tons

MERCURY (Hg)

The only metal that is liquid at normal temperatures. Named for the speedy messenger of the Roman gods; also known as quicksilver. Poisonous and a potential environmental threat. But vital for thermometers, barometers and other instruments. Major uses, though, in manufacture of chlorine, in batteries, mercury-vapor lights. Also recovery of gold and silver. Condensed from its heated ore, cinnabar, which is getting scarce. World reserves thought to be just a few million flasks. Found around the world, but Soviets have lion's share and U. S. precious little. Price, however, fixed by producers about $400 a flask. Could be a bargain.

Price 1970-1980	U.S. $ per flask
1970	475.00
1971	325.00
1972	210.00
1973	250.00
1974	275.00
1975	175.00
1976	90.00
1977	150.00
1978	125.00
1979	200.00
1980	400.00
Nov. 1980	390.00

World Production	Percentage
Soviet Union	31
Spain	17
Algeria	15
China	10
Canada	6
Rest of the world	21

Total World Production:

206,220 flasks

MOLYBDENUM (Mo)

Your broker will call this one "Molly." It is heavily traded, quite difficult to substitute, and for once, U.S. is biggest producer of something important. A refractory metal like titanium or vanadium. (Refractory is a word we define when you get to tantalum.) The great thing about Molly is the fact that its price has gone from $1.50 to over $9.00 a lb., in just this decade. No reason to expect inflation won't continue to keep it higher'n Grandpa on Saturday night. Almost indispensable for certain oil pipeline manufacture (when vanadium was used in the alloy in the steel to build the Alaskan pipeline, the permafrost cracked hundreds of miles of it, and it all had to be dug up and replaced with steel made from molybdenum alloy) and a biggy in aerospace manufacture. Not the number one free market trader by any means, but if you can get into this market somehow on a pronounced pullback, it could be a good idea.

Price 1970-1980	U.S. $ per lb. Mo contained
1970	1.60
1971	1.70
1972	1.80
1973	1.90
1974	2.20
1975	2.50
1976	3.00
1977	3.40
1978	5.90
1979	5.80
1980	6.00
Nov. 1980	9.20

World Production	Percentage
United States	57
Canada	18
Chile	11
Soviet Union	10
Rest of the world	4

Total World Production:

157,000 metric tons

OSMIUM (Os)

Only seldom traded on the open market. Another platinum
by-product, but about the least important of all precious
metals. Nobody really knows the true extent of Russia's
platinum-bearing sands behind the Ural Mountains, so, like
all platinum products, the world supply is in question.
Densest known form of matter and can be highly poisonous.
Major uses: some very complex industrial uses, also foun-
tain pen tips, electrical contacts, etc. Could still jump in price
if significant big use could be found for it. Market's generally
drier than a 1907 prune. Not worth spending a lot of time on if
you are a beginner.

Price 1970-1980	U.S. $ per Troy ounce
1970	215.00
1971	215.00
1972	215.00
1973	200.00
1974	200.00
1975	200.00
1976	200.00
1977	175.00
1978	150.00
1979	150.00
1980	150.00
Nov. 1980	135.00

World Production	Percentage
South Africa	88
Russia	12

Total World Production:

Figures not available.

RHENIUM (Re)

Major use as a catalyst in the oil industry. A catalyst is something that alters the chemical properties of one or more other substances. Other important uses: in high-octane gas and other petroleum products, lamp filaments, thermocouples, electrical contacts. A metal getting more and more important. Definitely substitutable for platinum. By-product of molybdenum. Has gone from $2700 per kilo to $5500 per kilo in just a year. Has fallen back now from its $5500 high. Writer blew an opportunity to buy it back then. Mobil apparently tried to buy half a ton of rhenium, but no producer had that much stock. Oil companies would rather use rhenium as a catalyst than any possible substitute such as platinum group metals. Reason is that rhenium is found wherever molybdenum occurs, and U.S. has lots of molybdenum. A quite brilliant metal, incorruptible, clean to work with. Keep talking to your broker about rhenium since its price is having a real sinking spell now.

Price 1973-1980	U.S. $ per kilogram
1973	700.00
1974	650.00
1975	600.00
1976	550.00
1977	500.00
1978	550.00
1979	1200.00
1980	5000.00
Nov. 1980	1800.00

World Production	Percentage
United States	38
West Germany	20
Chile	15
Soviet Union	12
Sweden	8
Belgium	4
Rest of the world	3

Total World Production:

12,000 kilograms

RHODIUM (Rh)

Some would-be brokers trying to furnish advice without sufficient expertise got their clients into this one way too early. A platinum metal. Most expensive of all metals at this time and pretty as a red heifer in a flower bed. So shiny it reflects more clearly than a mirror; thin rhodium coat will keep silver from tarnishing; good use in searchlights and motion picture projectors. Steel and brass may be rhodium clad to avoid corrosion. Here's another one where South Africa and Russia could shut off U. S. water. Would make great jewelry if you are Bunker Hunt. Although I'd never go completely overboard on buying such an expensive metal, naturally, it's always the first one that people like to substitute for when at all possible. It has the advantage, for those emotionally requiring same, of being portable enough for stashing. Worth a constant price check with your broker.

Price 1970-1980	U.S. $ per Troy ounce
1970	210.00
1971	200.00
1972	200.00
1973	225.00
1974	330.00
1975	340.00
1976	350.00
1977	450.00
1978	650.00
1979	590.00
1980	800.00
Nov. 1980	700.00

World Production	Percentage
Soviet Union	51
South Africa	41
Canada	7
Rest of the world	1

Total World Production:

151,000 Troy ounces

RUTHENIUM (Ru)

Cheapest of all platinum group metals. That's because it has few essential uses. Very scarce. One of the rarest ever. Principal uses: jewelry and electrical contacts. A few minor uses; however, a .1% alloy makes titanium 100 times more corrosion resistant. Seldom traded and the market tiny. Even though a precious metal, it is at this writing in great over-supply. I wouldn't be surprised to see new uses for ruthenium, since it is so much cheaper than other platinum group metals. Industry would like to use more if it could find out how. Until that time, no big winner.

Price 1970-1980	U.S. $ per Troy ounce
1970	56.00
1971	53.00
1972	52.00
1973	52.00
1974	59.00
1975	60.00
1976	60.00
1977	60.00
1978	45.00
1979	45.00
1980	45.00
Nov. 1980	45.00

World Production	Percentage
Soviet Union	77
Canada	16
South Africa	7

Total World Production:

200,000 Troy ounces

SELENIUM (Se)

The Xerox companies around the world eat selenium for their copying machines. This is a "must watch" element, one of the four "metalloids," an alkali metal like calcium. Metalloid is just a four-bit word for a strategic element like silicon, arsenic or tellurium, all of which are about halfway between a metal and an earth substance in their chemical composition. A metalloid is any substance that can be combined with a metal to form a useful industrial alloy (mixture). If anyone wanted to corner a market (something never to try), selenium is the type of product you'd start with, since annual world production is in such low tonnage. Selenium price no factor in price of end product; tripling price would add only few cents to most products requiring selenium. Used to de-color glass and big in electronics, plastics, not to mention an important use in forging stainless steel. A few minor uses too—like explosives.

Price 1970-1980	U.S. $ per lb.
1970	27.00
1971	8.00
1972	9.00
1973	9.00
1974	15.00
1975	11.00
1976	10.00
1977	18.00
1978	9.00
1979	13.00
1980	10.00
Nov. 1980	5.75

World Production	Percentage
Japan	30
Canada	27
United States	15
Belgium	11
Mexico	3
Rest of the world	14

Total World Production:

1,490,000 kilograms

SILICON (Si)

U. S. in good shape here, since silicon is as unlimited as sand in the sea. Biggest part of its cost is in energy required to make it, same problem as with magnesium. Second most abundant element. In practically every rock, all natural waters, atmosphere, plants, animals—just everywhere. Space instruments even show it present in the sun and other stars. Very big in all sorts of aluminum products, like window frames, doors, ladders, etc., and has some uses in many steels. There's a huge free market with occasional years of price volatility. As energy prices increase with inflation, so should silicon. Yet it's a strategic that you're going to want to trade, so read up on it.

Price 1970-1980	U.S. $ per metric ton
1970	500.00
1971	400.00
1972	400.00
1973	400.00
1974	1500.00
1975	1500.00
1976	800.00
1977	1000.00
1978	750.00
1979	1100.00
1980	1400.00
Nov. 1980	1175.00

World Production	Percentage
United States	24
Soviet Union	22
Norway	11
Canada	10
Japan	8
South Africa	6
Rest of the world	19

Total World Production:

550,000 metric tons

SODIUM (Na)

You use a sodium compound every day—sodium chloride—table salt. But you can forget about ever trading in sodium. It's the sixth most abundant element on earth and neither price nor production figures are available. The pure element is touchy stuff and reacts violently with water. Most sodium is used to make the gasoline additives that stop your car's engine from knocking: tetraethyl and tetra-methyl lead. It's also useful for making titanium (see titanium) and in cooling atomic power piles. Compounds in common use include sodium hydroxide for soapmaking and the sodium bicarbonate in fire extinguishers and stomach acid remedies. However, the element itself is not too valuable because of its abundance. How abundant is it?—Is the sea salty?

TANTALUM (Ta)

It's important in assembling refractories, among other things. (Refractory is just a big word for any of many materials that don't change chemically at high temperatures.) Biggest use of tantalum is in electronics industry in manufacture of capacitors. (A capacitor stores energy for minute periods of time, unlike longer lasting battery.) Very little trading but demand ought to continue big. Reason is big producers control it in an iron vise and can thus freeze prices at high levels. Again, U.S. would be out of business in this metal without foreign supply. Tantalum is also on Russia's shopping list, along with titanium, vanadium, beryllium, lithium and even nickel, though Russia is its major producer. Suffer, poor proletarian, so the generals can have their *dachas*. Tantalum's price has skyrocketed in last 18 months. Discovery of a new use could make this one take off.

Price 1970-1980	*U.S. $ per lb. tantalum pentoxide*
1970	9.00
1971	9.00
1972	6.00
1973	9.00
1974	10.00
1975	15.00
1976	17.50
1977	20.00
1978	25.00
1979	40.00
1980	95.00
Nov. 1980	110.00

World Production	*Percentage*
Thailand	37
Canada	10
China	10
Australia	7
Nigeria	6
Brazil	6
Zaire	3
Rest of the world	21

Total World Production:

1,235 metric tons

TELLURIUM (Te)

Not worth much for making electronic refrigerators. In fact, tellurium readily substitutable in all uses. Only advantage is that it sometimes is cheaper than the next best thing. Comes as by-product of copper—mostly copper in fact—but also zinc and lead. Industry is not yet going wild over tellurium. I am going to follow closely because of possible new developments in the offing. Major use is an alloy to a few copper and steel mixtures. Addition of less than one-tenth percent greatly increases strength of lead. Used as a coloring agent to give glass a blue to brown color. The inhalation of the vapors of tellurium produces a very offensive "tellurium breath." A little chemical use, not much. In fact, until a big new use comes along, tellurium's not much more vital than a lifeguard at a birdbath.

Price 1970-1980	U.S. $ per lb.
1970	6.00
1971	6.00
1972	6.50
1973	6.00
1974	7.00
1975	8.00
1976	11.50
1977	14.50
1978	20.00
1979	23.00
1980	20.00
Nov. 1980	16.50

World Production	Percentage
United States	41
Canada	26
Japan	19
Peru	14

Total World Production:

146,000 kilograms

TITANIUM (Ti)

Again, some early brokers trying to jump the gun in the strategics game recommended physical titanium and prematurely cost their clients a bundle. Titanium *stocks* have gone up but the physical stuff is in over-production for the time being and has had a big sinking spell in 1980. A fundamental now, in defense and civilian aircraft industries, not to mention many other military uses such as submarines and missiles. Russians building all-titanium hull attack subs; can go to far greater depths since titanium four times stronger than steel. Called titanium sponge because the metal is porous. Uses by industry increasing each day. Requires magnesium and sodium to produce. For some reason, Rolls-Royce, now back in car business, chooses only titanium made from sodium. Big, active market. Like all major strategics, good bet against inflation unless substitute quite unexpectedly found. Just don't get carried away.

Price 1970-1980	U.S. $ per kilogram
1970	2.50
1971	3.00
1972	3.00
1973	3.00
1974	4.00
1975	5.50
1976	6.50
1977	7.00
1978	9.00
1979	9.00
1980	42.00
Nov. 1980	17.50

World Production	Percentage
Soviet Union	38
United States	35
Japan	22
Great Britain	5

Total World Production:

93,000 metric tons

TUNGSTEN (W)

A real yes. Its symbol, "W," is for Wolfram, which is German for tungsten. Almost completely non-substitutable in steel making. Terribly hard and has high melting point, like molybdenum. In fact, highest melting point outside platinum group. Big use in more sophisticated armor-plating—tanks, armored cars, shells, drill tips—anything that requires an incredibly hard and tough cutting point. So hard in fact that "Carboloy," a tungsten derivative, sometimes used instead of diamonds for core drilling. Hope that China and Russia never get together and form a tungsten cartel, because U.S. steel industry would turn to jelly. Tungsten is a strategic metal staple, always a profit opportunity, so don't let your broker fail to keep you up to date. And watch the Chinese.

Price 1970-1980	U.S. $ per metric ton unit
1970	71.00
1971	60.00
1972	16.00
1973	16.00
1974	20.00
1975	37.00
1976	42.00
1977	130.00
1978	170.00
1979	135.00
1980	148.00
Nov. 1980	135.00

World Production	Percentage
China	23
Soviet Union	21
United States	7
South Korea	7
Australia	6
Bolivia	6
North Korea	5
Thailand	5
Rest of the world	20

Total World Production:

50,000 metric tons

VANADIUM (V)

One of the important metals. Name comes from Vanadis, the flawlessly beautiful Scandinavian goddess. U. S. might be in tough shape militarily if it couldn't get some from South Africa and Russia, and even Russia is trying to import vanadium now. Highly important as an additive in producing structural steel, and steadily becoming bigger in oil and gas pipeline manufacture. Really important in various steels that need to be double tough. Used in the contact process for the manufacture of sulfuric acid. Major producers control the price closer than a bird dog's spots, particularly the South Africans. They recognize that other refractory metals, especially molybdenum and columbium, are price rivals in the making of the same kind of steels that vanadium does. Some countries stockpiling it; other countries have to start doing same.

Price 1974-1980	U.S. $ per lb.
1974	6.03
1975	8.41
1976	8.41
1977	9.73
1978	8.86
1979	5.55
1980	7.32
Nov. 1980	2.90

World Production	Percentage
South Africa	36
Soviet Union	29
United States	24
Finland	6
Rest of the world	5

Total World Production:

30,000 metric tons

ZIRCONIUM (Zr)

Biggest producer appears to be South Africa, with Australia and Brazil also factors. Major use is in foundries for making casting molds. Number of minor uses such as deodorants, weather repellents, wax-making, tanning, and also anywhere pipes and pumps are used because it resists corrosion so well. Like titanium, zirconium requires either magnesium or sodium to make. A light, strong metal that is even alloyed with titanium in some special uses. A rare metal, with zircon, one of its offshoots, a diamond-like gem. Japanese report they have just recently developed new way to produce it at half the former cost. We'll keep an eye on it because it has lots of potential for nuclear industry, and if nuclear industry expands, so can zirconium use. Our atomic submarine, the Nautilus, could not have been launched without zirconium.

Price 1970-1980	Pounds Sterling per metric ton ore
1970	27.00
1971	28.00
1972	30.00
1973	31.00
1974	55.00
1975	150.00
1976	93.00
1977	75.00
1978	50.00
1979	43.00
1980	43.00
Nov. 1980	22.00

World Production	Percentage
South Africa	53
Australia	23
Brazil	9
Malaysia	9
Rest of the world	6

Total World Production:

32,500 metric tons

Three Strategic Metal Transactions

These are the kinds of documents and paperwork you can expect when buying and selling strategic metals with a traditional merchant broker. The papers cover three full transactions—one in lead, one in palladium ingots, one in germanium metal.

TRANSACTION 1:

COPYRIGHT   Authorised 27th February, 1979

STANDARD LEAD CONTRACT FORM

Approved by the Board of Directors and by the
Committee of the London Metal Exchange

———— SOLD ———— 60304

Contract **B** № 60304

LONDON,.............. 19 NOV79

M ....THE MCLENDON CO.,......

$\frac{I}{We}$ have this day $\frac{\text{sold to}}{\text{bought from}}$xxxxxxx you, according and subject to the Rules and

Regulations of the London Metal Exchange,

........*TWENTY FIVE 00TONS.............................

...................................25............Tonnes (two per cent. either more or less and
subject to Rule 3 below) of

STANDARD LEAD

Price £ ....579.00...........................per tonne net $\frac{\text{plus}}{\text{minus}}$ 1/04% % to us
xxxxxxx

*FIVE HUNDRED AND SEVENTY NINE 00POUNDS

Prompt.................................19 FEBRUARY 1980

We have the right at any time on demand to require you to pay us such a sum (hereinafter referred to as a "margin") in cash and/or to deposit with us security in such other form and of such amount not exceeding the value of the contract as we in our discretion require and in order to secure the due fulfilment by you of your obligations under this contract and to the intent that the value of the margin in relation to the contract shall at all times during the currency of the contract be maintained by you we have the further right on demand and whether in one or more calls to require you to pay to us the difference between the value of the contract at the time of entering into the same and the current market value at any time thereafter as we in our discretion require. In the event of any failure by you to fulfil your obligations we have an immediate right of appropriation of any such cash and/or to sell any security to satisfy our rights as above in addition to all other rights reserved to us by this contract.

This contract is made between ourselves and yourselves as principals, we alone being liable to you for its performance. The percentage (if any) charged by us to you is to be regarded simply as part of the price and may be shared by us with agents introducing the business, whilst we reserve the right also to charge a percentage or commission to any person from or to whom we may have bought or sold to cover our liability hereunder.

In the event of your failing to meet your engagements arising out of this or any other outstanding contract or contracts between us which are subject to the Rules and Regulations of the London Metal Exchange whether by failing to provide on the due date documents to meet sales or money to take up documents (as the case may be) or otherwise howsoever or of your failing to supply or maintain such margin (if any) for which we are entitled to call and have called or in the event of your suspending payment or becoming bankrupt or committing any act of bankruptcy or (being a Company) in the event of your going into liquidation whether voluntary or otherwise, we reserve the right to close this contract and any other said outstanding contract or contracts if as and when we in our sole discretion shall so decide by selling out or buying in against you (as the case may be) and any differences arising therefrom shall be payable forthwith notwithstanding that the prompt day or other day originally stipulated for settlement may not have arrived.

Any delay in our enforcing any of our rights under this contract shall not be deemed to constitute a waiver thereof.

Members of the London Metal Exchange

SPECIAL RULES FOR STANDARD LEAD

1. Quality.—The Lead delivered under this contract must be Refined Pig Lead (minimum 99·97 per cent. purity).

All Lead delivered must be:—

(*i*) of brands approved by and registered with the Committee.

(*ii*) in Pigs weighing not more than 55 kgs each.

2. Settlement.—Contracts shall be settled on exact quantities of 25 tonnes at the official Settlement price quoted by the Committee operative on the prompt date, Buyer and Seller paying or receiving, as the case may be, the difference, if any, between the Settlement price and the contract price.

3. Delivery.—Warrants tendered in fulfilment of contracts shall be invoiced at the Settlement price mentioned in Rule 2 above in parcels each of 25 tonnes or a multiple thereof (each 25 tonnes to be treated as a separate contract). Warrants shall be for 25 tonnes each (two per cent. either more or less). Warrants issued prior to the 1st January, 1970 for long tons shall constitute good delivery provided that their weights are within a 2% tolerance of 25 long tons. Each parcel of 25 tonnes and/or 25 long tons shall be of one brand and shall consist of pigs of one size, subject to the necessity of including different shapes and sizes at the bottom of each parcel for the purpose of palletisation, shall lie at one warehouse and the number of pigs comprising each parcel must be shown on the warrant. Rent shall be allowed on the invoice.

The Lead shall be delivered on the prompt date in any warehouse listed for this purpose with the Committee at listed delivery points in seller's option. (Names of such warehouses can be obtained from the London Metal Exchange Office.)

4. Weights.— In the case of warrants where weights are shown in long tons conversion shall be at the rate of 1 long ton to 1016 kilogrammes. Warrant weights in all cases shall be accepted as between buyer and seller.

5. Disputes.—Any question concerning formation and any dispute under this contract shall be notified to the Secretary of the London Metal Exchange in writing by the seller or the buyer or both of them jointly. Such question or dispute if not settled by agreement shall be referred to arbitration in accordance with the Rules and Regulations of the London Metal Exchange. The decision in writing of the Appeal Committee from the Award of the Arbitrators shall be a condition precedent to a Notice of Motion to remit or set aside the Award of the Arbitrators and the decision of the Appeal Committee or to an action being brought. The Uniform Law concerning the formation of contracts for the International Sale of Goods and the Uniform Law regulating the International Sale of Goods shall not apply.

6. Exchange Control Regulations.—In the event of a resident of the United Kingdom taking delivery of warrants in L.M.E. registered warehouse outside the United Kingdom, the buyer must conform with the Bank of England Metals Scheme C.M. Procedure currently in force.

(In the above Rules "The Committee" means the Committee of the London Metal Exchange.)

For Contract Rules see over.

Printed by Heffers Printers Ltd Cambridge England

CONFIRMATION NOTE

PROMPT 19/02/80

PRICE 579.00

19

J. H. RAYNER (MINCING LANE) LTD.

B № 60304

$\dfrac{I}{We}$ *beg to acknowledge receipt of your Contract,*

dated 19 NOV 79 *for the* $\dfrac{\text{sale to}}{\text{purchase from}}$ *me/us of*

25 *tonnes STANDARD LEAD which* $\dfrac{I}{We}$ *hereby confirm.*

CONTRACT RULES

Rule A. Members of the London Metal Exchange, in their dealings with other Members, shall be responsible to and entitled to claim against one another, and one another only, for the fulfilment of every Contract for Metals.

Rule B. In these Rules the expression "Members of the London Metal Exchange" includes Firms and Companies who, although not themselves Subscribers to the Exchange, are represented and deal thereon by and through "Representative Subscribers" to the Exchange acting as the representatives or Agents of such Firms or Companies.

Rule C. If any Member of the Metal Exchange fails to meet his engagements to another Member, whether by failing to provide on the due date documents (*i.e.* Bills of Lading, Warrants or Delivery Orders according to the metals dealt in) to meet sales made or money to pay for metals bought, or by making default in fulfilling any other obligation arising out of dealings made subject to the Rules and Regulations of the London Metal Exchange, notice of the default shall be given at once in writing to the Committee of the Exchange and the Committee shall immediately fix and publish a settlement price or prices as at the date of such communication to them for all contracts which the defaulter may have open under these Rules, whether with Members or with parties who are not Members. All such contracts shall forthwith be closed and balanced, by selling to or buying from the defaulting Member such metals as he may have contracted to deliver or take, at the settlement prices fixed for this purpose by the Committee, and any difference arising whether from or to the party in default shall become payable forthwith notwithstanding that the prompt day or other day originally stipulated for the settlement of the transaction may not have arrived. In fixing settlement prices under this Rule the Committee may in their discretion take into consideration the extent and nature of the transactions which the defaulting Member has open and any other circumstance which they may consider should affect their decision. In any case where the Committee shall be of opinion that the default is not due to the insolvency of the defaulter the Committee shall by resolution negative the application of this rule. Any claim arising out of a default not due to insolvency shall be settled by arbitration in the usual manner. This rule shall apply to cases in which at or after the decease of a Member the engagements entered into by him are not duly met.

Rule D. In any Contract made subject to the Rules and Regulations of the London Metal Exchange between a Member and a non-Member, in the event of the Non-Member failing to meet his engagement arising out of any such contract whether by failing to provide on the due date documents to meet sales or money to take up documents (as the case may be) or otherwise howsoever or of his failing to supply or maintain such margin (if any) for which the Member is entitled to call and has called, or in the event of the Non-Member's suspending payment or becoming bankrupt or committing any act of bankruptcy or (being a Company) in the event of its going into liquidation whether voluntary or otherwise, the Member shall have the right to close all or any such Contracts outstanding between them by selling out or buying in against the Non-Member (as the case may be) and any differences arising therefrom shall be payable forthwith notwithstanding that the prompt day or other day originally stipulated for settlement may not have arrived.

Rule E. Payments for Warrants or other documents (when deliverable under the Contracts) unless otherwise stipulated on the contract, shall be made by cash in London, or by cheque on a London *clearing* bank, either mode in Seller's option. The documents shall be tendered in London against the cash or cheque, as the case may be, and not later than 2.30 p.m. on the prompt or settling day.

Rule F. Contracts wherein Buyer or Seller (as the case may be) has the option to uplift or to deliver, prior to the prompt or settlement date by giving previous notice of his intention, shall have the notice reckoned by market days; such notices, unless otherwise stipulated at time of purchase or sale, shall be as follows: On a Contract with the option to uplift or to deliver during one calendar month or less, one day's notice shall be given; on a Contract with the option beyond one and up to two calendar months two days' notice shall be given; and on a Contract with the option beyond two and up to three calendar months three days' notice shall be given previous to the date on which delivery is required, or will be made. Notice shall be given for the whole quantity stated in the contract and shall be tendered in writing and delivered at the office of the seller of the option not later than noon on the day of notice. Rent shall only be allowed to Buyer to actual day of settlement; and there shall not be any allowance of interest for a payment made prior to the prompt date.

Rule G. Prompt or settlement dates falling on Saturday, Sunday, or a Bank Holiday which days are not market days, shall be settled as follows. Prompts falling on Saturday shall be settled on the Friday previous; but should the preceding Friday be a Bank Holiday the prompt shall be extended to the Monday following· should both the Friday preceding and the Monday following be Bank Holidays, the prompt shall be settled on the Thursday previous. Prompts falling on Sunday should be extended to the Monday following, but should that Monday be a Bank Holiday the prompt shall be extended to the Tuesday following; should both the following Monday and Tuesday be Bank Holidays, the prompt shall then be extended to the Wednesday following. Prompts falling on a Bank Holiday shall be extended to the day following; and if the Bank Holiday fall on Friday the prompts shall be extended to the Monday following; but should the Friday be Good Friday, prompts falling on that day shall be settled on the Thursday previous. If Christmas Day falls on Monday, prompts falling on that day shall be extended to the Wednesday following, but if Christmas Day falls on Tuesday, Wednesday, Thursday, or Friday, prompts falling on that day shall be settled on the day previous.

Rule H. The establishment, or attempted establishment of a "corner", or participation directly or indirectly in either, being detrimental to the interest of the Exchange, the Committee shall, if in their opinion a "corner" has been or is in the course of being established, have power to investigate the matter and to take whatever action it considers proper to restore equilibrium between supply and demand. Any member or members may be required to give such information as is in his or their possession relative to the matter under investigation.

Rule J (OPTIONS). On the day on which notice is due, the holder of the option shall, except in cases to which Rule C applies, declare in writing before 12 o'clock noon whether he exercises or abandons the option, and if he fails to make such declaration the option shall be considered as abandoned. Options (subject to Rule F above) may be declared for less than the total optional quantity in quantities of 25 tonnes for Copper-Electrolytic Wirebars, H.C.F.R. Wirebars, Cathodes or Fire Refined, 5 tonnes for Standard Tin, High Grade Tin, 25 tonnes for Standard Lead, 25 tonnes for Standard Zinc, 25 tonnes for Aluminium, 6 tonnes for Primary Nickel and 10,000 ounces for Silver or multiples thereof, only one declaration against each contract being allowed. In cases to which Rule C applies the prices fixed by the Committee, at which outstanding contracts are to be closed, shall equally apply to all option contracts; and all options shall be automatically determined, and be deemed to have been either exercised or abandoned according as the prices may be in favour of or against the defaulter and whether the defaulter be the Seller or the Buyer of an option, and the option money shall be brought into account. In contracts with optional prompts, the price which shall be taken as the basis of settlement shall be the settlement price fixed by the Committee under Rule C for the prompt most favourable to the holder of the option.

Rule K (CLEARING). All contracts made between Members of the London Metal Exchange who are entitled to deal in the Ring, either for Copper-Electrolytic Wirebars, H.C.F.R. Wirebars, Cathodes or Fire Refined, Standard Tin, High Grade Tin, Standard Lead, Standard Zinc, Aluminium, Primary Nickel or Silver, shall be settled through the Clearing, except when a Member insists on his right to receive cash instead of cheque from the Member to whom he has sold, in which case the Seller shall give notice to his Buyer before noon on the market day preceding the settling day, and such transactions shall then be exempted from settlement through the Clearing. The Rules governing the Clearing of all contracts shall be those in existence at the time fixed for the fulfilment of the contract. Copies of such rules may be obtained from the Secretary of the Exchange.

Rule L. In case of strikes, lock-outs, or other unforeseen contingencies in London, or other authorised port or point of delivery, which prevent or delay the discharge and/or warehousing of Copper-Electrolytic Wirebars, H.C.F.R. Wirebars, Cathodes or Fire Refined, Standard Tin, High Grade Tin, Standard Lead, Standard Zinc, Aluminium, Primary Nickel and/or Silver, the Seller may be allowed to postpone delivery if he can prove to the satisfaction of the Committee (of which proof the Committee shall be the sole judge) that he does not hold available metal in warehouse or vault with which to fulfil his contracts and that he has metal of the requisite quality which has arrived in London or any other authorised port or point of delivery at least ten days prior to the earliest prompt for which relief is asked, or has metal of the requisite quality in his works, but the delivery, discharge and/or warehousing of which is prevented or delayed as aforesaid. He must also deposit with the Secretary of the Exchange such sums as the Committee may require but not exceeding £5 per tonne in the case of Copper, Lead, Zinc and Aluminium, £10 per tonne in the case of Tin and Primary Nickel and £5 per thousand ounces in the case of Silver. No interest will be allowed on deposits, which will be returned after delivery of Warrants. Should his application be passed by the Committee, he shall deposit documents or other proof to the satisfaction of the Committee with the Secretary of the Exchange, who shall issue Certificates for Copper, Lead, Zinc and Aluminium in quantities of 25 tonnes, Certificates for Tin in quantities of 5 tonnes, Certificates for Nickel in quantities of 6 tonnes and Certificates for Silver in quantities of 10,000 ounces. The Seller shall deliver these Certificates to his Buyer. The Certificates will then constitute a good delivery on the Clearing within the period stated thereon and differences must be settled on the prompt day. The holder of a Certificate must present it to the firm named thereon not later than 2.30 p.m. on the day following that on which he receives notice in writing from his Seller that the Warrant for the actual Copper, Tin, Lead, Zinc, Aluminium, Nickel or Silver is ready. He must take up the War ant against payment at the settlement price fixed on the preceding market day, receiving or paying any difference between this and the price mentioned on the Certificate. In the event of the price on the Certificate being above or below the settlement price operative on the day of delivery the receiver shall pay or be paid the amount of any difference. No other payments shall pass except against delivery of the actual Warrant. In case of any dispute, the Committee's ruling to be final. A fee of £5 to be paid by the Applicants for each Certificate issued.

ARBITRATION

Rule 1. All disputes arising out of or in relation to contracts subject to the Rules and Regulations of the London Metal Exchange shall be referred to arbitration as hereinafter provided. The Executive Secretary of the Committee of the London Metal Exchange (hereinafter referred to as "the Secretary") shall be notified of such disputes in writing and the party first notifying the difference shall at the time of such notification deposit with the Metal Market & Exchange Co. Ltd., the sum of £100. All such disputes shall be referred to two arbitrators, one to be appointed by each party to the difference from the Arbitration Panel of the London Metal Exchange, such arbitrators having power to appoint a third arbitrator from the Panel and having all the powers conferred on arbitrators by the Arbitration Act 1950 or any statutory modifications thereof for the time being in force. The Secretary shall be notified in writing by each party of the appointment of the arbitrators. The arbitration and any Appeal made pursuant to Rule 8 of these Rules from the Award of the Arbitrators to the Committee shall take place at the London Metal Exchange (unless mutually agreed by the Arbitrators and the parties to the dispute that the venue should be elsewhere in England or Wales) and English procedure and law shall be applied thereto.

Rule 2. Persons eligible for appointment to the Arbitration Panel shall be members of the Exchange, their partners or co-directors (as the case may be) or members of their staff. Appointment to and removal from the Panel shall be made, at their sole discretion, by the Committee of the London Metal Exchange who will also be responsible for maintaining a panel of sufficient size.

Rule 3. In the event of either party to the difference (*a*) failing to appoint an arbitrator, or (*b*) failing to give notice in writing or by cable of such appointment to reach the other party within 14 days after receiving written or cabled notice from such other party of the appointment of an arbitrator (any notice by either party being given to the other either by cable or by registered post addressed to the usual place of business of such other party), or (*c*) in the case of death, refusal to act, or incapacity of an arbitrator, then, upon written or cabled request of either party an arbitrator shall be appointed from the said Arbitration Panel by the Committee of the London Metal Exchange.

Rule 4. In case the two arbitrators appointed as aforesaid, whether originally or by way of substitution, shall not within three calendar months after the appointment of the arbitrator last appointed deliver their Award in writing, or choose a third arbitrator, then the said Committee on the written request of either party shall appoint a third arbitrator selected from the said Arbitrators Panel to act with the two aforesaid arbitrators.

Rule 5. The Award in writing of the arbitrators or any two of them shall be made and delivered in triplicate to the Secretary within a period of three calendar months from the date of the acceptance of the appointment by the arbitrator last appointed.

Rule 6. Every Award made pursuant to any provision of this Rule shall be conclusive and binding on the parties to the arbitration, subject to appeal as hereinafter mentioned.

Rule 7. The procedure upon an arbitration shall be as follows:

(a) Within a period of 21 days after the appointment of the second of the two arbitrators so appointed, each party shall deliver to the arbitrators and to each other a statement of case in writing with the originals, or copies, of any documents referred to therein. All such documents to be in the English language or accompanied by certified translations into English.

(b) If either party shall make default in delivering such statements and documents (due consideration being given to time occupied by mails) the arbitrators shall proceed with the case on the statement before them, provided always that, in the sole discretion of the arbitrators, an extension of time may be allowed for the delivery of such statements and documents.

(c) The arbitrators shall appoint a day for a hearing within 28 days, or such further time as the arbitrators shall in their sole discretion allow, after the expiry of the 21 days in accordance with Rule 7(a), and shall give due notice in writing thereof to the parties, who may, and if required by the arbitrators shall, attend and shall submit to examination by the arbitrators and produce such books and documents as the arbitrators may require. Each party shall be entitled to produce verbal evidence before the arbitrators.

(d) Neither Counsel, nor Solicitor shall be briefed to appear for either party without the consent of the arbitrators.

(e) The arbitrators may engage legal or other assistance.

(f) The arbitrators may adjourn the hearing from time to time, giving due notice in writing to the parties of the resumed hearing, and the arbitrators may, if they think fit, proceed with such a resumed hearing in the absence of either party or of both parties.

(g) Where any change takes place in the constitution of the tribunal of arbitrators, either by substitution or otherwise, the new tribunal shall appoint a day for the hearing which shall be not later than 28 days, nor earlier than 7 days, after the change. Each party, if desiring to do so, may submit an Amended Statement of Case, with a copy to the other party, which must reach the new tribunal within seven days of its appointment.

(h) In the event of a third arbitrator being appointed, the provisions contained in Section 9 Sub-Section 1 of the Arbitration Act 1950 shall not apply to any reference.

(i) The cost of the arbitration shall be at the sole discretion of the arbitrators. The arbitrators shall fix the amount of their remuneration. The Award shall state separately the amount of such costs and remuneration and by whom they shall be paid and whether the whole or any part of the deposit referred to in Rule 1 of these Rules shall be returned to the party lodging the same or be forfeited. In the event of either or both parties having been granted permission by the arbitrators to be legally represented at the hearing the arbitrators may take into consideration any legal costs which have been incurred.

(j) The Award shall be deposited with the Secretary who shall forthwith give notice of receipt thereof in writing to both parties, and a copy of such Award shall be delivered to both parties on payment by either party of the costs specified in the Award, which payment shall not affect any provision of the Award.

(k) In the event that after the deposit referred to in Rule 1 of these Rules has been made the parties to the arbitration shall (i) settle their differences (ii) fail to proceed as directed by the arbitrators under sub-clause (c) of this Rule (iii) fail to take up the Award within 28 clear days of notification being given under sub-clause (j) of this Rule, such deposit shall be forfeited.

(l) At the time of issuing their Award, all statements and all documents lodged with the arbitrators shall be delivered by them to the Secretary, by whom they shall be retained until the expiration of the time for giving notice of appeal, as hereafter mentioned, after which the Secretary shall, unless there shall be such appeal, return them to the parties concerned.

Rule 8. Either party shall have the right to appeal against the Award to the Committee of the London Metal Exchange.

Rule 9. The method of appeal against the Award shall be as follows:

(a) The party making the appeal shall (i) within 21 days of the date of the Award give notice in writing of such appeal to the Secretary, and to the other party and shall at the same time state the grounds for appeal. (ii) Deposit with the Secretary the sum of £200, and in addition the sum, if any, which shall be payable under the Award by the Appellant.

(b) Upon the receipt of such Notice of Appeal the Committee shall within 4 weeks nominate not less than five members, (hereinafter called "the Appeal Committee") to hear the Appeal. Members of the Appeal Committee shall be members of the Committee of the London Metal Exchange and/or members of the Board of the Metal Market & Exchange Co. Ltd.

(c) The procedure on appeal shall as far as possible be similar to that above provided for the original hearing, except that all statements and documents delivered to the Secretary under Rule 7(l) shall be laid before the Appeal Committee, who may, however, require such further statement or statements or other information or documents from either or both of the parties as the Appeal Committee may think necessary. The provisions of Rule 7(k) shall apply in like manner to the deposit referred to in sub-paragraph (a) (ii) of this Rule as the deposit in connection with the original hearing.

(d) The decision in writing of the majority of the Appeal Committee (which latter shall not at any time number less than five) shall be final and binding on all parties, and the Appeal Committee shall also decide whether the whole or any part of the said deposit of £200 shall be returned to the Appellant or be forfeited.

(e) The Appeal Committee shall have the same discretion regarding costs as is given to the arbitrators under Rule 7(i) and shall fix the amount of their remuneration and direct by whom it shall be paid.

(f) All statements and all documents lodged with the Appeal Committee shall together with the Award, be deposited by them with the Secretary by whom they shall be retained until the costs and fees specified in the Award have been paid by either party. On payment, which shall not affect any provision of the Award, a copy of the Award shall be delivered to both parties and all documents returned to the parties concerned.

J. H. RAYNER (MINCING LANE) LTD.

50 MARK LANE
LONDON
EC3R 7RJ

Telegraphic Address: RAYMAR LONDON TELEX
Telephone. 01-488 3211 (ADMIN.)
01-623 1411
01-709 9144
Telex: LONDON 883461-2-3-4

STATEMENT OF OPEN POSITION

THE MCLENDON CO.
1917 ELM STREET
DALLAS
TEXAS 75201
CLIENT NO. 1510

MARKET	COMMODITY	POSITION AS AT
L. M. E.	LEAD	31 NOV79

Contract Date	REF	PROMPT DATE	BT	SD	PRICE	BOUGHT VALUE	SOLD VALUE	COM
19 NOVEMBER 79	060304	19 FEBRUARY 80	1		579 00	14475 00		36 18
E. & O. E.			1	0		14475 00	0 00	
AVERAGE PRICE					579 00	0 00		

When in agreement kindly sign and return the attached copy.

APPENDIX C

COPYRIGHT

Authorised 27th February, 1979

STANDARD LEAD CONTRACT FORM

Approved by the Board of Directors and by the
Committee of the London Metal Exchange

————SOLD————60605

Contract **B** № 6060⁵

LONDON,————14 JAN 80

M   THE MCLENDON CO.

$\frac{I}{We}$ have this day $\frac{\text{sold to}}{\text{bought from}}$ you, according and subject to the Rules and
XXXXXXXX
Regulations of the London Metal Exchange,

*ONE HUNDRED AND TWENTY FIVE 00 TONS

————————————1 25————————Tonnes (two per cent. either more or less and
subject to Rule 3 below) of

STANDARD LEAD

Price £————436.00————————per tonne net $\frac{\text{plus}}{\text{minus}}$ 1/16% % to us
XXXXXXX

*FOUR HUNDRED AND THIRTY SIX 00 POUNDS

Prompt————————14 APRIL————19 80

We have the right at any time on demand to require you to pay us such a sum (hereinafter referred to as a "margin") in cash and/or to deposit with us security in such other form and of such amount not exceeding the value of the contract as we in our discretion require and in order to secure the due fulfilment by you of your obligations under this contract and to the intent that the value of the margin in relation to the contract shall at all times during the currency of the contract be maintained by you we have the further right on demand and whether in one or more calls to require you to pay to us the difference between the value of the contract at the time of entering into the same and the current market value at any time thereafter as we in our discretion require. In the event of any failure by you to fulfil your obligations we have an immediate right of appropriation of any such cash and/or to sell any security to satisfy our rights as above in addition to all other rights reserved to us by this contract.

This contract is made between ourselves and yourselves as principals, we alone being liable to you for its performance. The percentage (if any) charged by us to you is to be regarded simply as part of the price and may be shared by us with agents introducing the business, whilst we reserve the right also to charge a percentage of commission to any person from or to whom we may have bought or sold to cover our liability hereunder.

In the event of your failing to meet your engagements arising out of this or any other outstanding contract or contracts between us which are subject to the Rules and Regulations of the London Metal Exchange whether by failing to provide on the due date documents to meet sales or money to take up documents (as the case may be) or otherwise howsoever or of your failing to supply or maintain such margin (if any) for which we are entitled to call and have called or in the event of your suspending payment or becoming bankrupt or committing any act of bankruptcy or (being a Company) in the event of your going into liquidation whether voluntary or otherwise, we reserve the right to close this contract and any other said outstanding contract or contracts if as and when we in our sole discretion shall so decide by selling out or buying in against you (as the case may be) and any difference arising therefrom shall be payable forthwith notwithstanding that the prompt day or other day originally stipulated for settlement may not have arrived.

Any delay in our enforcing any of our rights under this contract shall not be deemed to constitute a waiver thereof.

Members of the London Metal Exchange

SPECIAL RULES FOR STANDARD LEAD

1. Quality.—The Lead delivered under this contract must be Refined Pig Lead (minimum 99·97 per cent. purity).

All Lead delivered must be:—

(i) of brands approved by and registered with the Committee.

(ii) in Pigs weighing not more than 55 kgs each.

2. Settlement.—Contracts shall be settled on exact quantities of 25 tonnes at the official Settlement price quoted by the Committee operative on the prompt date, Buyer and Seller paying or receiving, as the case may be, the difference, if any, between the Settlement price and the contract price.

3. Delivery.—Warrants tendered in fulfilment of contracts shall be invoiced at the Settlement price mentioned in Rule 2 above in parcels each of 25 tonnes or a multiple thereof (each 25 tonnes to be treated as a separate contract). Warrants shall be for 25 tonnes each (two per cent. either more or less). Warrants issued prior to the 1st January, 1970 for long tons shall constitute good delivery provided that their weights are within a 2% tolerance of 25 long tons. Each parcel of 25 tonnes and/or 25 long tons shall consist of pigs of one brand and shall consist of pigs of one size, subject to the necessity of including different shapes and sizes at the bottom of each parcel for the purpose of palletisation, shall lie at one warehouse and the number of pigs comprising each parcel must be shown on the warrant. Rent shall be allowed on the invoice.

The Lead shall be delivered on the prompt date in any warehouse listed for this purpose with the Committee at listed delivery points in seller's option. (Names of such warehouses can be obtained from the London Metal Exchange Office.)

4. Weights.— In the case of warrants where weights are shown in long tons conversion shall be at the rate of 1 long ton to 1016 kilogrammes. Warrant weights in all cases shall be accepted as between buyer and seller.

5. Disputes.—Any question concerning formation and any dispute under this contract shall be notified to the Secretary of the London Metal Exchange in writing by the seller or the buyer or both of them jointly. Such question or dispute if not settled by agreement shall be referred to arbitration in accordance with the Rules and Regulations of the London Metal Exchange. The decision in writing of the Appeal Committee from the Award of the Arbitrators shall be a condition precedent to a Notice of Motion to remit or set aside the Award of the arbitrators and the decision of the Appeal Committee or to an action being brought. The Uniform Law concerning the formation of contracts for the International Sale of Goods and the Uniform Law regulating the International Sale of Goods shall not apply.

6. Exchange Control Regulations.—In the event of a resident of the United Kingdom taking delivery of warrants in L.M.E. registered warehouse outside the United Kingdom, the buyer must conform with the Bank of England Metals Scheme C.M. Procedure currently in force.

(In the above Rules "The Committee" means the Committee of the London Metal Exchange.)

For Contract Rules see over.

Printed by Heffers Printers Ltd Cambridge England

CONFIRMATION NOTE

PROMPT 14/04/80   PRICE 435.00
                                                            19

J. H. RAYNER (MINCING LANE) LTD.

№ 60605

$\frac{I}{We}$ beg to acknowledge receipt of your Contract,

dated   14 JAN 80   for the $\frac{\text{sale to}}{\text{purchase from}}$ me/us of

125   tonnes STANDARD LEAD which $\frac{I}{We}$ hereby confirm.

FROM THIS POINT WE HAVE DELETED THE CONTRACT RULES.

APPENDIX C

COPYRIGHT

Authorised 27th February, 1979

STANDARD LEAD CONTRACT FORM

Approved by the Board of Directors and by the
Committee of the London Metal Exchange

SOLD   60606

Contract **B** № 60606   LONDON, ...14 JAN 80.........

M THE MCLENDON CO.

$\frac{I}{We}$ have this day $\frac{\text{sold to}}{\text{bought from}}$ xxx you, according and subject to the Rules an

Regulations of the London Metal Exchange,

*TWO HUNDRED AND FIFTY 00 TONS

.... 250 .... Tonnes (two per cent. either more or less an
subject to Rule 3 below) o

STANDARD LEAD

Price £ ....438.00............ per tonne net $\frac{\text{plus}}{\text{minus}}$ xxxxxxx   1/16% % to u

*FOUR HUNDRED AND THIRTY EIGHT 00 POUNDS

Prompt .... 14 APRIL 19 80

We have the right at any time on demand to require you to pay us such a sum (hereinafter referred to as "margin") in cash and/or to deposit with us security in such other form and of such amount not exceeding the val of the contract as we in our discretion require and in order to secure the due fulfilment by you of your obligatio under this contract and to the intent that the value of the margin in relation to the contract shall at all times duri the currency of the contract be maintained by us we have the further right on demand and whether in one or mo calls to require you to pay to us the difference between the value of the contract at the time of entering into the same a the current market value at any time thereafter as we in our discretion require. In the event of any failure by you fulfil your obligations we have an immediate right of appropriation of any such cash and/or to sell any security satisfy our rights as above in addition to all other rights reserved to us by this contract.

This contract is made between ourselves and yourselves as principals, we alone being liable to you for performance. The percentage (if any) charged by us to you is to be regarded simply as part of the price and m be shared by us with agents introducing the business, whilst we reserve the right also to charge a percentage commission to any person from or to whom we may have bought or sold to cover our liability hereunder.

In the event of your failing to meet your engagements arising out of this or any other outstanding contra or contracts between us which are subject to the Rules and Regulations of the London Metal Exchange wheth by failing to provide on the due date documents to meet sales or money to take up documents (as the case may or otherwise howsoever or of your failing to supply or maintain such margin (if any) for which we are entitled call and have called or in the event of your suspending payment or becoming bankrupt or committing any act bankruptcy or (being a Company) in the event of your going into liquidation whether voluntary or otherwise, reserve the right to close this contract and any other said outstanding contract or contracts if as and when we our sole discretion shall so decide by selling out or buying in against you (as the case may be) and any differen arising therefrom shall be payable forthwith notwithstanding that the prompt day or other day originally stipula for settlement may not have arrived.

Any delay in our enforcing any of our rights under this contract shall not be deemed to constitute a wai thereof.

Members of the London Metal Exchan

SPECIAL RULES FOR STANDARD LEAD

1. Quality.—The Lead delivered under this contract must be Refined Pig Lead (minimum 99·97 per cent. purity).

All Lead delivered must be:—

(*i*) of brands approved by and registered with the Committee.

(*ii*) in Pigs weighing not more than 55 kgs each.

2. Settlement.—Contracts shall be settled on exact quantities of 25 tonnes at the official Settlement price quoted by the Committee operative on the prompt date, Buyer and Seller paying or receiving, as the case may be, the difference, if any, between the Settlement price and the contract price.

3. Delivery.—Warrants tendered in fulfilment of contracts shall be invoiced at the Settlement price mentioned in Rule 2 above in parcels each of 25 tonnes or a multiple thereof (each 25 tonnes to be treated as a separate contract). Warrants shall be for 25 tonnes each (two per cent. either more or less). Warrants issued prior to the 1st January, 1970 for long tons shall constitute good delivery provided that their weights are within a 2% tolerance of 25 long tons. Each parcel of 25 tonnes and/or 25 long tons shall be of one brand and shall consist of pigs of one size, subject to the necessity of including different shapes and sizes at the bottom of each parcel for the purpose of palletisation, shall lie at one warehouse and the number of pigs comprising each parcel must be shown on the warrant. Rent shall be allowed on the invoice.

The Lead shall be delivered on the prompt date in any warehouse listed for this purpose with the Committee at listed delivery points in seller's option. (Names of such warehouses can be obtained from the London Metal Exchange Office.)

4. Weights.— In the case of warrants where weights are shown in long tons conversion shall be at the rate of 1 long ton to 1016 kilogrammes. Warrant weights in all cases shall be accepted as between buyer and seller.

5. Disputes.—Any question concerning formation and any dispute under this contract shall be notified to the Secretary of the London Metal Exchange in writing by the seller or the buyer or both of them jointly. Such question or dispute if not settled by agreement shall be referred to arbitration in accordance with the Rules and Regulations of the London Metal Exchange. The decision in writing of the Appeal Committee from the Award of the Arbitrators shall be a condition precedent to a Notice of Motion to remit or set aside the Award of the Arbitrators and the decision of the Appeal Committee or to an action being brought. The Uniform Law concerning the formation of contracts for the International Sale of Goods and the Uniform Law regulating the International Sale of Goods shall not apply.

6. Exchange Control Regulations.—In the event of a resident of the United Kingdom taking delivery of warrants in L.M.E. registered warehouse outside the United Kingdom, the buyer must conform with the Bank of England Metals Scheme C.M. Procedure currently in force.

(In the above Rules "The Committee" means the Committee of the London Metal Exchange.)

For Contract Rules see over.

Printed by Heffers Printers Ltd Cambridge England

CONFIRMATION NOTE

PROMPT 14/04/80   PRICE 19   438.00

J.H.RAYNER(MINCING LANE) LTD.

B № 60606

$\dfrac{I}{We}$ *beg to acknowledge receipt of your Contract,*

dated 14 JAN 80 *for the* $\dfrac{sale\ to}{purchase\ from}$ *me/us of*

250 *tonnes STANDARD LEAD which* $\dfrac{I}{We}$ *hereby confirm.*

FROM THIS POINT WE HAVE DELETED THE CONTRACT RULES.

APPENDIX C

COPYRIGHT Authorised 27th February, 1979

STANDARD LEAD CONTRACT FORM

Approved by the Board of Directors and by the
Committee of the London Metal Exchange

———— SOLD ———— 60607

Contract **B** № 60607

LONDON, 14 JAN 30

M THE MCLENDON CO.

$\frac{\text{I}}{\text{We}}$ have this day $\frac{\text{sold to}}{\text{bought from}}$ you, according and subject to the Rules and

xxxxxxxx

Regulations of the London Metal Exchange,

*TWO HUNDRED AND FIFTY 00 TONS

250 Tonnes (two per cent. either more or less and

subject to Rule 3 below) of

STANDARD LEAD

Price £ 439.00 per tonne net $\frac{\text{plus}}{\text{minus}}$ 1/16% % to us

xxxxxxx

*FOUR HUNDRED AND THIRTY NINE 00 POUNDS

Prompt 14 APRIL 1980

We have the right at any time on demand to require you to pay us such a sum (hereinafter referred to as a "margin") in cash and/or to deposit with us security in such other form and of such amount not exceeding the value of the contract as we in our discretion require and in order to secure the due fulfilment by you of your obligations under this contract and to the intent that the value of the margin in relation to the contract shall at all times during the currency of the contract be maintained by you we have the further right on demand and whether in one or more calls to require you to pay to us the difference between the value of the contract at the time of entering into the same and the current market value at any time thereafter as we in our discretion require. In the event of any failure by you to fulfil your obligations we have an immediate right of appropriation of any such cash and/or to sell any security to satisfy our rights as above in addition to all other rights reserved to us by this contract.

This contract is made between ourselves and yourselves as principals, we alone being liable to you for its performance. The percentage (if any) charged by us to you is to be regarded simply as part of the price and may be shared by us with agents introducing the business, whilst we reserve the right also to charge a percentage or commission to any person from or to whom we may have bought or sold to cover our liability hereunder.

In the event of your failing to meet your engagements arising out of this or any other outstanding contract or contracts between us which are subject to the Rules and Regulations of the London Metal Exchange whether by failing to provide on the due date documents to meet sales or money to take up documents (as the case may be) or otherwise howsoever or of your failing to supply or maintain such margin (if any) for which we are entitled to call and have called or in the event of your suspending payment or becoming bankrupt or committing any act of bankruptcy or (being a Company) in the event of your going into liquidation whether voluntary or otherwise, we reserve the right to close this contract and any other said outstanding contract or contracts if as and when we in our sole discretion shall so decide by selling out or buying in against you (as the case may be) and any differences arising therefrom shall be payable forthwith notwithstanding that the prompt day or other day originally stipulated for settlement may not have arrived.

Any delay in our enforcing any of our rights under this contract shall not be deemed to constitute a waiver thereof.

Members of the London Metal Exchange

SPECIAL RULES FOR STANDARD LEAD

1. Quality.—The Lead delivered under this contract must be Refined Pig Lead (minimum 99·97 per cent. purity).

All Lead delivered must be:—
    (*i*) of brands approved by and registered with the Committee.
    (*ii*) in Pigs weighing not more than 55 kgs each.

2. Settlement.—Contracts shall be settled on exact quantities of 25 tonnes at the official Settlement price quoted by the Committee operative on the prompt date, Buyer and Seller paying or receiving, as the case may be, the difference, if any, between the Settlement price and the contract price.

3. Delivery.—Warrants tendered in fulfilment of contracts shall be invoiced at the Settlement price mentioned in Rule 2 above in parcels each of 25 tonnes or a multiple thereof (each 25 tonnes to be treated as a separate contract). Warrants shall be for 25 tonnes each (two per cent. either more or less). Warrants issued prior to the 1st January, 1970 for long tons shall constitute good delivery provided that their weights are within a 2% tolerance of 25 long tons. Each parcel of 25 tonnes and/or 25 long tons shall be of one brand and shall consist of pigs of one size, subject to the necessity of including different shapes and sizes at the bottom of each parcel for the purpose of palletisation, shall lie at one warehouse and the number of pigs comprising each parcel must be shown on the warrant. Rent shall be allowed on the invoice.

The Lead shall be delivered on the prompt date in any warehouse listed for this purpose with the Committee at listed delivery points in seller's option. (Names of such warehouses can be obtained from the London Metal Exchange Office.)

4. Weights.— In the case of warrants where weights are shown in long tons conversion shall be at the rate of 1 long ton to 1016 kilogrammes. Warrant weights in all cases shall be accepted as between buyer and seller.

5. Disputes.—Any question concerning formation and any dispute under this contract shall be notified to the Secretary of the London Metal Exchange in writing by the seller or the buyer or both of them jointly. Such question or dispute if not settled by agreement shall be referred to arbitration in accordance with the Rules and Regulations of the London Metal Exchange. The decision in writing of the Appeal Committee from the Award of the Arbitrators shall be a condition precedent to a Notice of Motion to remit or set aside the Award of the Arbitrators and the decision of the Appeal Committee or to an action being brought. The Uniform Law concerning the formation of contracts for the International Sale of Goods and the Uniform Law regulating the International Sale of Goods shall not apply.

6. Exchange Control Regulations.—In the event of a resident of the United Kingdom taking delivery of warrants in L.M.E. registered warehouse outside the United Kingdom, the buyer must conform with the Bank of England Metals Scheme C.M. Procedure currently in force.

(In the above Rules "The Committee" means the Committee of the London Metal Exchange.)

For Contract Rules see over.

Printed by Heffers Printers Ltd Cambridge England

CONFIRMATION NOTE

PROMPT 14/04/80   PRICE 19   439.00

J. H. RAYNER (MINCING LANE) LTD.

$\frac{I}{We}$ beg to acknowledge receipt of your Contract,

B № 60607

dated   14 JAN 80   for the $\frac{\text{sale to}}{\text{purchase from}}$ me/us of

250   tonnes STANDARD LEAD which $\frac{I}{We}$ hereby confirm.

FROM THIS POINT WE HAVE DELETED THE CONTRACT RULES.

COPYRIGHT   Authorised 27th February, 1979

STANDARD LEAD CONTRACT FORM

Approved by the Board of Directors and by the
Committee of the London Metal Exchange

~~LCHT~~   68923

Contract **B** № 68928

LONDON,............18...JAN80..........

M ~~THE McLENDON CO.~~ ....

$\frac{I}{We}$ have this day $\underset{\text{bought from}}{\overset{\text{sold to}}{\text{~~sold to~~}}}$ you, according and subject to the Rules and

Regulations of the London Metal Exchange,

~~*SIX HUNDRED AND FIFTY 00TONS~~

..................................650.................... Tonnes (two per cent. either more or less and
subject to Rule 3 below) of

STANDARD LEAD

Price £............490.00............ per tonne ~~net~~ $\overset{\text{plus}}{\underset{\text{minus}}{\times\times\times}}$ 1/16% % to us

*FOUR HUNDRED AND NINETY 00POUNDS

Prompt...............14 APRIL   1980............

We have the right at any time on demand to require you to pay us such a sum (hereinafter referred to as a "margin") in cash and/or to deposit with us security in such other form and of such amount not exceeding the value of the contract as we in our discretion require and in order to secure the due fulfilment by you of your obligations under this contract and to the intent that the value of the margin in relation to the contract shall at all times during the currency of the contract be maintained by us we have the further right on demand and whether in one or more calls to require you to pay to us the difference between the value of the contract at the time of entering into the same and the current market value at any time thereafter as we in our discretion require. In the event of any failure by you to fulfil your obligations we have an immediate right of appropriation of any such cash and/or to sell any security to satisfy our rights as above in addition to all other rights reserved to us by this contract.

This contract is made between ourselves and yourselves as principals, we alone being liable to you for its performance. The percentage (if any) charged by us to you is to be regarded simply as part of the price and may be shared by us with agents introducing the business, whilst we reserve the right also to charge a percentage or commission to any person from or to whom we may have bought or sold to cover our liability hereunder.

In the event of your failing to meet your engagements arising out of this or any other outstanding contract or contracts between us which are subject to the Rules and Regulations of the London Metal Exchange whether by failing to provide on the due date documents to meet sales or money to take up documents (as the case may be) or otherwise howsoever or of your failing to supply or maintain such margin (if any) for which we are entitled to call and have called or in the event of your suspending payment or becoming bankrupt or committing any act of bankruptcy or (being a Company) in the event of your going into liquidation whether voluntary or otherwise, we reserve the right to close this contract and any other said outstanding contract or contracts if as and when we in our sole discretion shall so decide by selling out or buying in against you (as the case may be) and any differences arising therefrom shall be payable forthwith notwithstanding that the prompt day or other day originally stipulated for settlement may not have arrived.

Any delay in our enforcing any of our rights under this contract shall not be deemed to constitute a waiver thereof.

Members of the London Metal Exchange

SPECIAL RULES FOR STANDARD LEAD

1. Quality.—The Lead delivered under this contract must be Refined Pig Lead (minimum 99·97 per cent. purity).

All Lead delivered must be:—
    (*i*) of brands approved by and registered with the Committee.
    (*ii*) in Pigs weighing not more than 55 kgs each.

2. Settlement.—Contracts shall be settled on exact quantities of 25 tonnes at the official Settlement price quoted by the Committee operative on the prompt date, Buyer and Seller paying or receiving, as the case may be, the difference, if any, between the Settlement price and the contract price.

3. Delivery.—Warrants tendered in fulfilment of contracts shall be invoiced at the Settlement price mentioned in Rule 2 above in parcels each of 25 tonnes or a multiple thereof (each 25 tonnes to be treated as a separate contract). Warrants shall be for 25 tonnes each (two per cent. either more or less). Warrants issued prior to the 1st January, 1970 for long tons shall constitute good delivery provided that their weights are within 2% tolerance of 25 long tons. Each parcel of 25 tonnes and/or 25 long tons shall be of one brand and shall consist of pigs of one size, subject to the necessity of including different shapes and sizes at the bottom of each parcel for the purpose of palletisation, shall lie at one warehouse and the number of pigs comprising each parcel must be shown on the warrant. Rent shall be allowed on the invoice.

The Lead shall be delivered on the prompt date in any warehouse listed for this purpose with the Committee at listed delivery points in seller's option. (Names of such warehouses can be obtained from the London Metal Exchange Office.)

4. Weights.—In the case of warrants where weights are shown in long tons conversion shall be at the rate of 1 long ton to 1016 kilogrammes. Warrant weights in all cases shall be accepted as between buyer and seller."

5. Disputes.—Any question concerning formation and any dispute under this contract shall be notified to the Secretary of the London Metal Exchange in writing by the seller or the buyer or both of them jointly. Such question or dispute if not settled by agreement shall be referred to arbitration in accordance with the Rules and Regulations of the London Metal Exchange. The decision in writing of the Appeal Committee from the Award of the Arbitrators shall be a condition precedent to a Notice of Motion to remit or set aside the Award of the Arbitrators and the decision of the Appeal Committee or to an action being brought. The Uniform Law concerning the formation of contracts for the International Sale of Goods and the Uniform Law regulating the International Sale of Goods shall not apply.

6. Exchange Control Regulations.—In the event of a resident of the United Kingdom taking delivery of warrants in L.M.E. registered warehouse outside the United Kingdom, the buyer must conform with the Bank of England Metals Scheme C.M. Procedure currently in force.

(In the above Rules "The Committee" means the Committee of the London Metal Exchange.)

For Contract Rules see over.

Printed by Heffers Printers Ltd Cambridge England

CONFIRMATION NOTE

PROMPT 14/04/80   PRICE 490.00
                                                             19

J.H.RAYNER(MINCING LANE) LTD.

$\frac{I}{We}$ *beg to acknowledge receipt of your Contract,*

B № 68928

dated 18 JAN80 *for the* ~~XXsalextaxX~~ *me/us of*
$\frac{}{purchase\ from}$

650 ....*tonnes STANDARD LEAD which* $\frac{I}{We}$ *hereby confirm.*

FROM THIS POINT WE HAVE DELETED THE CONTRACT RULES.

APPENDIX C

J. H. RAYNER (MINCING LANE) LTD.

50 MARK LANE
LONDON
EC3R 7RJ

Telegraphic Address: RAYMAR LONDON TELEX
Telephone: 01-488 3211 (ADMIN.)
01-623 1411
01-709 9144
Telex: LONDON 883461-2-3-4

STATEMENT OF OPEN POSITION

```
THE MCLENDON CO.
1917 ELM STREET,
DALLAS
TEXAS 75201
CLIENT NO  1510
```

MARKET	COMMODITY	POSITION AS AT
L. M. E.	LEAD	31 JAN8

Contract Date	REF	PROMPT DATE	BT	SD	PRICE	BOUGHT VALUE	SOLD VALUE	COM
18 JANUARY 8	068928	14APRIL 80		26	490.00		318500.00	199.06
14 JANUARY 8	060605	14APRIL 80	5		436.00	54500.00		34.06
14 JANUARY 8	060606	14APRIL 80	10		438.00	109500.00		68.43
14 JANUARY 8	060607	14APRIL 80	10		439.00	109750.00		68.59
19 NOVEMBER 79	060304	19FEBRUARY 80	1		579.00	14475.00		36.18

E. & O. E.

| | | 26 | 26 | | 288225.00 | 319500.00 | |

AVERAGE PRICE   443 42   490.00

When in agreement kindly sign and return the attached copy.

TRANSACTION 2:

GERALD METALS LIMITED

EUROPE HOUSE, WORLD TRADE CENTRE
ST. KATHARINE BY THE TOWER, LONDON EI 9AA

DIRECTORS
P. BOURDEIX (FRENCH)
    - MANAGING
RALPH KESTENBAUM
G. L. LENNARD (U.S.)
W. S. LINNELL
J. W. PARDOE, M.A.

AFFILIATED COMPANIES
NEW YORK, N.Y.
LAUSANNE   SANTIAGO
TOKYO   LIMA

Telephone: 01 - 481 0681
Telex: 884377
Cables: GERALDMET, LONDON

RING DEALING MEMBER OF THE LONDON METAL EXCHANGE

The McLendon Company Ltd.,
1917 Elm Street
Dallas 75201
Texas
U S A

CONTRACT No. S5709 A

This cancels our
previous contract

11th January , 19 80

We hereby confirm having ~~PURCHASED from you~~ and your having ~~SOLD to us~~ the below material at the
                          SOLD to you   PURCHASED from us
following terms and conditions:

MATERIAL: U.S.S.R. Palladium Ingots 99.95% min. Pd.

QUANTITY: 261 Troy ounces

PRICE: $194.00   (One hundred and ninety four U S dollars)
                      per troy ounce

PLACE OF DELIVERY: Loco Zurich SBC

TIME OF DELIVERY: Prompt

PAYMENT: Payment by Nett cash/telegraphic transfer to be
                      received at our Bankers prior to release of material

WEIGHING & QUALITY DETERMINATION:

OTHER CONDITIONS: Sellers weights and assays final

LAW/CLAIMS/ARBITRATION

This contract shall be governed by the laws of England. Any claim whatsoever by either party shall be notified in writing to the other
so that such notice shall be received within twenty-one days of the date of delivery or of the time for delivery as specified in this contract
and in default of such written notice of claim any claim shall be absolutely barred. Any dispute arising out of or under this contract shall
be settled by Arbitration in London in accordance with the Rules and Regulations of the London Metal Exchange.

FORCE MAJEURE: Should any circumstances arise preventing either party from wholly or partially carrying out its obligations
                     under the contract, namely fire, acts of God, elements, war, military operations of any nature, shortages
of transportation, blockade or prohibitions of export or import, the period stipulated for the performance of this contract shall be
extended for as long as the circumstances prevail.

In the event of these circumstances proceeding for more than three months, the party not declaring Force Majeure shall have the right
to refuse to fulfil its obligations under this contract, and in such case neither party shall be entitled to indemnification of any losses
it may sustain.

The party unable to carry out its obligations under the contract shall immediately advise the other party of the commencement and
termination of the circumstances preventing performance of this contract. A certificate issued by the Chamber of Commerce of the
Seller's or Buyer's country shall be sufficient proof of the operation and the duration of such circumstances, and any objection to
such certification supplied by the party declaring Force Majeure by the party not declaring Force Majeure can only be upheld by
resorting to arbitration as specified above.

We are pleased to have concluded this business with you and kindly ask you to return duplicate copy of this contract duly signed.

Accepted: GERALD METALS LIMITED

....   J. MCLEAN   W S LINNELL

GM13

GERALD METALS LIMITED

EUROPE HOUSE, WORLD TRADE CENTRE
ST. KATHERINE BY THE TOWER, LONDON E1 9AA

DIRECTORS:
RALPH KESTENBAUM (MANAGING)
G. LENNARD (U.S.)
W.S. LINNELL
J.W. PARDOE, M.A., M.P.

AFFILIATED COMPANIES
NEW YORK, N.Y.
MEXICO, D.F.
TOKYO

Telephone: 01-481 0681
Telex: 884377
Cables   GERALDMET, LONDON
VAT Registration No 243 3411 96

The McLendon Company Ltd.,
1917 Elm Street
Dallas 75201
Texas
U S A

Date 11th January Invoice **No.** 9548
1980

Our Contract No.	Your Order No.	Terms		Payment	
S-5709 A		LOC ZURICH SBC		PROMPT NETT CASH	
Shipped From	Shipped To	Via		Shipped Date	

Units & Marks	Description	Weight	Price	Total
	U.S.S.R. PALLADIUM INGOTS 99.95% MIN. PD.			
	Nett Weight	261 T/O	$194.00 p T/O	US$ 50,634.00
	Please remit to: CITIBANK N A 336 Strand London WC2R 1HB U S Dollar Merchanting Account 990027 GERALD METALS LIMITED			
P-4966			GERALD METALS LIMITED	

GM 7

GERALD METALS LIMITED

EUROPE HOUSE, WORLD TRADE CENTRE
ST. KATHARINE BY THE TOWER, LONDON E1 9AA

DIRECTORS
P. BOURDEIX (FRENCH)
— Managing
RALPH KESTENBAUM
G. L. LENNARD (U.S.)
W. S. LINNELL
J. W. PARDOE. M.A.

AFFILIATED COMPANIES
NEW YORK, N.Y.
MEXICO, D.F.
TOKYO

Telephone: 01-481 0681
Telex: 884377
Cables: GERALDMET, LONDON

RING DEALING MEMBER OF THE LONDON METAL EXCHANGE

The McLendon Company Ltd.,
1917 Elm Street
Dallas 75201
Texas
U S A

CONTRACT No. P5335 A

This cancels our
previous contract

4th March , 1980

We hereby confirm having PURCHASED from you ~~SOLD~~ and your having ~~PURCHASED~~ SOLD to us the below material at the
following terms and conditions:

MATERIAL: U.S.S.R. Palladium Ingots 99.95% min. Pd.

QUANTITY: 261 Troy ounces

PRICE: $291.00 (Two hundred and ninety one U Sdollars)
per troy ounce

PLACE OF DELIVERY: In vault, KLM Amsterdam

TIME OF DELIVERY: Prompt

PACKING:

PAYMENT: Net cash by telegraphic transfer immediately upon
release of material and advice by Sellers of full
weights and assays

WEIGHING & QUALITY DETERMINATION:

OTHER CONDITIONS:

LEGAL JURISDICTION: In England, according to the Laws of England.

ARBITRATION: In London according to the rules and regulations of the LONDON METAL EXCHANGE

FORCE MAJEURE: Should any circumstances arise preventing either party from wholly or partially carrying out its obligations under the contract, namely fire, acts of God, elements, war, military operations of any nature, shortages of transportation, blockade or prohibitions of export or import, the period stipulated for the performance of this contract shall be extended for as long as the circumstances prevail.

In the event of these circumstances proceeding for more than three months, the party not declaring Force Majeure shall have the right to refuse to fulfil its obligations under this contract, and in such case neither party shall be entitled to indemnification of any losses it may sustain.

The party unable to carry out its obligations under the contract shall immediately advise the other party of the commencement and termination of the circumstances preventing performance of this contract. A certificate issued by the Chamber of Commerce of the Seller's or Buyer's country shall be sufficient proof of the operation and the duration of such circumstances, and any objection to such certification supplied by the party declaring Force Majeure by the party not declaring Force Majeure can only be upheld by resorting to arbitration as specified above.

We are pleased to have concluded this business with you and kindly ask you to return duplicate copy of this contract duly signed.

Accepted:

GERALD METALS LIMITED

I MCLEAN

W/S/ LINNELL

GM13 x

GERALD METALS LIMITED

EUROPE HOUSE, WORLD TRADE CENTRE
ST. KATHERINE BY THE TOWER, LONDON E1 9AA

DIRECTORS
RALPH KESTENBAUM (MANAGING)
G. LENNARD (U.S.)
W. S. LINNELL
J. W. PARDOE, M.A., M.P.

AFFILIATED COMPANIES
NEW YORK, N.Y
MEXICO, D.F
TOKYO

Telephone 01-481 0681
Telex: 884377
Cables   GERALDMET, LONDON
VAT Registration No 243 3411 96

Purchase
PURCHASED FROM: Date 4th March   Invoice XXXX
The McLendon Company Ltd.,   1980
1917 Elm Street
Dallas 75201
Texas
U S A

Our Contract No.	Your Order No.	Terms		Payment	
P-5335 A		KLM AMSTERDAM			
Shipped From	Shipped To	Via		Shipped Date	
Units & Marks	Description	Weight	Price	Total
	U.S.S.R. PALLADIUM INGOTS 99.95% MIN. Pd.			
	Nett Weight	261 T/O	$291.00 p T/O	US$75,951.00

GERALD METALS LIMITED

GM 7

TRANSACTION 3:

WOGEN RESOURCES LIMITED 17 Devonshire St. London W1N 1FS

The McLendon Company
2119 Southland Centre
400 N. Olive Street
Dallas
Texas 75201
U.S.A.

CONTRACT OF SALE

No. ...... 03707S ......

Telephone: 01-580 5762/3/4/5
Administration: 01-637 1178
Cables Wogenmet London W.1
Telex 28820

19 June 1980

We hereby confirm having this day SOLD to you subject to the conditions
printed overleaf.

Quantity   100 (One Hundred) kilos

Description   Germanium Metal
                    50 ohms

Price US$645 (U S Dollars Six Hundred and Forty Five) kg

Package

Place of Delivery   In warehouse Rotterdam

Time of Delivery/Shipment   July 1980

Terms of Payment Prompt nett cash on receipt of confirmed, unconditional
release by warehouse to buyer, or against warehouse warrant, plus the
following documents:- 1. Signed commercial invoice, stating origin of
Special Remarks   material.
          2. Seller's or producer's detailed weight certificate showing
             individual gross and nett weights of each unit of packing.
        ·3. Seller's or producer's Quality Certificate.

P.T.O.   WOGEN RESOURCES LTD.

CONFIRMATION NOTE

WOGEN RESOURCES LTD.   Date.................................
17 Devonshire Street, London, W1N 1FS

We acknowledge receipt of your Contract

·No. ...... 03707S ...... dated ... 19 June 1980 ... for 100 Kgs. Germanium Metal.
which we hereby confirm.

                              Signed.......................................

```
T
WUI GA
844 28823"*
MCLENCO DAL

0185179 1126 12/08

17.25
28823 OSVOS NL
OOSTEROM WAREHOUSE
ROTTERDAM
844 28823
DECEMBER 3 1980
ATTENTION R. FRINGS

PLEASE TELEX RELEASE TODAY TO WOGEN
RESOURCES LONDON (ATTENTION G.
ALCOTT) 6 CASES (NOS. 101/6)
GERMANIUM METAL 100.647 KILOS
NETT/142.400 KILOS GROSS YOUR
REF. F. 2555.
THANKS
GORDON MCLENDON
THE MCLENDON COMPANY
T DALLAS TEX
73 2761 MCLENCO DAL
*

28823 OSVOS NL
```

Telex/TWX

western union

Telex/T.WX

western union

```
RCA DEC 03 1240*
MCLENCO DAL

28820 WOGEN G

3.12.80  NF/MW    1742H

ATTN:  MR GORDON MCLENDON

CONFIRM OUR PURCHASE FROM YOU TODAY
100 KGS CZCH GERMANIUM METAL FOR
PROMPT RELEASE IN WAREHOUSE ROTTERDAM
AT USD860/KG OUR CONTRACT REF NO.
04141P REFERS.  WE WOULD APPRECIATE
YOUR GIVING HOLDING WAREHOUSE IN
ROTTERDAM THE APPROPRIATE
INSTRUCTIONS AND LOOK FORWARD TO
RECEIVING YOUR INVOICE ENABLING US
TO MAKE FULL PAYMENT.

AS DISCUSSED GERMANIUM MARKET SHOWS
EVERY SIGN OF RISING FURTHER AND
WILL KEEP YOU IN TOUCH.

REGARDS
N FRENCH

*

MCLENCO DAL

28820  WOGEN G

WOGEN CONTRACT OF PURCHASE No. 04141P
```

THE McLENDON COMPANY

---INVOICE---

December 8, 1980

From: The McLendon Company
      2119 Southland Center
      Dallas, Texas 75201

To: Wogen Resources, Ltd.
      17 Devonshire St.
      London, W1N 1FS
      England

Re: Your Contract Of Purchase No. 04141

Please pay The McLendon Company the sum of US$ 86,556.42
(Eighty Six Thousand Five Hundred Ffifty Six & 42/100 Dollars)
for 100.647 kilos of Germanium Metal at US$860 per Kilo.
Reference your contract above.

Terms: Cash due prompt

Acknowledgments

Beyond those mentioned in the dedication, there are too many to remember down through these years. Therefore, my first acknowledgment of appreciation—and it will run very deep in many cases—is to all of those friends and associates whose names and particular contributions I shall have forgotten to include in the writing of these words of heartfelt thanks.

Dr. George Christy, the able and pragmatic economist at North Texas State University in Denton, Texas, has offered me such assistance and friendship, both in this book and in many other endeavors, that he deserves first mention as much as anyone. But one of his protégées, Jerry Lewis, who happens to be much more my friend than merely my personal broker, is for my money one of the best things that ever happened to Merrill-Lynch, not to mention he is no mean professor of practical economics and history, with an uncanny analytical ability and the gift to speak in plain English.

Four dear friends, Sy Weintraub, Col. Frank Brandstetter, Jack Schatz, and Forrester Mashbir, have given me enormous support and supplied invaluable advice, and another dear friend. Walter Hagan has transmitted something beautiful that God gave him.

Without the enormous drive, talent, and encouragement of Jim Blanchard, Dale Piret, and their staff—not to mention their time and counsel—I should probably never have gotten this book written at all. But when Jim insisted, and Sy Weintraub somehow sold the President of Pocket Books, Ron Busch, on taking this chance by so generously agreeing to publish the first book yet written for the general public in the heretofore almost dark literary continent of strategic metals, I agreed. Mr. Busch has given me every assistance any author could desire. I do not know many publishers, but he must be the best. It was he who introduced me to my editor, Harris Dienstfrey, for whose talent I have not only developed a special appreciation but who, with another, deserves perhaps the most important gratitude of all: Without Harris and Billie Odom, my devoted secretary of many summers, I might very well on many occasions have been tempted by exhaustion or frustration, or both, to jump from the seventeenth floor of the Yale Club in New York, where most of this book has been written.

I acknowledge with pleasure the contributions of three talented gentlemen from Tienjin, China—Han Wen Hsu, Liu Bao Qi, and Tian Jun Lin—whose ability in their field is becoming more internationally known with each month.

Bob Hudspeth, Bob Williams, Robert Stewart, Elvis Mason, David Vining, and too many others to mention at First International Bancshares have left their own imprints upon this work, as have Dr. Leo Mildenberg and Sylvia Hurter of the Bank Leu in Zurich, Bruce McNall of Numismatic Fine Arts, Wong Nang Jang of the Oversea-Chinese Banking Corporation in Singapore, and Dr. Eric Stoeger of the Bankhaus Deak in Vienna; also Nicholas Deak and Otto Roethenmund, and Dick Becker and Richard Willstatter, the latter two among the ablest metal men in the business. My friend Ray Zauber in his field, too. And, of course, Peter Robbins, who is the learned author of what almost certainly is the first book ever printed on this subject whose services were engaged in our very earliest research and were extremely helpful.

Louis W. Ingram, Jr., has proved once more his authority in the field of Constitutional law.

And, of course, deep gratitude to that dean of Constitutional scholars, former Senator Sam Ervin, who gave us a long time out of his busy day in Morganton, N.C., concluding with an Ervinesque observation:

"I say an activist judge is a judge who interprets the Constitution to mean what it would have said if he, instead of the founding fathers, had written it."

Our principal photographer, Charles Petrovitch, has done excellent work.

In Australia, the writer had superlative aid from his friend and attorney, Charles Kerry; the fine, old-line Sydney brokerage house of Hordern Utz and Bode could not have offered more comprehensive advice; and both the Bank of New South Wales and the Hong Kong-Shanghai Banking Corporation.

I owe thanks to so many financial newsletter writers that I dare not mention even one.

Dorothy Manning, the Treasurer of the McLendon Company, I put by herself here at the last because her friendship and advice down through the years, not to mention her help with this book, are deserving of a very special thanks.

Not only had I better stop before I offend any more people by leaving them out, but my publisher, Ron Busch, has just had the good sense to tell me that I cannot use any more space for this section.

New York City   GORDON McLENDON
January 13, 1981

Recommended Readings

I make no pretense here to an exhaustive listing of all the works relevant to the subjects on which this book has tried to throw new light. Such a listing would be a project at least as large as the writing of the text itself. Instead, I furnish below the title, author and publisher of a few of the important books and other publications dealing with some of the general subjects covered in this volume.

Anderson, Benjamin M. *Economics and the Public Welfare,* Van Nostrand, New York.

Bar, Hans J. *The Banking System of Switzerland.* Schulthess Polygraphischer Verlag, AG, Zurich, Switzerland.

Bastiat, Frederic. *The Law.* The Foundation for Economic Education, New York.

Blanchard, James U. III. *Alternative Investment Handbook.* Alexandria House, Washington, D. C.

———. *Gold Newsletter.* 8422 Oak Street, New Orleans, La.

Brown, Susan Love; Keating, Karl; Mellinger, David; Post, Patrea; Smith, Stuart; and Tudor, Catriona. *The Incredible Bread Machine.* Ward Ritchie Press, Pasadena, California.

Browne, Harry. *How You Can Profit from the Coming Devaluation.* Avon Books, New York.

———. *You Can Profit from a Monetary Crisis.* Macmillan, New York.

Burger, Albert E. "The Monetary Economics of Gold." Federal Reserve Bank of St. Louis Review; St. Louis, Mo.

Chase, Stuart. *A New Deal*. Macmillan, New York.

Christy, George A., and Roden, Peyton W. *Finance, Environment and Decisions*. Harper and Row, New York.

———— and Clendenin. *Introduction to Investments*. McGraw-Hill, New York.

Colt, C. C.; and Keith, N. *28 Days*. Greenberg Publishers, New York.

Curtiss, W. M. *The Tariff Idea*. The Foundation for Economic Education, New York.

Durant, Will. *Lessons of History*. Simon and Schuster, New York.

————. *The Story of Civilization III: Caesar and Christ*. Simon and Schuster, New York.

Edwards, John; and Robbins, Peter. *Guide to Non-Ferrous Metals and their Markets*. Nichols Publishing Co., New York.

Federal Reserve Bulletin, July 1974. Federal Reserve System, Washington, D. C.

Federal Reserve System, Purposes and Functions. Board of Governors, Federal Reserve System, Washington, D. C.

Fehrenbach, T. R. *The Swiss Banks*. McGraw-Hill, New York.

Friedman, Milton. *Capitalism and Freedom*. University of Chicago Press, Chicago.

————; and Schwartz, Anna Jacobson. *A Monetary History of the United States, 1867-1960*. Princeton University Press, Princeton, N. J.

Hargis, Anthony L. *In Gold I Trust*. Steck-Warlick Company.

Hayek, F. A. *Capitalism and the Historians*. University of Chicago Press, Chicago.

Hazlitt, Henry. *What You Should Know About Inflation*. Van Nostrand, New York.

————. *Economics in One Lesson*. Harper and Row, New York.

————. *Man vs. the Welfare State*. Arlington House; New Rochelle, N. Y.

Hebling, Hans H.; and Turley, James E. "A Primer on Inflation: Its Conception, Its Costs, Its Consequences." Federal Reserve Bank of St. Louis Review; St. Louis, Mo.

Hoppe, Donald J. *How to Invest in Gold Stocks and Avoid the Pitfalls.* Arlington House; New Rochelle, N. Y.

Kennedy, John F. *Why England Slept.* Wilfred Funk, New York.

Kolko Gabriel. *Railroads and Regulation, 1877-1916.* Princeton University Press, Princeton, N. J.

————. *The Triumph of Conservatism.* Quadrangle Books, Chicago.

Marx, Karl; and Engels, Friedrich. *The Communist Manifesto.* Washington Square Press, New York.

Matthews, Herbert L. *Fruits of Fascism.* Harcourt, Brace and World; New York.

Metal Bulletin. 708 Third Avenue, New York, N.Y. 10017.

Metals Week. 1221 Avenue of the Americas, New York, N.Y. 10020.

Meyer, Alfred G. *Marxism. The Unity of Theory and Practice.* Harvard University Press, Cambridge, Mass.

Mises, Ludwig von. *Human Action.* Yale University Press; New Haven, Conn.

————. *The Theory of Money and Credit.* Yale University Press; New Haven, Conn.

Pugsley, John A. *Common Sense Economics.* Common Sense Press; Costa Mesa, California.

Rand, Ayn. *The Fountainhead.* New American Library; New York.

————. *Atlas Shrugged.* Random House, New York.

Read, Leonard E. *Anything That's Peaceful.* Foundation for Economic Education; Irvington-on-Hudson, N. Y.

Rickenbacker, William F. *Wooden Nickels.* Arlington House; New Rochelle, N. Y.

Riegel, E. C. *The New Approach to Freedom.* The Heather Foundation; San Pedro, Calif.

Robbins, Peter; and Lee, Douglass. *Guide to Precious Metals and their Markets.* Nichols Publishing Co., New York.

Rothbard, Murray N. *America's Great Depression.* Van Nostrand, New York.

Schmidt, Emerson P. *Union Power and the Public Interest.* Nash Publishing, Los Angeles.

Schultz, Harry. *Panics and Crashes . . . and How You Can Make Money Out of Them*. Pinnacle Books, New York.

Simon, William E. *A Time for Truth*. McGraw-Hill, New York.

"Smith, Adam." *The Money Game*. Random House, New York.

Smith, Jerome F. *Silver Profits in the Seventies*. ERC Publishing Co.; West Vancouver, B.C., Canada.

Tier, Mark. *World Money Analyst*. 302 Tung Sun Commercial Centre, 200 Lockhart Rd., Wanchai, Hong Kong.

Tocqueville, Alexis de. *Democracy in America*. Knopf, New York.

Vacca, Roberto. *The Coming Dark Age*. Anchor Press/Doubleday; Garden City, N. Y.

ABOUT THE AUTHOR

Born in Paris, Texas, McLendon was once described in *Coronet* Magazine as "a multi-talented genius of almost labyrinthine versatility." He is a world-recognized authority on economics and business and a frequent speaker at international financial seminars in such diverse cities as Zurich, Vienna, Acapulco, Montreal, New York and Hong Kong. A gifted performer, he has appeared on such national television programs as the Mike Douglas, Tom Snyder, Art Linkletter, Irv Kupcinet and Mike Wallace programs. He is Executive Producer of "Escape to Victory," a major 1981 United Artists' film directed by John Huston, and starring Sylvester Stallone, Michael Caine, Max von Sydow and Péle.

After being graduated from Yale as a major in Oriental languages and serving as a Japanese language officer in United States Naval Intelligence in many Pacific battle areas (Saipan, Palau, Tinian, Yap, Ulithi, Guam, etc.), for which service he received, at War's end, special commendation from the Joint Intelligence Center of the Pacific area, he quickly won fame as both a network sports broadcaster and radio/TV station owner. Between 1947 and 1952, he created and owned, with his father, the nationwide 458-station Liberty Broadcasting System where, known as "The Old Scotchman," he was named (in 1951) America's Outstanding Sports Broadcaster. His nationwide "Game of the Day" baseball and "Game of the Week" professional football broadcasts, particularly his re-creations, were hailed as masterpieces of the sports broadcasting art. His broadcasts with Dizzy Dean are legend, and he brought to network radio such prominent names as Lindsey Nelson, Jerry Doggett, Don Wells and many others.

He is generally credited with being the first U.S. broadcaster to editorialize following the Federal Communications Commission's historic "Mayflower" decision of June 1, 1949. A renowned innovator, he is generally credited with originating the modern Top 40 format (music and news), the modern good-music format (KABL), the all want-ad format, and he is the undisputed father of the all-news format. In good music, his famous "Love Songs for the Good Times," an M-G-M album by the Gordon McLendon Singers, is still regarded as a classic by good music radio stations.

McLendon is a member of the Association of Former Intelligence Officers as well as the Special Forces Club, an organization of former O.S.S. Intelligence agents based in London. As a recognized authority and writer on intelligence matters, McLendon covered the so-called "U.S. War Crimes Tribunal" in Stockholm, from which he and a fellow journalist were physically expelled; the Vietnamese war; the crises in Rhodesia and South Africa; the Russo-Chinese bitterness from remote Outer Mongolia; and he has editorialized frequently from such world capitals as Moscow, Irkutsk, Ulan Bator, Sydney, Singapore, Vienna, East Berlin, Paris, London, Rome, Athens, Bahrain and Belgrade.